Paths to Inclusion

MIGRATION AND REFUGEES
Politics and Policies in the United States and Germany
General Editor: Myron Weiner

Volume 1
Migration Past, Migration Future
Germany and the United States
Edited by Klaus J. Bade and Myron Weiner

Volume 2
Migrants, Refugees, and Foreign Policy
U.S. and German Policies Toward Countries of Origin
Edited by Rainer Münz and Myron Weiner

Volume 3
Immigration Admissions
*The Search for Workable Policies in Germany and the
United States*
Edited by Kay Hailbronner, David A. Martin and Hiroshi Motomura

Volume 4
Immigration Controls
*The Search for Workable Policies in Germany and the
United States*
Edited by Kay Hailbronner, David A. Martin and Hiroshi Motomura

Volume 5
Paths to Inclusion
The Integration of Migrants in the United States and Germany
Edited by Peter H. Schuck and Rainer Münz

Paths to Inclusion

The Integration of Migrants in the United States and Germany

Edited by
Peter H. Schuck and Rainer Münz

Published in association with the
American Academy of Arts and Sciences

Berghahn Books
NEW YORK · OXFORD

First published in 1998 by

Berghahn Books

Editorial Offices:
165 Taber Avenue, Providence, RI 02906, USA
3, NewTec Place, Magdalen Road, Oxford, OX4 1RE, UK

© 1998 American Academy of Arts & Sciences

Library of Congress Cataloging-in-Publication Data

Paths to inclusion : the integration of migrants in the United States and Germany /
  edited by Peter H. Schuck and Rainer Münz.
       p.   cm. – (Migration and refugees ; v. 5)
    Includes bibliographical references and index. ISBN 1-57181-091-9 (alk. paper)
       1. United States--Emigration and immigration--Social aspects. 2. American-
ization. 3. Assimilation (Sociology) 4. United States--Emigration and immigra-
tion--Government Policy. 5. Immigrants--Government Policy--United States. 6.
Germany--Emigration and immigration. 7. Germanization. 8. Germany--Ethnic
relations. I. Schuck, Peter H. II. Münz, Rainer, 1954- . III. Series.
JV6483.M54 1998 vol. 5
[JV6475]
304.8'73–dc21   97-30105
                                                                                        CIP

British Library Cataloguing in Publication Data

A catalogue record for this book is available from the British Library.

Printed in the United States on acid-free paper.

Contents

Introduction

Peter H. Schuck and *Rainer Münz*

The United States and Germany are now the world's two largest recipients of immigrants. This commonality, which only emerged in the postwar period, provides a rich opportunity to compare the ways in which the two countries think about and approach the problem of inclusion and integration of migrants. Most Americans view themselves as descendants of immigrants, and large-scale immigration is an integral part of the United States' history, culture, politics, and self-understanding. For Germany, immigration marks a sharp departure from—indeed a reversal of—the historical pattern. Most Germans still see their country as an ethnically defined nation-state. This is one reason why ethnic Germans from the former Soviet Union are still admitted despite other policies designed to limit the current inflow of new immigrants.

Immigration thus poses an old challenge for the United States and an altogether new one for Germany. Moreover, the social, legal, economic, and political institutions for dealing with these challenges in the two countries are quite different. In this volume, we shall explore these differences and their implications for the integration of migrants in the United States and Germany. In the course of doing so, however, we shall also find some important and perhaps surprising areas of convergence.

During the nineteenth century and the first half of the twentieth, Germany was a country of mass emigration, sending some 90 percent of its overseas migrants to the United

States (approximately 5.5. million between 1800 and 1930). Temporary labor migration and internal migration from non-German-speaking peripheries to the emerging industrial centers of the country (e.g., ethnic Poles to the Ruhr region) exceeded by far permanent immigration from other countries. In contrast, the United States during this period was a country of immigration (38 million between 1800 and 1930), although the numbers of immigrants and their countries of origin changed significantly over time. Between 1924 and 1945 the United States experienced a sharp decline in immigration because of the introduction of annual admission quotas, restrictive admission procedures, the Depression, and the country's reluctance to accept refugees from Europe or Asia before and during World War II. During the interwar period, Germany had almost no normal immigration, but shortly before World War II several hundred thousand German and Austrian citizens fled Nazi Germany, whereas during the war millions of foreigners were brought to Germany as forced labor. (These patterns are traced in Klaus J. Bade, "From Emigration to Immigration: The German Experience in the Nineteenth and Twentieth Centuries," and Reed Ueda, "An Immigration Country of Assimilative Pluralism: Immigrant Reception and Absorption in American History," chs. 1 and 2 in vol. 1 of this series.) In the immediate postwar period, both the United States and Germany became the destinations of large numbers of refugees, and Germany also had to absorb millions of expellees of German origin.

In the United States, as Frank Bean, Robert Cushing, and Charles Haynes show in "The Changing Demography of U.S. Immigration Flows: Patterns, Projections, and Contexts" (ch. 4 in vol. 1 of this series), both the quantity and characteristics of the flow changed again after 1965, when Congress passed new immigration legislation. During the 1990s between 750,000 and 1,000,000 legal immigrants (including refugees) were settling in the United States annually, approximating the record levels reached before World War I, while only 200,000 left the country each year. Today, nearly 85 percent of all legal migrants to the United States are from Asia or Latin America. The majority of them are admitted for family unification reasons or as political asylees and refugees.

In 1997 approximately 26 million people legally residing in the United States were foreign-born (9 percent of the total population); this share, which is likely to continue to grow, represented a distinct increase over 1970 (when the proportion was 5 percent) but is still much lower than the share of the foreign-born population in the early 1900s (14 percent) and lower than the share today in some other countries, such as Canada (22 percent). Nearly one-eighth of the U.S. population is now of Hispanic or Asian origin. Because of declining U.S. citizen fertility rates, migration now accounts for more than a third of the annual population increase, which will have important long term effects on the ethnodemographic composition of the U.S. population. According to projections of the U.S. Bureau of the Census reported by Frank Bean, Robert Cushing, and Charles Haynes, the four largest racial/ethnic minority groups (Asians, Hispanics, African Americans, and Native Americans) are projected to increase from nearly 25 percent of the total population in 1990 to 38 percent in 2020.

These figures do not include illegal migration. An estimated 200,000 to 300,000 illegal migrants settle in the United States each year, more than cross the borders illegally, and the remainder overstay the residence periods authorized on their visas. Following the passage of the Immigration Reform and Control Act in 1986, which granted amnesty to most migrants who had resided in the United States in illegal status since 1981 or earlier, 2.6 million of them were given legal residency rights. Many of these have now completed the requirements to become naturalized U.S. citizens. Nevertheless, by 1998 another estimated 5 million more undocumented aliens resided in the country.

Migration and refugee issues in Germany differ from those of the United States. In the United States, the integration of immigrants begins with their admission as legal permanent residents. Rapid naturalization is encouraged as a major step toward absorption into the mainstream of American society. But in a highly deregulated economy (by German standards) that in principle offers economic opportunities for everyone, socioeconomic integration is perceived as the migrants' own responsibility. American society increasingly sees itself as a salad bowl rather than a melting pot, so this integration does not necessarily entail complete cultural assimilation. In Germany, far more

than in the United States, migration is interpreted as a temporary change of residence and as a reversible decision, with
return migration to countries of origin playing a more prominent role. But even long-term immigrants and their children are
not perceived as full members of German society if they did not
arrive as ethnic Germans (*Aussiedler*). Germany is reluctant to
naturalize foreign residents without ethnic German background. As a result, most foreign immigrants and their descendants have not become German citizens and play a more
marginal role in Germany's economy and society than U.S.
immigrants do on the other side of the Atlantic. At the same
time, a highly regulated economy and an ethnonationally
defined society offer fewer opportunities for non-German residents, conferring more responsibility for the success or failure of
socioeconomic integration on the government.

Today, in both countries, about a tenth of the legal resident
population is foreign born (11 percent in Germany; 9 percent in
the United States). Both countries admit new immigrants primarily within the framework of family unification but to a
lesser extent also as new labor migrants. In the United States,
annual quotas apply to regular immigrants from all parts of
the world who do not qualify as immediate family members
(spouses, parents, and minor children) of U.S. citizens, whereas
in Germany such quantitative limits only regulate the immigration of ethnic Germans from the former Soviet Union. Both
countries in principle accept the immigration of refugees, but
since the fall of communism they try in practice to restrict their
number legally and through administrative procedure. Therefore both countries have introduced "temporary protection" in
addition to a more permanent "refugee" status. Both have succeeded in limiting the ability of potential asylum seekers to
claim asylum on their territory. But for different historical reasons both countries accept Jewish immigrants from the former
Soviet Union as "refugees."

In the United States, all governmental decision making about
immigration and naturalization is centralized at the federal
level. Legislation in Congress concerning immigration and the
absorption of legal and illegal immigrants is heavily influenced
by political groups, including business associations that rely on
high- or low-skill immigrants, and ethnic lobbies interested in

broadening their constituencies. In contrast to Germany, the United States has a largely deregulated labor market, low minimum wages, and no national register of employees or residents, and it has not introduced a national identification system either for its own citizens or for aliens residing in the United States. Under these circumstances, both legal and illegal migrants are relatively free to pursue economic opportunities without much governmental interference. Most immigration control takes place at U.S. borders and at embassies and consulates abroad rather than in the interior.

In contrast to the United States, immigration decision making in Germany is highly decentralized. Only the recognition of asylum seekers as political refugees and of ethnic Germans as *Aussiedler* is handled by a federal agency. But in the absence of annual quotas at the national level for other categories of immigrants, decisions about family unification and the admission of new labor migrants are taken by state (*Länder*) and local authorities. Even the deportation of illegal immigrants or rejected asylum seekers is organized and also decided in part by state rather than federal authorities. The only influential ethnic lobbies are so-called expellees' associations and compatriots' associations (*Vertriebenenverbände* and *Landsmannschaften*) set up by expellees of the postwar era and ethnic German immigrants from East Central Europe, the Balkans, and the former Soviet Union.

In Germany, all citizens and legal resident aliens are registered by local authorities. In addition, a national register of foreigners has been set up at the federal level. All foreigners must carry an ID at all times. In combination with a highly regulated labor market, this situation provides very little economic opportunity for illegal immigrants, and thus large-scale illegal migration to Germany has not yet occurred and is unlikely to become a major problem. This system, however, also restricts the job opportunities of certain legal immigrants. Only Germans and citizens of other member countries of the European Union (EU) enjoy free access to the labor market. As a result of the Schengen agreement among many of the EU states, Germany has abolished systematic border control with most other EU member countries. But citizens of neighboring non-EU countries (the Czech Republic, Poland, and Switzerland) also need no visa when traveling to or through Germany.

In both countries, the migration debates are highly contentious. In their analysis in volume 1 of this series (ch. 3, "Changing Patterns of Immigration to Germany, 1945–1995: Ethnic Origins, Demographic Structure, Future Prospects"), Rainer Münz and Ralf Ulrich describe three major migrant flows into Germany since World War II. The first flow involved mostly Germans: With the redrawing of the German borders after World War II and large-scale ethnic cleansing ordered or at least approved by the Allies, approximately 7 million German citizens living in the former eastern part of the Reich and 5 million ethnic Germans living in Czechoslovakia, Hungary, Poland, and Yugoslavia were expelled from their traditional settlement areas and resettled in parts of occupied Germany that later became the Federal Republic of Germany (FRG) and the German Democratic Republic (GDR), both established in 1949, and in Austria, already reestablished in 1945. Other ethnic Germans were allowed to stay in their traditional settlement areas (in Romania and to some extent in Poland and Hungary) or internally displaced (within the Soviet Union) and later became the source of a constant migration flow. Between 1950 to 1997 approximately 3.8 million *Aussiedler*, mainly from Poland, Romania, Russia, Kazakhstan, and Kyrgyzstan, were first invited and later at least allowed to migrate to (West) Germany. Between 1988 and 1997 more than 2.4 million ethnic Germans arrived, but in 1997 only 134,000 were admitted. A distinctive feature of these ethnic German flows, analyzed by Rainer Münz and Rainer Ohliger in this volume, is that the migrants, if officially recognized as *Aussiedler*, are automatically accorded German citizenship and become eligible for a series of absorption and integration measures, including special housing allowances, vocational training, and German language courses. In this particular respect, the German case has more in common with the Israeli one than with U.S. experience.

The second flow of migrants to Germany has consisted of labor migrants and their family members. In the mid-1950s, as reported by Klaus Bade and Rainer Münz and Ralf Ulrich in volume 1, West Germany started to recruit workers from several Mediterranean countries to meet the labor shortages of its high-growth economy. The government initially planned to rotate the guest workers so that West Germany would not have a permanent foreign immigrant population. But as Wolfgang Seifert shows in his chapter in this volume, the originally conceived rotation system was partly abolished to enable German employers to recruit labor migrants for longer periods. Many foreign workers also showed an interest in staying for extended periods of time and in bringing family members along. The one-millionth foreign worker arrived in 1964, and by 1973—the year that recruitment was halted for economic and demographic reasons—2.6 million foreign workers and 1.4 million other foreigners were living on West German territory. Most of the labor migrants recruited between 1955 and 1973 returned to their countries of origin, but others remained and brought their family members or started new families. Although only a small number of new labor migrants (mainly from Central and Eastern Europe) are formally admitted today, the flow continues through the free access of EU nationals to the German labor market, as well as through family unification and the formation of new families by people living in Germany and members of their ethnic or religious communities living abroad.

Refugees and asylum seekers constitute the third major influx into Germany. The German Constitution (Art. 16 and 16a) declares that people persecuted for political reasons have the right to asylum. During the cold war, this provision enabled Hungarians, Czechs, and Poles to be recognized as political refugees in the Federal Republic. Beginning in the 1980s a growing number of asylum seekers arrived from developing countries, especially from Iraq and Iran, but most came from Poland, Romania, Turkey, and former Yugoslavia. The number of asylum seekers rose sharply with the fall of the iron curtain, because individuals were then able to travel freely and use legal asylum opportunities provided by Germany, while sharp economic decline, political violence, interethnic tensions, and civil wars started to make life more difficult and even very dangerous in parts of the Balkans and the former Soviet Union.

Since 1993, when the German Constitution was amended, access to asylum in Germany has been severely reduced. In principle, persons who arrive from "safe countries" of origin or who have traveled through "safe transit countries" are no longer entitled to claim asylum. Because all of Germany's neighbors are considered to be safe countries, the number of persons being able to apply for asylum sharply declined (from 436,000 in 1992 to 127,000 in 1995). At the same time, Germany introduced temporary protection status for refugees from Bosnia with the expectation that these victims of ethnic cleansing would return home after the end of the war and the implementation of the Dayton agreement.

By 1997 approximately 7.3 million foreigners resided in the Federal Republic (constituting 9 percent of the total population), the largest number being citizens of Turkey, the former Yugoslavia, Italy, and Greece. Of these, 1.3 million were born as foreigners in Germany. In fact, its large foreign population has made Germany, like the United States, an ethnically diverse country. And because of the low fertility in Germany, which has caused an excess of deaths over births, population growth (or decline) depends entirely on international migration.

As projected by Rainer Münz and Ralf Ulrich, the continuation of naturalization rates and the net immigration of foreigners at present levels (190,000 per year) would increase the size of foreign population in Germany from 7 million in 1995 to 11.3 million (14 percent of the total population) in 2015, and 13.6 million in 2030. In this demographic context, Germany must reconsider both its integration and its naturalization policies.

The contrasts between the historical experience and self-understandings of Germany and the United States are reflected in their different traditions concerning the basis of national identity, membership in the polity, and law enforcement. The chapter by Klaus Bade in volume 1 and those by Gerald Neuman and Peter H. Schuck in this volume explore these differences. Since the 1870s Germany has viewed itself as an ethnic nation-state based on a common Germanic culture, history, language, and ancestry.

Germany's citizenship law, introduced in 1913, has drawn most directly from the rule of jus sanguinis (the law of descent), which defines national citizenship in terms of parentage. Such rules do not provide additional incentives to migrants and their children to naturalize. But recent changes in the German citizenship law removed some of the barriers. The law now gives foreigners after ten years of legal residence an option and after fifteen years a legal claim to become citizens and, in addition, gives some recognition to jus soli (law of the soil) principles by facilitating the naturalization of young foreigners who were born (or at least grew up) in Germany and attended school there. As shown by Münz and Ulrich, these changes led to a distinct increase in naturalization rates. However, the large majority of those eligible for naturalization have not naturalized and thus still remain foreign nationals.

In the United States, public attitudes emphatically reject any ethnocentric conception of its polity (although a smattering of Anglophiles, including some nativists, vigorously advocate it). Instead, the American political identity is more fluid and abstract; it is based on an acceptance of liberal democratic and constitutional principles. Nevertheless, widespread concern exists about the emergence of non-English-speaking immigrant minorities and the use of languages other than English in everyday life, especially in interactions between individuals and government officials. Almost half of the states have declared English to be their official language—a change of largely symbolic significance—and the U.S. House of Representatives passed a similar provision in 1996.

U.S. citizenship law has since 1868 been marked by a thoroughgoing commitment to the common law principle of jus soli, which extends national (and state) citizenship to all who are born on the territory of the United States. The law grants automatic citizenship even to those who are born to parents who have no real link (other than mere presence) to American society, including those who possess other nationalities and are only in the country temporarily or illegally. In addition, U.S. law gives limited recognition to jus sanguinis principles by conferring citizenship on many foreign-born children of U.S. citizens. Finally, immigrants can become naturalized citizens much more easily and quickly in the United States than in Germany; indeed, they are now doing so in record numbers: the 1996 total of one million was more than double that in 1995 and four times higher in 1990.

Until a change in the federal welfare law in 1996, these liberal features of U.S. citizenship law were coupled with an array of welfare benefits, public services, and other rights for which all legal immigrants, and not just citizens, were eligible. This combination—easy access to citizenship and universal entitlements—had aroused some concern in the United States about what Peter Schuck had called the "devaluation" of citizenship, prompting policy proposals designed to reinvigorate the ideals of civic participation, sacrifice, and responsibility. The 1996 welfare reforms denied federally funded benefits to many legal immigrants and all illegal ones, as well as restricting some state-funded benefits. Although some of these benefits were restored in 1997 through new legislation, the 1996 law obviously signifies an effort to revalue U.S. citizenship. These restrictions—and similar ones in California and some other states—partly explain the rapid increase in naturalizations in 1995 and 1996.

Attitudes toward law enforcement are somewhat different in the two countries. Although both adhere to the rule of law and constitutionalism, Germany bases its legal system on a civilian statutory code tradition drawn from Roman law. It embraces the ideal of the *Rechtsstaat* —a government of clearly defined, comprehensive legal principles that rigorously observes and enforces its rules—although in practice, of course, it often falls short of that ideal. The United States—because of its relative social heterogeneity, its geographical fragmentation, its ideological suspicion of a strong state and entrenched bureaucracy, its traditions of common law and of independent constitutional courts, and various other reasons—prefers a legal regime of ambiguity, broad administrative discretion, and compromised, even lax, law enforcement. One notorious example in the United States is the fact that many employers continue to employ undocumented aliens illegally despite sanctions contained in the 1986 immigration reform law. Other examples are the government's reluctance to apprehend and repatriate most of the deportable aliens who are not already in government custody, and its failure to deport most criminal aliens.

Germany and the United States also take somewhat different views of the nature and desirability of migrant integration and the forces that should shape it. The chapters by Peter H. Schuck, Nathan Glazer, Alejandro Portes, and Richard Alba develop the U.S. perspective on these questions, while those by Wolfgang Seifert; Richard Alba, Johann Handl, and Walter Müller; and Rainer Münz and Rainer Ohliger present the German perspective.

In both countries, the national governments expected the flow of labor migrants to be temporary, controllable, and reversible. As noted earlier, postwar Germany admitted its guest workers (*Gastarbeiter*) on a rotational basis, while the bracero program in the United States recruited Mexican farmworkers on a seasonal basis from World War II to the 1960s. In both countries, however, many of the guest workers put down deep roots, managed to remain, and were often encouraged by their employers to do so. In reality, they became immigrants and established recurrent patterns of migration from their communities of origin. In 1983/84, Germany offered financial incentives to induce labor migrants and their families to return to their countries of origin. The program was not very successful. Economic growth and political stability in the countries of origin proved to be a much more powerful incentive for the return migration of Italian, Greek, or Portuguese labor migrants and their families. In the United States, numerous Mexican workers who were recruited during the 1940s, 1950s, and 1960s through the bracero program did not return to Mexico, and in most cases no systematic efforts were made to repatriate them. But the U.S. government's inability or reluctance to repatriate "temporary" migrants has extended not only to labor migrants but also to recipients of temporary protected status and unsuccessful asylum seekers.

The United States, while deploying a rhetoric of vigorous border control and law enforcement similar to Germany's, has—unlike Germany—both acquiesced in a high level of illegal aliens in the country and encouraged (albeit grudgingly, given the tension with law enforcement goals) their assimilation into the mainstream of American life. In addition to its birthright citizenship rule and its toleration of dual citizenship, the most dramatic example of this was the massive amnesty program in the 1986 immigration control law, which conferred legal status on more than 2 million undocumented aliens, many of them former temporary labor migrants, and thus placed them on a path of integration that has already culminated in citizenship for many and will produce additional naturalizations in the near future. A new amnesty for 400,000 illegal aliens from Central America was enacted in late 1997. Other programs permit still other illegal aliens to regularize their status. In addition, school districts in the United States, aided by federal grants, spend billions of dollars to educate migrant children with limited or no English-language proficiency. In any case, immigrants and their children are encouraged to identify themselves as Americans.

Germany has traditionally resisted this approach. First, its citizenship policy does not encourage identification of regular immigrants with German society. Only ethnic German immigrants who were given *Aussiedler* status, and their accompanying family members, are naturalized on arrival. Unlike in the United States, with its jus soli rule, children born in Germany are not accorded citizenship unless at least one of their parents is a German citizen. In most cases so far, both parents (and thus the children as well) are foreign nationals. Currently 13 percent of all children born in Germany remain foreigners by law. Although naturalizations have increased considerably since the late 1980s, Germany, with a naturalization rate of 1 percent (excluding naturalizations of ethnic German *Aussiedler*), still naturalizes a much smaller share of its legal foreign residents than do most other West European countries and the United States. In 1990 and 1993 legal changes were introduced in order to facilitate the naturalization of second-generation foreigners born and/or raised in Germany and of immigrants who have lived in Germany for more than ten years. Administrative discretion of local authorities was partly reduced, although it remains broader than the discretion of the federal naturalization officials in the United States. As a rule, foreigners in Germany must still renounce their original citizenship, but in a growing number of cases exceptions are granted, particularly to Turks, Afghans, Iranians, and other foreigners whose countries of origin actively discourage or prohibit their nationals from renouncing citizenship. Despite legal change and a more liberal administrative practice, authorities both at the federal and local levels do not encourage foreigners (other than ethnic German *Aussiedler*) to naturalize.

Second, German economic, social, and political policies limit and delay integration. While ethnic German immigrants and citizens of other EU member countries enjoy immediate access to the German labor market, other foreign nationals only become eligible for basic economic and social rights after a certain duration of stay in Germany. Although many labor migrants of the

1960s and 1970s have managed to become an integral part of Germany's labor market, they remain concentrated in lower socioeconomic groups and declining industries, as Wolfgang Seifert's chapter shows. At the same time, as Richard Alba, Johann Handl, and Walter Müller report, the children of labor migrants, on average, are less successful in Germany's educational system and less adapted to the needs of the labor market. As a result, the unemployment rate among young foreigners is more than twice as high as that among Germans of the same age.

The role of government in fostering the integration of migrants also differs in the two countries. In light of the United States' far-greater commitment to the integration of migrants, it may seem paradoxical that its governments bear little responsibility for promoting it, while Germany, which is less committed to integration, accords its governments a more prominent role in facilitating or discouraging it. The United States does not provide any special governmental assistance to newly arrived migrants (except for refugees, who are eligible for extensive income supports and special public services). Indeed, the eligibility for public benefits of even long-term legal resident aliens, a politically uncontroversial matter in Germany, is still hotly contested in the United States, where the questions of whether migrants use these services more than native-born Americans do and whether their taxes fully defray the attendant costs have been intensively debated both in Congress and in those states with large numbers of immigrants. In 1996 this debate culminated in a broad limitation of federal benefits for many legal resident aliens; the states and localities, moreover, are now freer to limit the benefits they fund.

Governments in the United States possess fewer levers of influence over the integration of migrants than German governments do. Migrants who arrive in the United States are (except for refugees) essentially on their own; whether, how, and when they assimilate is left largely to their own efforts, private nonprofit institutions, the market, and other informal processes of integration into mainstream society. The main agents of integration are an open society, a growing economy, large and upwardly mobile ethnic enclaves, immersion in the English language, and a deregulated labor market offering opportunities for most legal and illegal immigrants. In contrast to the United

States, German governments can regulate the ability of certain groups of migrants to reside in a given community, to occupy particular housing, and to take certain jobs. The conditions of their employment are controlled by employer-union arrangements. At the same time, high unemployment among both native and foreign-born populations, social and fiscal problems related to German unification, high minimum wages, and a highly regulated labor market reduce economic opportunities for immigrants.

In the United States, the question of whether Asian and Latin American migrants will assimilate into American society as earlier generations of migrants did is particularly contentious, perhaps because it is less clear what assimilation means now that the United States has embraced some aspects of multiculturalism. Many restrictionists (a broad category defined in Schuck's chapter) fear that the country has lost its capacity to·absorb migrants as a consequence of government multicultural policies, including bilingual classes aimed at reinforcing ethnic and cultural identities and affirmative action policies in education, employment, government contracting, and voting rights. They argue that these policies, along with a cultural norm that legitimates the maintenance of group identities, is further fragmenting a society already divided along racial lines. Others, restrictionists and expansionists alike, worry that children of new migrants may be recruited into the underclass population in U.S. cities, that conflicts between relatively well-educated migrants and the native African-American population will intensify, and that the public school system may not assimilate immigrant children as well as it did in the past (see chapt. 2). On the other hand, the rates of intermarriage—always a revealing index of assimilation—have risen, and the acquisition of English is quite high among the second generation, many of whose members perform exceedingly well in school. Indeed, the degree and speed of social mobility among some Asian immigrant groups may be even higher than those achieved by earlier migrant communities.

The United States has succeeded in effectively integrating these earlier generations of migrants into the U.S. labor market and the society as a whole. Income and occupational differences among white ethnic groups—descendants of migrants to the

United States of the late nineteenth and early twentieth centuries (Italians, Poles, Ukrainians, Greeks, Jews, etc.) —and between them and the rest of the country have virtually disappeared. The bitter conflicts between Catholics and Protestants and among the migrant communities themselves have long since dissipated. What remains are troubling racial divisions. Most African Americans are the descendants not of voluntary immigrants but of slaves who were forcibly brought to America in the eighteenth century. Their progress, which has been dramatic in recent decades and has created a large and dynamic black middle class, is affected by today's immigrants, although in ways that are still matters of dispute among researchers. In any event, the United States' ancient racial problems must not be conflated with the other difficult integration issues raised by today's migration, issues that this volume hopes to clarify and help resolve.

What does the future hold for the integration of migrants in Germany and the United States? Several chapters in this volume (for example, the one by Alba, Handl, and Müller) suggest that strong demographic and social pressures are pushing Germany to embrace a public philosophy that moves away from its traditional concept of the ethnic nation-state toward a more assimilationist ethos and the acceptance of a higher degree of heterogeneity within German society. This change must inevitably accompany a fundamental reassessment of the nation's traditional view of the transitory or marginal position of migrants within German society. In light of its historical experience since 1945, Germany should come to see itself as a nation strong enough to absorb migrants without losing its national identity and social cohesion.

Some of the chapters in this volume (for example, those by Schuck, Portes, and Alba) also presage changes in how the United States views, and seeks to integrate, migrants. Compared to the German situation, however, these changes are likely to be more gradual and incremental. They may alter, for example, the number of legal admissions, the composition of the various legal migration streams, the design of bilingual education and affirmative action programs, the eligibility of immigrants and their children for social programs, the enforcement of immigration controls, the design of refugee programs from the former Soviet Union, the role of courts in reviewing the administration of the immigration laws, and the rigor of the legal requirements for naturalization. Some of these issues are also discussed in volume 2.

It is unlikely that the movement we anticipate toward a more welcoming approach to the integration of migrants into German society and toward a reassessment of integration in the United States will produce a close convergence of German and U.S. ideological commitments, institutional arrangements, and policy choices. As the contributions to this volume demonstrate, the two countries are still too different in national ideology, history, culture, economy, politics, and self-understanding for that. Even today, few Germans regard the United States as a desirable model for the integration of migrants, while in the United States Americans retain a strong sense of exceptionalism with regard to their immigrant society.

The rich distinctiveness of the two nations, however, does not prevent them from learning from each other's experiences with large-scale immigration and the integration of newcomers. In this exploratory spirit, the present volume analyzes and compares the U.S. and German immigration experiences and their rather different paths to inclusion, while seeking to identify desirable policy changes in both countries.

We are grateful to the German-American Academic Council Foundation for its financial support for the project and to its director, Dr. Joseph Rembser; the Gottlieb Daimler- and Karl Benz-Foundation for its support for a meeting of the participants in Ladenburg, Germany; our editor Sarah St. Onge; Lois Malone, who prepared the index; and Corinne Schelling of the American Academy of the Arts and Sciences, who has had principal responsibility for the management of this project since its inception.

Chapter 1

Assimilation, Exclusion, or Neither?

Models of the Incorporation of Immigrant Groups in the United States

Richard D. Alba

In *Birds of Passage*, Michael Piore notes that, during their initial phase in the host society, immigrants are "probably the closest thing in real life to the *Homo economicus* of economic theory" (1979, 54). They work much of the time, frequently at jobs they would reject at home, and sleep in shifts in apartments occupied by large groups of fellow immigrants; their behavior is entirely oriented toward the goal of earning as much money to send home as possible. But fairly rapidly a change sets in: they work less and enjoy their leisure time more, and they consume more of the money they earn. A process of incorporation has begun that, for many, will not end in their own lifetimes but instead continue into the lives of their children and grandchildren. Incorporation here refers to the processes by which immigrants and their descendants change from being outsiders-in-residence, whose participation in the host society is limited to its labor market and who remain in many respects oriented toward their homelands, to natives.

U.S. scholars draw on two bodies of historical experience in their formulation of abstract models of incorporation. On the

Notes for this chapter begin on page 26.

one hand, there are the experiences of the various ethnic groups emerging from mass European immigration; on the other are those of racially defined groups, above all, African Americans. The conceptual models that have been abstracted from and now define these experiences contrast strongly. From the first set has come the family of models covered by the term *assimilation*. It is largely these models that provide the dominant motif in the way the immigrant-ethnic experience has been interpreted; this becomes clearer when one considers not only the writing of historians, sociologists, and other scholars but also the understandings of ethnicity that exist in the larger society. (The assimilationist bent implicit in so-called common sense about ethnicity is epitomized by then-president Ronald Reagan's 1988 remark to a Moscow audience that Americans may have "made a mistake" in "humoring" Native Americans' desire to maintain their cultures, which he characterized as "that kind of primitive lifestyle.") Assimilation has not been the only note to be sounded, of course; interpretations that stress the persistence of ethnic elements, especially cultural ones, have been a recurring counterpoint. Greater consistency can be found at the core of interpretations of the experiences of racially identified minorities, where the prevailing note has been one of racial exclusion. Attempts to recast those experiences into the mold of immigration groups have failed to take hold (Omi and Winant 1994).

A key question is: which set of models is more appropriate for the new immigrant groups, i.e., those that began to come in large numbers after the 1965 reform of immigration law?[1] From the fact that they share the status of immigrants with earlier arrivals from Europe, one might conclude that their experiences will fit the outlines of the assimilation models. Students of immigration, however, have underscored features that distinguish contemporary immigration from that of the past, such as the shift in geographic sources of immigration to Asia, Latin America, and the Caribbean; the radically changed technologies of transportation and communication that allow immigrants and their families to maintain close links to their homelands; and the absence of any foreseeable caesura in the immigrant flow comparable to the closing of the gates during the 1920s, induced by restrictive immigration legislation followed by the Depression (Portes and Rumbaut 1990). Because of these differences, the direct application of models of absorption developed from the experiences of European groups appears problematic. It can accordingly be argued that the more appropriate set of models is that of racial exclusion, inasmuch as the new immigrant groups come mostly from outside of Europe and frequently differ in skin color and other physical features from the white European norm. This set of models is also problematic, however, for it is attuned primarily to the experiences of nonimmigrant groups, whose entry to U.S. society was forced through conquest or enslavement. Thus one has to ask: is there yet a third set of possibilities, now only beginning to be glimpsed?

An examination of the major models of the past should provide some clues to the ways in which they may or may not apply to new immigrant groups. One must of course be attentive to the specific group experiences that provide the fundament for different models. The models applied to immigrant groups derive mainly from the experiences of the groups most numerous in the century of mass immigration starting around 1820, especially the experiences of those immigrants who settled in large numbers in U.S. cities, such as the Irish, Italians, East European Jews, and Poles. Other groups, some of them quite large (e.g., Germans), have received less attention from scholars, even though in some ways (e.g., persistence of the German language until the World War I period [Kamphoefner 1994]) their experiences challenge standard elements in the assimilation model. The models of racial exclusion in the main seem most specifically attuned to the African-American experience, although generalization to other nonwhite immigrant groups or even to all non-European immigrant groups ("peoples of color") is often claimed (e.g., Blauner 1972). This extrapolation is problematic even in application to other nonimmigrant groups, such as Native Americans, whose high rate of intermarriage with whites and astonishing rise in numbers since 1960 challenge a facile application of the concept of a stigmatized minority (Snipp 1989).

Assimilation Models

The assimilation family of models is usually traced back to such writers as Robert E. Park, but the canonical statement for contemporary scholarship is that of Gordon (1964; see also Hirschman 1983). Gordon advanced assimilation theory by presenting a carefully defined, multidimensional concept of assimilation. Though he envisioned seven dimensions in all, the critical distinction in his account lay between acculturation and what he termed "structural" assimilation, by which he meant the entry of members of a minority into primary-group relationships with others (whether these others had to be members of the ethnic majority, however defined, or just members of other groups, possibly of other minorities, was never clear). Of additional importance for the issues that have arisen in the application of the assimilation model is Gordon's concept of "identificational assimilation," which he formulated as the erasure of any ethnic identity smaller than the national identity of the society ("development of [a] sense of peoplehood based exclusively on [the] host society [Gordon 1964, 71]).

Acculturation, Gordon argued, typically came first and was inevitable, to a large degree. Yet his concept of acculturation was so broad, ranging from such externals as dress to the subtleties of value systems pertaining to private spheres, that there is room for doubt about its inevitability. With respect to the more or less necessary accommodations to the host society, research strongly supports him. For instance, the evidence shows that high-fertility immigrant groups, such as the Italians and East European Jews, converted within a generation to the low-fertility patterns characteristics of other white Americans in urban areas (Femminella and Quadagno 1976; Morgan, Watkins, and Ewbank 1994). Perhaps most important, given the role of language as a seedbed for other aspects of culture, is the evidence on linguistic acculturation: this appears to show that, for virtually all groups, a three-generation model of conversion to English monolingualism holds (Veltman 1983; Stevens 1992). Even here, though, there is room for skepticism, because, by and large, the European immigrant groups did not bring the elite cultures of their home societies with them (Portes and Rumbaut

1990); many, in fact, spoke dialects, which were sometimes mutually unintelligible within the same nationality group (among the Italians, for example) and were unlikely candidates for second languages in a bilingual pattern. Thus it can be argued that the new immigrant groups, some of whom come from the highly educated strata of their home societies (e.g., Indians, Koreans), have a better chance of developing true bilingualism. On different grounds—namely, that Spanish is a lingua franca for a plurality of the new immigrants (Stevens 1994)—the argument can be pressed on behalf of Spanish.

Some scholars also see limits to the factual extent of acculturation among European-ancestry Americans and point especially to values and behavior patterns in the family realm as the domain where distinctive ethnic cultural patterns persist (e.g., Greeley and McCready 1975). This empirical challenge feeds into cultural pluralist alternatives to the assimilation model, which will be discussed below. There is also debate about whether the common culture that arises from acculturation is that of the dominant group or is more syncretic, blending elements contributed by different groups. Gordon's view was that acculturation was decidedly a one-way process, except for a cosmopolitanism with regard to such matters as food and music. Whether this is true can be questioned, but more commonly by multiculturalists seeking to make room for non-European contributions than on behalf of non-British Europeans.

In Gordon's view, structural assimilation was far from inevitable—Gordon, in fact, characterized the U.S. pattern as one of structural pluralism, rather than cultural pluralism—but once it occurred, then all other forms would run to completion. Recent research, however, indicates that a strong form of structural assimilation—namely, intermarriage—is occurring at a robust level (Alba 1990; Lieberson and Waters 1988). Roughly three-quarters of all marriages of non-Hispanic whites involve some degree of ethnic-boundary crossing. The acid test of intermarriage among European-ancestry Americans is the Jewish case. While intermarriage between Jews and Gentiles has occurred at low levels for most of the twentieth century, it has surged in the most recent decades: data from the 1990 National Jewish Population Survey reveal that almost 60 percent of Jews marrying since 1985 have married partners raised in other religions; just two decades earlier, the figure had been only about 10 percent (Steinfels 1992). This rapid rise in intermarriage is suggestive of a broad and deep decline in the role of ethnoreligious origins in determining the choice of marriage partners by whites (Kalmijn 1991).

The growing extent of acculturation and structural assimilation among whites has led to a shift in the research frontier to questions concerned with the subjective dimension of ethnicity: ethnic identity. Some scholars have seen the persistence of some forms of ethnic identity among intermarried whites as a direct challenge to, indeed a refutation of, a central principle in Gordon's scheme: namely, that structural assimilation implies all other forms (Novak 1971). Others have elaborated a concept of ethnic identity, generally labeled "symbolic ethnicity" after Gans (1979), that is more consonant with assimilation (Alba 1990; Waters 1990). This is a form of limited-liability ethnicity that allows whites to feel ethnic occasionally in family and leisure-time activities but carries few commitments in everyday social life. Gans argues that it is consistent with what he describes as the "straight-line" theory of assimilation, the view that each generational remove from immigration represents an additional step in assimilation. But he is agnostic about whether symbolic ethnicity can persist indefinitely. Alba (1990) argues that it can, because symbolic ethnicity is the identificational expression of a European-American group in the process of formation.

One kind of assimilation that is overlooked in Gordon's account is socioeconomic assimilation, which can be defined as participation in mainstream socioeconomic institutions (e.g., the labor market, education) on the basis of parity with the majority. This form of assimilation is of considerable significance, because entry to the mainstream has undoubtedly provided a motive for other kinds of assimilation. In other words, the desire to compete on an equal footing with the majority has inspired many ethnics, at least those of the second and third generations, to shed their ethnic languages and accents and other external vestiges of their ethnicity. (A generation ago, this desire also led many South and East European ethnics to anglicize their names in the hope of gaining greater acceptance.) Moreover, the social mobility that accompanied participation in the mainstream economy promoted equal-status contact across ethnic lines in schools and workplaces and thus paved the way for the initial stages of structural assimilation.

Recent research has demonstrated a growing and impressive convergence in the average socioeconomic life chances of the members of white ethnic groups. Convergence here means in particular that the disadvantages that were once quite evident for some groups of largely peasant European origins, such as the Italians, have mostly faded and their socioeconomic attainments increasingly resemble, if not even surpass, those of the average white American. This convergence has not necessarily diminished the exceptional achievements of some relatively small groups, such as East European Jews, however. This convergence is evident in the increasing parity in the educational attainments across birth cohorts (from older to younger) of different European ancestry groups (Alba 1995), the decline of white ethnic differences in average occupational standing by the third generation (Neidert and Farley 1985), and the gradual erosion of ethnic economic niches, such as the Italian concentration in barbering (Lieberson and Waters 1988). These indicators of convergence do not imply, however, that the different ethnic groups followed identical routes to parity, that there was a single process of assimilation for all groups (Steinberg 1989). Groups with peasant origins in Europe that settled in urban settings in the United States, such as the Irish and Italians, entered the labor force at much lower levels than did groups that brought urban experience and industrial skills with them, East European Jews being perhaps the preeminent example. The latter, in particular, made effective use of entrepreneurial inclinations and the availability of skilled labor to develop ethnic subeconomies that served as a platform for the large-scale entry of subsequent generations into professional occupations. The groups with peasant origins worked their way upward more slowly and by ethnically different routes, for instance, the Irish were more concentrated than the Italians in political offices and in government employment more generally. Perhaps the critical point is that the dynamism of the U.S. economy at key intervals in this century gave these groups the opportunity to rise through the socioeconomic ranks.

Another form of assimilation that Gordon's scheme slights has to do with residential context. This is an odd omission in a way, because the settlement of immigrants in compact ethnic communities, from which there was a gradual dispersal, usually only after a generation or two, was one of the most prominent observations of the Chicago school of sociologists (Wirth 1965); more recently, Massey (1985) formalized these observations into what he called a "model of spatial assimilation." In any event, residential context can be seen as a crucial determinant of everyday social contacts, especially for the generation growing up, and thus of the level of structural assimilation, the keystone in Gordon's arch of assimilation.

Here, too, the evidence generally tells a tale of growing assimilation on the part of European-ancestry ethnics. Research has generally supported the hypothesis that generational progression weakens the residential segregation of ethnic groups (Lieberson 1963; Guest and Weed 1976). Indeed, residential assimilation has probably strengthened in recent decades because of the profound transformation in the residential settings of the majority wrought by growing suburbanization. About two-thirds of non-Latino whites who live in metropolitan areas now reside outside of large (i.e., central) cities and thus in suburban communities. The opening up of the suburbs siphoned off many socially mobile families whose adults had grown up in urban ethnic neighborhoods but now sought less congested circumstances in which to raise their own children. Even if parents did not move expressly to promote assimilation, relocating probably had that effect in many cases, because suburban communities tend to be more ethnically intermixed than do urban neighborhoods, and thus children had ethnically diverse playmates.

The depiction of assimilation as the master trend among European-ancestry whites has not been without critics. As a perpetually incomplete process, it is vulnerable to the charge that it is the glass half-filled. Two predominant strands can be recognized in the extensive literature that asserts the persistence, or in some cases the revival, of ethnicity. According to one, ethnic solidarity, the self-conscious recognition of ethnic origin as a social bond, crystallizes under certain conditions: namely, where ethnic group membership overlaps substantially with occupation and neighborhood. Under these conditions, it has been argued, the interests held in common by individuals who share more than ethnicity alone come into play in support of ethnicity (Glazer and Moynihan 1970; Yancey, Ericksen, and Juliani 1976; Morawska 1985). These were once seen as widespread conditions, bolstering the conclusion that ethnicity retained its potency among whites. As Glazer and Moynihan pithily describe the New York City of the 1950s and 1960s, "to name an occupational group or class is very much the same thing as naming an ethnic group" (1970, lvii). But research as well as common observation suggest that this description is less valid today. This is not to deny that some economic niches remain among white ethnic groups nor that ethnic neighborhoods can still be found in the large cities where immigrants settled in great numbers at the beginning of the century. But these traces of persistence, however remarkable they seem nearly three-quarters of a century after the end of the era of European immigration, do not appear to characterize the situations of a large fraction of whites.

The other strand of counterargument points to cultural differences coincident with ethnic origin as evidence that ethnicity continues to matter. A common form of this argument holds that the assimilation required to take advantage of the opportunities for social mobility in U.S. society leaves ample room for a distinctive cultural ethos in private realms, particularly those touching on the family. Andrew Greeley (1971; Greeley and McCready 1975) has probably done the most to develop evidence supportive of this argument. It finds resonance also in the imaginative literature on ethnicity, which emphasizes its frequently subtle influences in family settings (e.g., Gordon 1989; McDermott 1992). (Often, however, the action in these novels takes place in a past era, thus highlighting the difficulty of imagining a vital contemporary role for ethnicity.) A corollary argument holds that a straight line of descent need not connect ethnic cultural distinctions of the present to the cultures immigrants brought from the homelands, for unpredictable ethnic reinventions can supply the necessary distinctions even after assimilation has eroded the immigrant cultures (Conzen et al. 1992). Implied is that cultural assimilation need not be an irreversible process, for ethnic cultural distinctions are capable of reviving phoenixlike. The argument that cultural differences persist in some form is certainly credible, but it fails to answer questions about the significance of these differences: for example, how does their magnitude compare to that in that in the past? do the differences continue to set ethnically distinguishable groups apart or are they instead simply within the range of normal variation to be observed among white Americans? Given the high rates of intermarriage among all the major white ethnic groups, including those for whom the greatest distinctiveness is claimed (such as the Irish, Italians, and Jews), it is difficult to see these differences as salient, given that they pose so little difficulty in this sensitive area. Nevertheless, the claim that a voluntary pluralism best characterizes the incorporation of the descendants of European immigrants persists (Fuchs 1990).

Models of Racial Exclusion

An alternative framework for predicting and understanding the incorporation of new immigrant groups into U.S. society can be derived from the various models of exclusion arising from the experiences of some nonimmigrant groups, chiefly African Americans and, to a lesser extent, Native Americans, Puerto Ricans, and others. The distinctiveness of the African-American experience seems particularly marked. Recent research (e.g., Massey and Denton 1993; Farley and Frey 1994) documents that their level of residential segregation is considerably higher than that of other groups, including the Asian and Hispanic populations, to which the bulk of new immigrants belong. And new findings reveal that the level of intermarriage between African Americans and other groups is still at a low level compared to the intermarriage rates observed for other groups, even if black intermarriage has surged since the late 1960s to reach historic heights: 10 percent among young black men and roughly half that level among black women (Kalmijn 1993). Moreover, Hacker's (1992) comprehensive portrait of the African-American situation on a wide range of social indicators demonstrates that progress has been frustratingly slow on many fronts. Perhaps most tellingly, the ratio of black to white average family incomes, which climbed modestly in the decade or so following the civil rights legislation of the 1960s, has fallen back again to the level it maintained during the 1950s.[2]

The racial cleavage through the middle of U.S. society has proven to be one of the abiding problems for social science investigation, and a wide variety of approaches have been applied in the hope that successful explanation will produce effective policy recommendations (McKee 1993). The early sociology of these groups wavered on the fundamental question of whether the African-American situation could be understood with the same conceptual models applied to European-American immigrant groups. Robert E. Park, the preeminent early student of U.S. ethnic and race relations, is often seen as subscribing to the affirmative position, because of the seeming universality of his statement of the race relations cycle, but he also recognized the exceptional circumstances of African Americans (Lal 1990). One early model, the caste model associated with the names of W. Lloyd Warner and his associates (e.g., Dollard 1937), which depicted African Americans as occupying a hereditary and disadvantaged status, obviously took a conceptual approach opposite to the assimilation-oriented models applied to European-American immigrant groups.

Some other approaches, however, were more consonant with these models. The most important were those envisioning the causes of black disadvantage as extreme forms of prejudice and discrimination, an approach that reached its zenith in Gunnar Myrdal's *An American Dilemma* (1944). Myrdal's view of racial prejudice as a complex of unenlightened attitudes in contradiction to U.S. ideals epitomized a melioristic view of racial disadvantage, putting it on the same scale, though not at the same position, as the disadvantages suffered by some immigrant groups, such as Italians and Jews. This view suggested that racial disadvantage is ultimately resolvable, because it is anchored in subcultures of prejudice, themselves minority-group phenomena (e.g., southern whites), which give way before more modern outlooks, spread by assimilatory institutions such as education and the mass media.

The view that black disadvantage is linked to the prejudices and discriminatory acts of whites has not disappeared, but it has been overshadowed during the last quarter of a century by approaches that highlight the deep embedding of racial differences in basic social institutions. An exemplar is the approach taken by Robert Blauner (1972). Of particular significance for the new immigrant groups, Blauner's account placed great weight on the distinction between groups "of color" (a category in which he included Latinos, though many are phenotypically white) and white, or European-ancestry, groups, though at the same time he also stressed the fatefulness of each group's mode of entry to U.S. society and whether that entry was the result of conquest or enslavement or, instead, more or less voluntary immigration. In his view, however, the non-European groups that arrived in the United States through immigration have suffered under legal liabilities of a far more extreme cast than the disadvantages faced by the most disparaged of the European immigrant groups, examples being the Chinese Exclusion Act of 1882, which virtually ended Chinese immigration until the middle of the twentieth century and made Chinatowns into bachelor societies, or the California Alien Land Laws of the early twentieth century, which were intended to bar Japanese agriculturalists from land ownership.

Blauner's arguments are paradigmatic in several respects for models of racial exclusion. For one thing, he identified "racial privilege," which he defined as a "systematic 'headstart' in the pursuit of social values" (1972, 22), as an essential feature of U.S. society, deeply woven into its institutional fabric. This privilege is not reducible to strictly economic terms but includes an important status component, as racial minorities provide a form of social basement, to which whites, on the main and upper floors of the societal edifice, need not descend. For another, he stressed the institutional basis of racial exclusion, arguing that "institutional racism" is more important than individual-level prejudice and discrimination in accounting for racial disparities. He pointed in particular to institutions, such as schools and police forces, that have a salient presence in minority communities as those charged with keeping minorities in their place and, if possible, reconciling them to their lesser role in the larger society.

In Blauner's view, racism in the United States is a direct outgrowth of the worldwide hegemony of Europeans over non-Europeans and thus an expression of the same forces that gave birth to colonialism. Thus analytic models applying to the racial divisions within a society are analogous to those defining the relationship between colonizing and colonized nations: Blauner was among the first (along with Carmichael and Hamilton 1967) to apply the concept of "internal colonialism" to U.S. majority-minority relations. In his treatment, this concept had economic, political, and cultural aspects, all of which converged in minority communities. Thus the businesses and real estate in these communities remain largely in the hands of outsiders, and minority earnings in the mainstream economy flow out virtually as soon as they are brought home. As already noted, the institutional presence of the majority group in minority communities is concentrated in institutions of social control. Finally, the white majority has attempted to wipe out the psychological basis for further minority resistance to its hegemony by an all-out assault on the minority group's culture. Culture is one of the "vessels of a people's autonomy and integrity; when cultures are whole and vigorous, conquest, penetration, and certain modes of social control are more readily resisted" (Blauner 1972, 67). Hence, like colonizers everywhere, the white majority seeks to restrict the minority group's cultural practices and force Anglo conformity. Such attempts are exemplified in the nineteenth- and early-twentieth-century repression of Native American religious rites and in the use of boarding schools to weaken Native American languages and promote acculturation. (For a compelling fictional account of the confrontation between Native American and white cultures, see Erdrich 1988.)

A central ambiguity in Blauner's scheme lies in the pairing of the two factors determinative of group status: racial distinctiveness and colonized—i.e., nonimmigrant—entry. For non-European immigrant groups, which would be the more fateful? As noted earlier, Blauner found enough parallels between the experiences of groups whose entry was coerced and those of immigrant groups such as the Chinese and Japanese to argue that color was more predictive of ultimate fate; in any event, his vision was dominated by the division of the world into colonizing, i.e., European, and colonized, i.e., third world, peoples. But the fit of many contemporary immigrant groups into the internal colonialism concept is awkward and reveals some of the general problems arising when models of racial exclusion are applied to immigration experiences. Many of the new immigrants bring capital with them and have a strong entrepreneurial bent; they quickly own businesses and buildings in their communities and, in the manner of middleman minorities, in other minority communities besides. Moreover, the children from some of these groups do considerably better than do majority children in school, although school is supposed, according to the model, to be a site where subordination is reproduced in each new generation of minority children. Of course, Blauner wrote before the character of the new immigration was clear; had he first observed the gulf between the experiences of the post-1965 immigrants and those of earlier immigrants from the same areas, he might well have modified his account.

Some elements of Blauner's approach reappear in, and are refined by, the highly influential racial-formation theory developed by Michael Omi and Howard Winant (1994). The emphasis in Omi and Winant's account falls on the social construction and contestation of racial categories. These categories represent bulwarks of the privileges of the racial majority, but, far from being obvious at the outset, they usually have been painfully assembled over long periods. Omi and Winant's approach has inspired studies of the historical development of "whiteness": according to these, whiteness was not initially an obvious basis for the distinction between European immigrant laborers and blacks, free and slave; the racial majoritarian status of groups like the Irish, for example, required an effort lasting decades, during which they sought to create a sharp separation of their status from that of blacks, often employing cultural devices such as blackface minstrelsy (Roediger 1991). If racial categories are the sites of socially assembled meanings, then it follows that these categories can be altered by collective efforts. Thus one distinctive note sounded by this approach is the fluidity of racial dividing lines; Omi and Winant allow more room for minority groups to challenge and even to alter the significance and meaning of racial categories than is generally presupposed by models of racial exclusion. At the same time, they emphasize race as one of the deepest fault lines in U.S. society, implying that it is of inescapable consequence for new immigrants.

A very different approach explains minority-group disadvantage on a nonracial basis, namely, social class. The most noteworthy recent attempt along these lines is represented by

William J. Wilson's controversial thesis about African Americans. While Wilson accepts that the exclusion of blacks from the mainstream society in earlier eras was based on race, he argues that the life chances of contemporary African Americans are more determined by their social-class origins (Wilson 1978). His position implies that not all African Americans suffer disadvantages; some, in particular the highly educated, who are especially helped by affirmative action policies, have attained acceptance in largely white, middle-class arenas. They compete on equal terms with whites in the mainstream labor market and have left impoverished minority communities for more prosperous residential settings, though in some cases these are African-American, rather than white, suburbs (Dent 1992). (The residential mobility of middle-class African-Americans has been a particular point of contention between Wilson and his critics; see, e.g., Massey and Eggers 1990. That African Americans have access to suburban residential opportunities on a par with those of socioeconomically similar whites is doubtful [Alba and Logan 1991, 1993; Logan and Alba 1993].)

The extreme disadvantages borne by other African Americans are explained by Wilson in two distinct yet interrelated ways. One focuses on the interface between lower-class position and the larger socioeconomic environment in urban settings. Critical here is the segmented nature of the labor market, along with powerful changes in the socioeconomic landscape, such as the shift from a manufacturing industrial base to one dominated by service provision and the exodus of jobs from central cities, where African Americans and other minorities are concentrated, to suburbs, where most whites reside, or even farther afield. As a result of labor-market segmentation, lower-class African Americans tend to be confined to job sectors that are not desirable to members of the white majority, because the jobs typically offer some combination of unstable employment, low pay, little prospect for advancement, and difficult or dangerous working conditions. Since the manufacturing jobs that once represented to European immigrants and their children a portal to opportunities for decent wages and eventual mobility have mostly disappeared from the inner city, many African Americans have little chance to get good jobs, and this problem is especially severe for men.

These circumstances, especially when their impact is spatially concentrated as a result of the extreme racial segregation of many U.S. cities, promote the emergence of the underclass, the second and much-disputed strand in Wilson's explanatory scheme (Massey 1990). The underclass is composed of individuals who are permanently detached from the mainstream society and, in particular, from its economy. The underclass is conceived by Wilson and others who have employed the concept in terms of urban ghettos beset by multiple, interlinked social problems: heavy unemployment, single-parent families, high school dropout rates, crime, and the like (Wacquant and Wilson 1989). Wilson concentrates in particular on the implications of the shortage of marriageable black men, those with stable employment yielding earnings adequate to support a family, on black family life. The dearth of successful role models in underclass communities, whose middle-class residents have already left and which are largely bereft of supportive institutional infrastructures, has devastating consequences for the next generation.

Wilson's embrace of the underclass concept has proven highly controversial. Scholars have challenged the utility of the concept on the grounds of the apparently small size of the underclass by some measures, the flawed explanations Wilson offers for its rise (Massey and Eggers 1990), and, finally and perhaps most influentially, the ideological freight that the concept appears to bring with it (Gans 1990). In a recent statement, Wilson (1991) himself appears to accept that another term must be substituted, though without conceding any of what he sees as the substantive core of the concept.

Wilson's analysis leads him to advocate nonracial strategies for redressing black disadvantage, specifically, policies that ameliorate class-derived disadvantages and thus presumably have greater impact on racial minorities because of their concentration in lower classes. Such race-neutral strategies are, for obvious reasons, not the most likely of conclusions to be drawn from models of racial exclusion. Indeed, in recent years, one strategy that has grabbed much attention is at opposite poles from Wilson's, both in its race consciousness and cultural point of leverage: namely, multiculturalism. Multiculturalism is in a number of respects an amorphous concept, but it can be viewed as a project to affirm the worth of minority cultures and cultural contributions (Takaki 1993), one that fits rather neatly with Blauner's view that culture is the chalice of a people's autonomy and ability to resist oppression.

Although multiculturalism obviously shares some intellectual lineage with cultural pluralism, an early-twentieth-century version of a multicultural United States, it also brings a distinctive set of emphases. Cultural pluralism, as embodied in Horace Kallen's well-known metaphor of the orchestra constituted from the instruments contributed by different ethnic groups, stressed existing cultural diversity and urged its preservation for the sake of a richer society. While surely no present-day multiculturalist would deny this pluralist tenet, the focus of multiculturalist discussion is more narrowly on educational institutions and academic disciplines, especially in the humanities and social sciences. On this plane, there has been much discussion of the canon, the artistic and intellectual works deemed to represent the highest achievements of culture (the so-called classics) and constituting the backbone of the education of each new generation. (While some multiculturalists would reject the concept of a canon altogether, it is hard to see on a practical level how they can prevent its reemergence. Education, especially on its higher levels, involves introducing students to some standard set of works, acquaintance with which is presumed to give access to the culture of the educated classes.) The multicultural project aims to stretch the canon by incorporating non-European works on a basis of equality with those of the Western heritage.

Below the university level, the emphasis has been on devising curricula that give full—exaggerated, some would say—weight to the roles of non-European peoples in history and in the creation of culture. The greatest controversy has surrounded the development of Afrocentric curricula. This sort of project is easily disparaged as an attempt to distort history in order to enhance the self-respect of minority students (Schlesinger 1992), and perhaps it does at times degenerate to this level. But, as one of its most eloquent advocates has put it, multiculturalism is about the "politics of recognition," the recognition by the majority of the cultural and social value contributed by the minority, and is essential to the foundation of a democratic social order (Taylor 1992).

Despite the attention lavished on it, the status of multiculturalism as a model of incorporation is ambiguous. Insofar as it is limited to stretching the canon to include non-European contributions, it can be read as a corrective to a Eurocentric, and thus ethnocentric, bias in history and the arts and thus as similar to the efforts of earlier European groups to attain legitimate recognition for their cultural and historic achievements. Insofar as it has a larger ambition—to attain parity for the different ethnic cultures in U.S. society—then it has failed to spell out how such parity might be feasible. The main dilemma it fails to surmount is an asymmetry in expectations: while members of a minority culture are expected to be bi- (but not multi-) cultural if they are to be successful in the mainstream society, members of the majority culture face no similar normative expectation and, in general, reject such an expectation categorically.[3]

Is There a Third Alternative?

The models of incorporation to be derived from the experiences of earlier groups are polar contrasts: assimilation, the predominant pattern among groups of European origin, and exclusion, the pattern among groups introduced by routes other than immigration, with African and Native Americans the main exemplars for these models. Which, then, is it to be for the groups arising from the new immigration? With the European groups, the new groups share a common origin in immigration; with African and Native Americans, most share racial distinctiveness. Yet neither set of models seems a precise fit to the circumstances of the new immigration.

Doubts arise about the assimilation model because it appears to be rooted in the specific historical circumstances that prevailed during and shortly after mass immigration from Europe but no longer holds for the new immigration and the society that receives it. For one thing, the hiatus in large-scale immigration after the 1920s created by restrictionist legislation and the Depression is thought by many to be unreproducible. This hiatus virtually guaranteed that ethnic communities and indeed ethnicity itself would lose its strength and attractiveness over time, as the second and third generations experienced outward mobility and no new inflows compensated for these losses. But, according to a common argument, migration across borders is a hallmark of the contemporary era, and the nature of the flows is such that state policies are unlikely to be able to dam them (Massey forthcoming). Consequently, no comparable hiatus can be envisioned for the new immigration. Under these conditions, according to population projections by Edmonston and Passel (1994), the communities of the new immigrant groups will be dominated by the first and second generations, where the stamp of ethnicity is likely to be pronounced for many years to come.

Of equal importance, no one anticipates an expansive occupational structure like the one that prevailed in the centers of immigrant reception during much of this century. Not only were immigrants coming from peasant backgrounds and possessing few skills of value in an industrial economy able to find work, but over the course of a few generations their families experienced substantial upward mobility, in part as a function of the structural changes associated with upward shift in the occupational center of gravity (from blue- to white-collar work) combined with the arrival of other groups to take over the bottom jobs. But the contemporary occupational structure is more bifurcated than its predecessors, and this dims the prospects for immigrant groups entering on the bottom tiers to experience upward mobility in the same manner as the Irish and the Italians (Gans 1992; Portes and Zhou 1993). Without this opportunity, or at least the perception of it, the motivation to aim for the mainstream is reduced.

Other differences appear to point in the same direction: the greater ease of travel and communication back and forth between a homeland and the United States, presumably enhancing the self-conscious desire to preserve ethnic connections and generating, some claim, a widespread transnationalism in which immigrants and their children feel at home in two societies (Glick Schiller, Basch, and Blanc-Szanton 1992); the sharing of a common language, Spanish, by a plurality of the new immigrants coming from different countries, raising the possibility of assimilation to a Latino subsociety; and so on.

But models of racial exclusion also seem problematic in broad application to the new immigrant groups (though a case can be made that they apply to some groups). Immigrant status seems at least as important as racial distinctiveness in determining how groups fare in the United States. Immigrants tend to have a much more positive view of the opportunities open to them in U.S. society than do native-born minorities, and they are also more willing to take arduous jobs and make other sacrifices that they view as temporary expedients on the way to economic success (Ogbu 1991). As a result, they are able to exploit economic niches that native-born Americans disdain, and this allows them to gain a foothold, however modest, in the U.S. economy, avoiding the joblessness found at high levels in underclass communities. Some immigrant groups also have strong tendencies to engage in entrepreneurial behavior, and this gives them access in many cases to incomes well above the average for native minorities or even, in some cases, native-born whites (Light 1984). Finally, some groups, especially Asian ones such as Indians, bring high levels of human capital, reflected in educational attainments well above average, and enter professional occupations in the United States in substantial numbers.

The new immigration has reinvigorated the classical pluralist models of U.S. society. The clearest expression of this is Lawrence Fuchs's *The American Kaleidoscope: Race, Ethnicity, and the Civic Culture* (1990), in which Fuchs pays tribute to the strength of the United States' civic culture, whose genius in his eyes lies in its ability to allow new groups to participate in the society through the polity while maintaining their ethnic distinctiveness in private realms. "Voluntary pluralism" is the result. This conception builds on a long tradition in U.S. thinking about immigration; its roots can be seen, for instance, in Nathan Glazer's (1975) notion of an "American ethnic pattern," one of whose key elements was acceptance of the principle that groups could establish the institutional infrastructure necessary to maintain their ethnicity, even to the point of separate schools, so long as they committed themselves to the basic tenets of the political and civic order. (For an application of the pluralist model to the participation of Mexicans, the largest contemporary immigrant group, in the polity, see Skerry 1993.)

But so general an understanding of the possibilities arising from the new immigration is unsatisfactory in the end, because of one of the salient characteristics of the contemporary immigration stream: its diversity of countries, cultures, and socioeconomic origins. Such diversity suggests that there will not be uniformity in the manner of incorporation. Portes and Rumbaut (1990) have coupled this diversity with that of the receiving context to identify what they term the "mode of incorporation," which is hypothesized to exert a great deal of influence in determining future group trajectories in U.S. society. The context of reception is partly defined by factors exogenous to the group-government policy, which can range from financial and other help in resettlement to opposition to entry (in the case of Haitian boat people, for instance), and the attitudes of other Americans, from prejudice to sympathy. But it is also determined to a substantial degree by endogenous factors, the economic and human capital that immigrants bring with them and the economic and social strengths of the ethnic community that receives them. In both respects, there is a wide range of variation, with more or less predictable consequences for ultimate incorporation.

At one end of the spectrum lies the possibility of second-generation assimilation into the inner-city underclass, termed "segmented assimilation" by Portes and Zhou (1993). This is where models of racial exclusion become relevant. The segmented assimilation outcome would appear most likely when the new ethnics are phenotypically nonwhite (and especially when they are "black" according to North American standards), come from non-middle-class families, and are located in the inner city and when the protection afforded by the ethnic community is weak or nonexistent. Haitians in South Florida are one illustration; so are some Mexican Americans in California, those who are characterized by reactive identities, which constitute defenses against the prejudices of Anglo society and poor prospects in school and the job market. Portes and Zhou argue that this form of problematic assimilation—problematic in that it offers no access to the mainstream and its opportunities—is a special risk for new immigrants because of their racial diversity and also because the larger socioeconomic environment has become less favorable (see also Gans 1992). It should be kept in mind, however, that this sort of adaptation is also to be found among European immigrants and that the second generation of many South and East European groups reached maturity under the bleak economic conditions of the Depression. For the Italians in particular, an extensive literature describes the difficulties of the second generation in U.S. schools and documents its high rates of school failure and dropout (Covello 1972). One of the paragons of sociological fieldwork takes its name, *Street Corner Society*, from the groups of young second-generation Italian men who spent much of their time on street corners during the 1930s (Whyte 1955).

At another end of the spectrum lies the possibility of assimilation into the middle-class mainstream (Glazer 1993). According to the mode-of-incorporation concept, this outcome would appear most likely where the second generation has ethnic origins that hold some prestige in Anglo eyes (most Asian origins would qualify), comes from middle-class backgrounds, and does well in the U.S. school system. The children of Asian professional immigrants (e.g., Indian physicians and engineers) are presumed to be the best candidates for this pattern. This is made more likely by the geographical dispersion of Asian professionals, whose locations are determined by labor market exigencies rather ethnic community attachments, with the consequence that the second generation grows up in largely white, suburban settings rather than in ethnic neighborhoods (Portes and Rumbaut 1990; Alba and Logan 1991).

A very different form of incorporation suggests the possibility, however, of a third way, a route between the Scylla of assimilation in the mold of white ethnics and the Charybdis of racial exclusion and assimilation to the underclass. This third way is represented by the model of the ethnic enclave economy and by related models that imply that immigrants and their children can draw socioeconomic advantages from ethnic solidarity, social affiliation with and cultural loyalty to the ethnic group. An ethnic enclave economy represents the strongest and most protective of communal contexts for receiving immigrants, who can expect not only the usual help from kin and coethnics during the initial settlement process—e.g., finding a place to live—but even jobs in firms owned by coethnics, where working conditions are supportive of immigrant cultural and social needs.

These ethnic subeconomies are characterized by a special set of conditions, most notably, ethnic ownership of many firms in interrelated sectors of the economy. Portes and his coworkers

(Portes and Bach 1985; Portes and Manning 1986) have made strong assertions about the advantages that ethnics derive from subeconomies of this type. For one thing, immigrants are said to receive economic returns from their human capital on a par with those received by native-born workers in the primary sectors of the economy; the enclave economy allows the ethnic workers who participate in it to avoid the pitfalls of the secondary sectors in the segmented mainstream labor market (Portes and Bach 1985). (This economic advantage has been disputed for workers, as opposed to owners, by Sanders and Nee 1987.) For another, working in ethnic firms offers routes of mobility to immigrants, who can move into supervisory positions they would presumably be unlikely to achieve in mainstream firms or even learn the ropes of the business and open their own firms, perhaps with financial and other assistance from their former employers. Insofar as the enclave economy is a viable equivalent to the primary sectors of the mainstream economy, it provides an economic motive to remain within an ethnic social and cultural matrix and thus constitutes a disincentive to assimilation.

The enclave model, persuasive as it is regarding the compatibility of ethnic solidarity and socioeconomic success, appears nevertheless uncertain as a conceptual solution of broad application to new immigrant groups and their long-term place in the United States. Two issues stand out. One concerns whether the enclave remains the locale for future generations of the group or instead serves as a platform enabling them to climb into the mainstream economy at high levels. The issue is raised by the classic example of an enclave from earlier immigrations, that established by East European Jews in New York City during the late nineteenth and early twentieth centuries (Portes and Manning 1986). Jews dominated a number of industries and trades—the garment industry, most famously—but Jewish owners encountered difficulties in recruiting their progeny to take their place. The second and subsequent generations frequently preferred instead to acquire advanced educational credentials and enter more prestigious, if not necessarily more lucrative, professional occupations. The same fate may befall the future generations of current enclave groups, and there are indeed signs of this among the Koreans, who have carved out a niche in some demanding lines of business, such as fruit-and-vegetable stands in New York City, which are unlikely to prove appealing to U.S.-born generations.

Whether the model can be widely emulated is a second issue. As of this moment, research has turned up a handful or so of examples of the enclave phenomenon, such as the Cubans of Miami, the Koreans of Los Angeles, and the Chinese of New York City. No doubt there are others, but it would appear that some unusual conditions must come together for an enclave to emerge. The case of the Cubans, whose enclave is perhaps the best known, points up some of these features. Given its origins in the Castro revolution, Cuban immigration in its early years contained a large portion of the island's former political and business elites, some of whom brought considerable capital with them. As a refugee group, Cubans also benefited from government programs not available to ordinary immigrant groups, such as the Cuban Loan Program, which enabled many Cuban youths to attend U.S. colleges (Portes and Zhou 1993). It is doubtful that many other groups have the capacity to assemble as robust an ethnic subeconomy as have the Cubans in Miami, and research using 1980 census data sustains this impression. In a study of the sectoral concentrations of owners and workers from new immigrant groups, Logan et al. (1993) found virtually no other examples to rival the diversity of the Cuban subeconomy in Miami.

Conclusion

No model reigns supreme in the sense that its explanatory and predictive abilities clearly appear to be better grounded than are those of its competitors. Each model finds application to some portion of the experiences of some groups but is problematic elsewhere. Given the racial distinctiveness of many of the new immigrants, the diversity of the immigration itself, and the likelihood that it will continue largely unabated into the far future, it would be foolhardy to forecast the assimilation of the new immigrants as the sole or even predominant outcome. Given the human-capital advantages brought by a number of new immigrant groups, their rapid entry into mostly white suburban milieus, and the educational success of their children, it would be equally foolhardy to forecast a future of race-based exclusion from the mainstream. Yet, if a third way is to be found in the possibilities limned by models of the benefits of ethnic solidarity, not only will this mark a break with the main features of the U.S. past, but it will present imposing demands on immigrant groups in the long term: first, that they summon the economic, social, and cultural resources to make solidarity rewarding; and, second, that socioeconomically successful families, in defiance of what appear to be the laws of upward and outward mobility in the U.S. context, maintain their attachment to their ethnic communities across generations.

But perhaps these models should not be assessed on their scientific merits alone but also on their properties as visions of American society and its future and, more particularly, on what they imply about the place of minorities. In this respect, there is no longer parity among the models. Clearly, models of racial exclusion envision an inferior position for minorities. The contest, then, is between models of assimilation and those of ethnic solidarity, and it is one in which both can show advantages. The models of assimilation offer the possibility of equal access to the most valued social goods but demand as the price of admission to the mainstream that ethnic individuals surrender much of their ethnic cultural heritage and communal attachments. The models of ethnic solidarity appear to offer as much, at least in economic terms, and without requiring assimilation as an entry ticket, but they are not cost-free, either. For solidarity to be effective, a group must have the resources needed to develop an ethnic subeconomy, and much depends on its character. Moreover, individuals must remain loyal to the group, which may imply the surrender of other possibilities of personal development available in the mainstream society. The contest remains undecided.

Notes

1. As Douglas Massey (forthcoming) and others have noted, the rise in immigration by some of the groups counted as part of the new immigration— e.g., Mexicans—was already under way when the 1965 legislation was passed. Thus, the term *post-1965 immigrants*, which is frequently used as a synonym for the new immigration, is not wholly accurate.

2. Some commentators, to be sure, have ascribed the relative decline of black family income during the last few decades to changing family patterns, specifically, the rise in the number of female-headed households, and have pointed out that married-couple black families are much closer to parity with whites than the overall averages suggest. However, it seems equally plausible to attribute the changes in black families to the worsening labor-market situation of a large segment of the black population, as William J. Wilson (1987) has done. Without question, the decline in relative income has been translated into dire consequences for inner-city African-American communities as well as for black children, approximately half of whom live in poverty at present.

3. This problem emerges in Gibson's [1988] empirical treatment of the strategy of "additive acculturation," the selective acceptance of elements of American culture without a corresponding loss of ethnic culture; see her fascinating account of Punjabi Sikh children in a California school system.

References

Alba, Richard. 1995. "Assimilation's Quiet Tide." *The Public Interest* 119 (spring): 1–18.

_____. 1990. *Ethnic Identity: The Transformation of White America.* New Haven: Yale University Press.

Alba, Richard, and John Logan. 1993. "Minority Proximity to Whites in Suburbs: An Individual-Level Analysis of Segregation." *American Journal of Sociology* 98 (May): 1388–1427.

_____. 1991. "Variations on Two Themes: Racial and Ethnic Patterns in the Attainment of Suburban Residence." *Demography* 28 (Aug.): 431–53.

Blauner, Robert. 1972. *Racial Oppression in America.* New York: Harper and Row.

Carmichael, Stokely, and Charles Hamilton. 1967. *Black Power: The Politics of Liberation in America.* New York: Vintage.

Conzen, Kathleen, David Gerber, Ewa Morawska, George Pozzetta, and Rudolph Vecoli. 1992. "The Invention of Ethnicity: A Perspective from the U.S.A." *Journal of American Ethnic History* 12: 3–41.

Covello, Leonard. 1972. *The Social Background of the Italo-American School Child*. Totowa: Rowman and Littlefield.

Dent, David. 1992. "The New Black Suburbs." *New York Times Magazine*, 14 June, 18–25.

Dollard, John. 1937. *Caste and Class in a Southern Town*. New Haven: Yale University Press.

Edmonston, Barry, and Jeffrey Passel. 1994. "The Future Immigrant Population of the United States." In *Immigration and Ethnicity: The Integration of America's Newest Arrivals*, ed. Barry Edmonston and Jeffrey Passel, 317–53. Washington, D.C.: Urban Institute Press.

Erdrich, Louise. 1988. *Tracks*. New York: Harper and Row.

Farley, Reynolds, and William Frey. 1994. "Changes in the Segregation of Whites from Blacks during the 1980s: Small Steps Towards a More Integrated Society." *American Sociological Review* 59 (Feb.): 23–45.

Femminella, Frank, and Jill Quadagno. 1976. "The Italian American Family." In *Ethnic Families in America: Patterns and Variations*, ed. Charles Mindell and Robert Haberstein. New York: Elsevier.

Fuchs, Lawrence. 1990. *The American Kaleidoscope: Race, Ethnicity, and the Civic Culture*. Hanover: University Press of New England.

Gans, Herbert. 1992. "Second Generation Decline: Scenarios for the Economic and Ethnic Futures of Post-1965 American Immigrants." *Ethnic and Racial Studies* 15 (Apr.): 173–92.

———. 1990. "Deconstructing the Underclass: The Term's Danger as a Planning Concept." *Journal of the American Planning Association* 56 (summer): 271–77.

———. 1979. "Symbolic Ethnicity: The Future of Ethnic Groups and Cultures in America." *Ethnic and Racial Studies* 2 (Jan.): 1–20.

Gibson, Margaret. 1988. *Accommodation Without Assimilation: Sikh Immigrants in an American High School*. Ithaca: Cornell University Press.

Glazer, Nathan. 1993. "Is Assimilation Dead?" *The Annals* 530 (Nov.): 122–36.

———. 1975. *Affirmative Discrimination*. New York: Basic.

Glazer, Nathan, and Daniel Patrick Moynihan. 1970. *Beyond the Melting Pot: The Negroes, Puerto Ricans, Jews, Italians, and Irish of New York City*. 1963. Reprint, Cambridge: MIT Press.

Glick Schiller, Nina, Linda Basch, and Cristina Blanc-Szanton. 1992. *Towards a Transnational Perspective on Migration: Race, Class,*

and Ethnicity Reconsidered. New York: New York Academy of
Sciences.

Gordon, Mary. 1989. *The Other Side*. New York: Penguin.

Gordon, Milton. 1964. *Assimilation in American Life*. New York:
Oxford University Press.

Greeley, Andrew. 1971. *Why Can't They Be Like Us?* New York:
Dutton.

Greeley, Andrew, and William McCready. 1975. "The Transmission of
Cultural Heritages: The Case of the Irish and the Italians." In
Ethnicity: Theory and Experience, ed. Nathan Glazer and Daniel
Patrick Moynihan, 209–35. Cambridge: Harvard University Press.

Guest, Avery, and James Weed. 1976. "Ethnic Residential
Segregation: Patterns of Change." *American Journal of Sociology*
81 (Mar.): 1088–1111.

Hacker, Andrew. 1992. *Two Nations: Black and White, Separate,
Hostile, and Unequal*. New York: Ballantine.

Hirschman, Charles. 1983. "America's Melting Pot Reconsidered."
Annual Review of Sociology 9: 397–423.

Kalmijn, Matthijs. 1993. "Trends in Black/White Intermarriage."
Social Forces 72 (Sept.): 119–46.

_____. 1991. "Shifting Boundaries: Trends in Religious and
Educational Homogamy." *American Sociological Review* 56 (Dec.):
786–800.

Kamphoefner, Walter. 1994. "German-American Bilingualism: Cui
Malo? Mother Tongue and Socioeconomic Status among the Second
Generation in 1940." *International Migration Review* 28 (winter):
846–64.

Lal, Barbara Ballis. 1990. *The Romance of Culture in an Urban
Civilization: Robert E. Park on Race and Ethnic Relations in Cities*.
London: Routledge.

Lieberson, Stanley. 1963. *Ethnic Patterns in American Cities*. New
York: Free Press.

Lieberson, Stanley, and Mary Waters. 1988. *From Many Strands:
Ethnic and Racial Groups in Contemporary America*. New York:
Russell Sage Foundation.

Light, Ivan. 1984. "Immigrant and Ethnic Enterprise in North
America." *Ethnic and Racial Studies* 7 (Apr.): 195–216.

Logan, John, and Richard Alba. 1993. "Locational Returns to Human
Capital: Minority Access to Suburban Community Resources."
Demography 30 (May): 243–68.

Logan, John, Richard Alba, and Thomas McNulty. 1994. "Ethnic
Economies in Metropolitan Regions: Miami and Beyond." *Social
Forces* 72 (Mar.): 691–724.

McDermott, Alice. 1992. *At Weddings and Wakes*. New York: Dell.

McKee, James. 1993. *Sociology and the Race Problem: The Failure of a Perspective.* Urbana: University of Illinois Press.

Massey, Douglas. Forthcoming. "The New Immigration and the Meaning of Ethnicity in the United States." In *American Diversity: A Demographic Challenge for the Twenty-first Century,* ed. Stewart Tolnay and Nancy Denton. Albany: SUNY Press.

_____. 1990. "American Apartheid: Segregation and the Making of the Underclass." *American Journal of Sociology* 96 (Sept.): 329–57.

_____. 1985. "Ethnic Residential Segregation: A Theoretical Synthesis and Empirical Review." *Sociology and Social Research* 69: 315–50.

Massey, Douglas, and Nancy Denton. 1993. *American Apartheid: Segregation and the Making of the Underclass.* Cambridge: Harvard University Press.

Massey, Douglas, and Mitchell Eggers. 1990. "The Ecology of Inequality: Minorities and the Concentration of Poverty, 1970–1980." *American Journal of Sociology* 95 (Mar.): 1153–88.

Morawska, Ewa. 1985. *For Bread with Butter: Life-worlds of East Central Europeans in Johnstown, Pennsylvania, 1890–1940.* Cambridge: Cambridge University Press.

Morgan, S. Philip, Susan Watkins, and Douglas Ewbank. 1994. "Generating Americans: Ethnic Differences in Fertility." In *After Ellis Island: Newcomers and Natives in the 1910 Census,* ed. Susan Watkins, 83–124. New York: Russell Sage Foundation.

Myrdal, Gunnar, with the assistance of Richard Sterner and Arnold Rose. 1944. *An American Dilemma: The Negro Problem and Modern Democracy.* New York: Pantheon.

Neidert, Lisa, and Reynolds Farley. 1985. "Assimilation in the United States: An Analysis of Ethnic and Generation Differences in Status and Achievement." *American Sociological Review* 50 (Dec.): 840–50.

Novak, Michael. 1971. *The Rise of the Unmeltable Ethnics.* New York: Macmillan.

Ogbu, John. 1991. "Immigrant and Involuntary Minorities in Comparative Perspective." In *Minority Status and Schooling: A Comparative Study of Immigrant and Involuntary Minorities,* ed. Margaret Gibson and John Ogbu, 3–33. New York: Garland.

Omi, Michael, and Howard Winant. 1994. *Racial Formation in the United States: From the 1960s to the 1990s.* New York: Routledge.

Piore, Michael. 1979. *Birds of Passage: Migrant Labor and Industrial Societies.* Cambridge: Cambridge University Press.

Portes, Alejandro, and Robert Bach. 1985. *Latin Journey: Cuban and Mexican Immigrants in the United States.* Berkeley: University of California Press.

Portes, Alejandro, and Robert Manning. 1986. "The Immigrant Enclave: Theory and Empirical Examples." In *Competitive Ethnic*

Relations, ed. Susan Olzak and Joane Nagel. New York: Academic Press.

Portes, Alejandro, and Ruben Rumbaut. 1990. *Immigrant America: A Portrait*. Berkeley: University of California Press.

Portes, Alejandro, and Min Zhou. 1993. "The New Second Generation: Segmented Assimilation and Its Variants." *The Annals* 530 (Nov.): 74–96.

Roediger, David. 1991. *The Wages of Whiteness: Race and the Making of the American Working Class*. New York: Verso.

Sanders, Jimy, and Victor Nee. 1987. "Limits of Ethnic Solidarity in the Ethnic Enclave." *American Sociological Review* 52 (Dec.): 745–67.

Schlesinger, Arthur, Jr. 1992. *The Disuniting of America: Reflections on a Multicultural Society*. New York: Norton.

Skerry, Peter. 1993. *Mexican Americans: The Ambivalent Minority*. New York: Free Press.

Snipp, Matthew. 1989. *American Indians: The First of This Land*. New York: Russell Sage Foundation.

Steinberg, Stephen. 1989. *The Ethnic Myth: Race, Ethnicity, and Class in America*. Boston: Beacon.

Steinfels, Peter. 1992. "Debating Intermarriage, and Jewish Survival." *New York Times*, 18 Oct., 1, 40.

Stevens, Gillian. 1994. "Immigration, Emigration, Language Acquisition, and the English Language Proficiency of Immigrants in the U.S." In *Immigration and Ethnicity: The Integration of America's Newest Arrivals*, ed. Barry Edmonston and Jeffrey Passel, 163–85. Washington, D.C.: Urban Institute Press.

_____. 1992. "The Social and Demographic Context of Language Use in the United States." *American Sociological Review* 57 (Apr.): 171–85.

Takaki, Ronald. 1993. "Multiculturalism: Battleground or Meeting Ground?" *The Annals* 530 (Nov.): 109–21.

Taylor, Charles. 1992. "The Politics of Recognition." In *Multiculturalism and "The Politics of Recognition,"* ed. Amy Gutmann, 25–103. Princeton: Princeton University Press.

Veltman, Calvin. 1983. *Language Shift in the United States*. Berlin: Mouton.

Wacquant, Loic, and William J. Wilson. 1989. "The Cost of Racial and Class Exclusion in the Inner City." *The Annals* 501 (Jan.): 8–25.

Waters, Mary. 1990. *Ethnic Options: Choosing Identities in America*. Berkeley: University of California Press.

Whyte, William Foote. 1955. *Street Corner Society: The Social Structure of an Italian Slum*. 1943. Reprint, Chicago: University of Chicago Press.

Wilson, William J. 1991. "Studying Inner-City Dislocations: The Challenge of Public Agenda Research." *American Sociological Review* 56 (Feb.): 1–14.

_____. 1987. *The Truly Disadvantaged: The Inner City, the Underclass, and Public Policy.* Chicago: University of Chicago Press.

_____. 1978. *The Declining Significance of Race: Blacks and Changing American Institutions.* Chicago: University of Chicago Press.

Wirth, Louis. 1965. "The Ghetto." In *On Cities and Social Life,* 84–98. 1928. Reprint, Chicago: University of Chicago Press.

Yancey, William, Eugene Ericksen, and Richard Juliani. 1976. "Emergent Ethnicity: A Review and a Reformulation." *American Sociological Review* 41 (June): 391–403.

Chapter 2

Divergent Destinies: Immigration, the Second Generation, and the Rise of Transnational Communities*

Alejandro Portes

Contemporary immigration to the United States is seldom associated with the traumas of poverty. This is due not to the absence of objective indicators of poverty, such as low incomes, among recent immigrants but to the low incidence of those social pathologies commonly associated with the domestic underclass (Marks 1991). Instead, the areas where the foreign born concentrate are characterized by a different set of social traits, including the widespread use of languages other than English, great diversity in terms of both national origins and socioeconomic backgrounds, the large and semiopen presence of unauthorized aliens, and the rise of vibrant business enclaves. The research literature on immigration has focused on these and related topics rather than on the issues that most concern students of domestic poverty. Indeed, when the two literatures come together, it is commonly in the form of comparisons that

* I thank the project coordinators and participants of the German-American Project on Immigration and Refugees, in particular Peter H. Schuck, Gerald Neuman, Richard D. Alba, and Nathan Glazer for their comments and suggestions on earlier versions.

Notes for this chapter begin on page 53.

point to the relative progress of immigrants relative to native-born minorities despite initial disadvantages, such as lack of English knowledge and unfamiliarity with the host culture. These comparisons are notable because immigrants must often endure conditions every bit as harsh, if not worse, than those facing the domestic poor. The difference is that immigrants' poverty is embedded in a social context that makes it appear less hopeless and more transitory than the kind afflicting the native born. In the pages that follow, after an overview of the characteristics of contemporary immigration, I review some of the reasons for this contrast as well as the relative accuracy of these comparisons.

Immigration Today[1]

In 1990 the United States admitted 1,536,483 foreigners for legal permanent residence. This is the single largest annual total in the United States in the twentieth century, exceeding by 240,000 the total for the preceding record year of 1907 (INS 1991). The 1990 figure is an inflated indicator of new arrivals, however, since it is dominated by legalizations of formerly unauthorized aliens, as mandated by the 1986 Immigration Reform and control Act (IRCA).

Even after discounting the new legalizations, immigration has continued to climb steadily, reaching 656,111 in 1990, a 15 percent increase over the figure five years earlier. For the decade, and dis-counting legalizations, legal immigration added almost 6 million newcomers to the U.S. population, a total second only to the period from 1901 to 10 (INS 1991). To this figure must be added the unauthorized immigrant population. Although the legalization program of IRCA reduced that population, the deterrents built into this law for preventing new illegal entries have proven inef-fective, leading to a rebound in the unauthorized inflow.

A careful perusal of the figures in table 2.1 brings to light two additional findings. First, proportionally the most immigration, in particular unauthorized immigration to the United States, is from Mexico. That country alone accounted for over one-fifth of legal immigrants, three-fourths of legalization applicants, and over 90

Table 2.1 Sources of Immigration to the United States, 1981–1990

Country	Legal Permanent Residents, 1981–90[1] N(000s)	%	Legalization Applicants, 1988–90[2] N(000s)	%	Deportable Aliens, 1990[3] N(000s)	%	Refugees 1981–90[4] N(000s)	%
Mexico	1,656	22.6	2,268	74.7	1,092	93.3		
Philippines	549	7.5	29	1.0				
China/Taiwan	347	4.7						
South Korea	334	4.6						
Vietnam	281	3.8					324	32.0
Dominican Republic	252	3.4	28	1.0	6	0.5		
India	251	3.4	22	0.7				
El Salvador	214	2.9	168	5.5	17	1.4		
Jamaica	208	2.8						
United Kingdom	159	2.2						
Canada	156	2.1			6	0.5		
Cuba	145	2.0 (62.0)[5]					113	11.1
Guatemala			71	2.3	10	0.8 (96.5)[5]		
Haiti			59	1.9				
Colombia			35	1.2				
Pakistan			22	0.7				
Peru			20	0.7 (89.7)[5]				
Laos							143	14.1
Cambodia							114	11.2
Soviet Union							72	7.1
Iran							47	4.6 (80.1)[5]
TOTAL[6]	7,338	100.0	3,035	100.0	1,170	100.0	1,013	100.0

1. Includes aliens legalized under IRCA.
2. Includes applicants under both the regular legalization program and the Special Agricultural Workers (SAW) program. As of 12 May 1991, 94.4 percent of regular applicants and 93.1 percent of SAW applicants who had received a final decision had been approved for legal residence.
3. These are workload figures and not persons since the same individual can be apprehended more than once.
4. Refugees and asylees granted lawful permanent resident status.
5. The figure in parentheses is the total of percentages listed in the column thus far.
6. Totals are for all countries, not just those specifically listed in the table.
Source: U.S. Immigration and Naturalization Service (1991)

percent of apprehended aliens during the last decade.[2] Second, every country sending large numbers of immigrants or refugees has been closely entangled with the United States at some point during its recent history, each having been subject to extensive U.S. political and economic influence during that period. Although this is not the place to develop this argument in detail, a brief review of the history of the top five countries sending legal immigrants (Mexico, the Philippines, China/Taiwan, South Korea, and Vietnam); the top two senders of unauthorized immigrants (Mexico and El Salvador); and the four main sources of refugees (Vietnam, Laos, Cambodia, and Cuba) will support this conclusion.[3]

Table 2.2 States and Cities of Preferred Destination of Legal Immigrants

States of Destination, 1980–90	N	%	Metropolitan Areas of Destination, 1990	N	%
California	2,331,000	35	Los Angeles-Long Beach	375,000	24
New York	959,000	14	New York	164,000	11
Texas	595,000	9	Chicago	73,000	5
Florida	440,000	7	Anaheim-Santa Ana	65,000	4
Illinois	401,000	6	Houston	58,000	4
New Jersey	266,000	4	Miami-Hialeah	38,000	3
Others	1,759,000	26	San Diego	37,000	2
			Riverside-San Bernardino	36,000	2
			Washington, D.C.	33,000	2
			San Francisco	29,000	2
			Dallas	29,000	2
			San Jose	26,000	2
			Others	491,000	32
			Nonmetropolitan areas	82,000	5

Sources: Fix and Passel 1991, 6–7; INS 1991, 82.

Just as the geographical origins of contemporary immigration are highly concentrated, so are its areas of destination. As during the turn of the century, immigrants today are overwhelmingly urban-bound, going to key metropolitan areas in a few states. As shown in table 2.2, the states and cities of destination of present-day immigrants differ, however, from the predominantly northeastern destinations of turn-of-the-century arrivals. California is by far the preferred state, and, within it, Los Angeles-Long Beach is overwhelmingly the most favored metropolis. In 1990 the 24 percent of legal immigrants intending to reside in Los Angeles exceeded the number going to any state other than California itself. Los Angeles also received more immigrants during that year than the next four most popular metropolitan destinations combined. Although the predominance of Los Angeles is somewhat exaggerated in 1990 because of the residential preferences of the newly legalized, figures for this year are representative of a trend observed during the entire decade. IRCA legalization brought into the open the absolute dominance of southern California and its displacement of New York as the prime destination of contemporary immigration, both legal and unauthorized.

As seen in table 2.2, just six states, including California, accounted for three-fourths of immigrant destinations during the 1980s, and just twelve cities, including Los Angeles, accommodated 60 percent. Past studies also show that individual immigrant nationalities tend to select different places of destination,

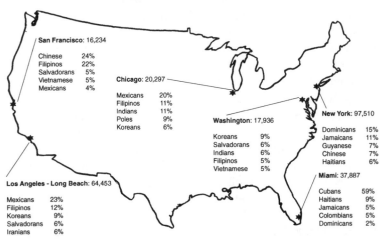

Figure 2.1 Composition of Immigrant Flows to Six Major Metropolitan Destinations, 1987

Note: Chinese include immigrants from mainland China only.
Source: U.S. Immigration and Naturalization Service 1987, table 16.

giving to each receiving city a different ethnic mix. This is illustrated in figure 2.1, which presents the composition of inflows going to the six major metropolitan destinations in 1987, the year before the IRCA legalization program started. Los Angeles-bound immigration is dominated by Mexicans, Filipinos, and Koreans; New York primarily receives flows from the Caribbean, as does Miami, where Cubans are dominant. Appropriately, given its midcountry location, Chicago is the most diverse of the major destinations, receiving large inflows from three continents.

By 1990 the foreign-born population of the United States stood at approximately 20 million, or 8 percent of the total. This is the largest absolute number of immigrants living in the United States ever. The previous peak of 14 million, recorded in the 1930 census, was surpassed sometime in the 1980s. As a percentage of the total population, however, contemporary immigration does not even come close to the peak years of the 1890s, when one of every seven people living in the country, or 15 percent, was foreign born (Fix and Passel 1991).

The surge of immigration during the last decade has produced two consequences of note. First, it has led to a doubling of the Asian population, to more than 7 million in 1990, and to a 53 percent increase, to 22.4 million, in the number of Hispanics (Rumbaut 1992). Neither group even existed as a statistical category before 1965. Second, immigration prevented serious declines in the population of some of the states where it has concentrated, while contributing to the extraordinary growth of others. An estimated 1 million immigrants to New York State helped compensate for its loss of 1.7 million people during the decade. Similarly, Illinois's 1 million population loss was partially balanced by a net immigration of 400,000. At the other end, rapid growth in Florida and California was fueled, in part, by the 439,000 immigrants going to the former and 2.33 million to the latter (Fix and Passel 1991).

Long-Term Determinants of Immigration[4]

Diversity in the modes of incorporation of contemporary immigrants takes place within a political economic framework that underlies the movement's fundamental continuity with earlier migrant waves. The countless literary sagas of immigration portray it as the journey of people struggling to leave behind political oppression and destitution and seeking to rebuild their lives in Freedom's shores. These stories reflect accurately many individual experiences, but they invert the actual causal sequence underlying U.S.-bound migrations. While individual motivations are undoubtedly important, a political economy analysis shows that what ultimately drives the process is not the dreams and needs of immigrants but the interests and plans of their prospective employers. Although geopolitical considerations have played a role in granting certain foreign groups access to U.S. territory, the fundamental reason for sustained immigration has been the labor needs of the economy (Piore 1979; Portes 1978; Rosenblum 1973).

As early as the 1830s, U.S. migration agents were sent to Ireland and the Continent to apprise people of "the better meals and higher wages" available for work in the Hudson and other canal companies (Lebergott 1964, 39). Similarly, labor migration from Mexico was initiated by recruiters sent by railroad companies into the interior of that country (Piore 1979, 23–24). Employer associations succeeded in keeping the immigration door open until World War I. When the war and rising nativist opposition prevented the continuation of European immigration during the 1920s, growers and industrialists resorted to three alternative sources of unskilled labor. First, the Mexican labor inflow was maintained and expanded. In addition, paid recruiters were sent to the island of Puerto Rico, and Puerto Rican peasants started leaving by the thousands to take industrial jobs in the Northeast and Midwest and agricultural jobs as far as the sugar plantations of Hawaii (Nieves-Falcon 1990; Portes and Grosfoguel 1994, 53). Southern blacks, however, represented the core labor pool to replace the dwindling European supply.

To tap this huge domestic reservoir, recruiters were sent to the South to advertise among black sharecroppers and urban artisans the high industrial wages and better living conditions awaiting them in the Northeast and Midwest. By 1916 major firms were already embarking on a policy of replacing European with black labor. During the 1920s important industrial sectors such as meatpacking and coalmining followed suit. The Ford Motor Company proved notably adept at using black workers to avoid unionization at its plants. As Sassen (1980, 3) reports: "Between 1900 and 1910, for every 75 foreigners that were added to the population of the Northeast, there was one black added, a ratio which not only contracted, but actually reversed in the next decade when for every new immigrant, there were three new blacks."

Black migrants continued migrating north well into the 1950s, but by then the labor needs of the economy had changed. Strong labor unions, increasingly tight labor markets, and growing competition from recovering Japanese and European producers led employers to turn once again to foreign sources of labor. Repeated extensions by Congress of the bracero agreement with Mexico kept western agriculture well supplied with low-wage labor. The termination of the agreement in 1964 was accompanied by a congressional proviso exempting employers from any legal liability for hiring illegal immigrants (Barrera 1980; Portes 1978). The surge of unauthorized immigration that followed went beyond the labor needs of agriculture, as Mexicans and other immigrants increasingly trekked to urban areas in search of industrial and service jobs. In 1965 a new immigration law officially reopened the immigration doors, and, as shown earlier, large flows, mostly from the third world, promptly ensued.

By the mid-1980s renewed domestic opposition to immigration, especially to unauthorized immigration, reached a fever pitch. In response, Congress passed the 1986 Immigration Reform and Control Act, a piece of legislation that reflected, with notable clarity, the resilient political power of growers and other employers of immigrant labor. Instead of reducing immigration, the new legislation stimulated it in three ways: first, by legalizing a total of 2.7 million formerly unauthorized immigrants; second, by allowing them to bring in relatives as legal immigrants after a relatively short waiting period; and third, by creating an innovative set of loopholes that allowed the continuation and even expansion of the unauthorized labor flow (Bach and Brill 1991; Papademetriou and Bach 1991; North 1990). The overriding force underlying an open-door immigration policy has thus been employer interests in an abundant source of labor to fuel economic growth and restrain the power of domestic workers. Before World War I, railroad construction, mining, and heavy manufacturing were the growth sectors attracting immigrant workers; today, agriculture and urban personal and business services fill this role. Although skilled and even professional labor has been in short supply at times, and qualified workers have been recruited abroad, immigration has for the most part increased the pool of unskilled labor. Today, needed skilled and professional immigrants generally arrive through the legal entry provisions of the 1965 and 1990 immigration acts, while the bulk of unskilled workers arrives through clandestine channels (Margolis 1994; Zhou 1992; Smith 1992).

Just as different sectors have fueled the demand for immigrant labor over time, different nationalities have responded to the call. Figure 2.2, taken from the most recent report of the U.S. Immigration and Naturalization Service, illustrates the gradual progression of nationalities attracted by the labor requirements of the U.S. economy, from the Germans and Irish in the early nineteenth century to the Mexicans, Filipinos, and Chinese today.

The Human Consequences of Immigration[5]

A political economic perspective clarifies the fundamental underpinnings of the immigration open door, but it commonly neglects an equally important fact, namely, that employers welcome immigrant workers but assume no responsibility for their future well-being or that of their children. Put differently, the benefits flowing from the abundance and low cost of immigrant labor are privatized, but the potential costs tend to be socialized. For example, today's growers and urban service firms employ unskilled third world workers, many of them unauthorized. The economic benefits of this strategy are undeniable (Galarza 1977; Waters 1994), yet the potential maladjustment of these immigrants and their children, who are growing up under conditions of disadvantage, is not seen in the least as the responsibility of employers. The costs of dealing with the subsequent problems are instead shifted toward society at large (Gans 1992).

Figure 2.2 Immigrants Admitted to the United States from the Top Five Countries of Last Residence, 1821–1993

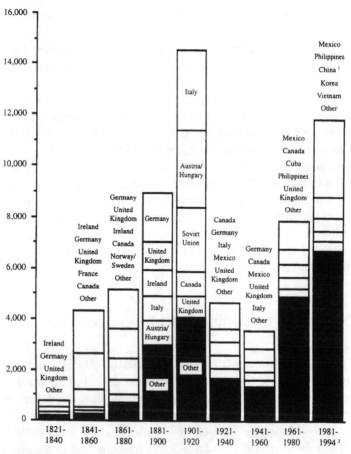

1. China includes mainland China and Taiwan.
2. Thirteen-year period.
Source: U.S. Immigration and Naturalization Service 1994.

Taking a broad historical view, the dominant policy underlying long-term immigration to the United States may thus be summarized as follows: the nation takes care of its immediate labor needs, as defined by powerful economic interests, and lets the future take care of itself. A fortunate combination of circumstances—an expanding economy and the scarcity of labor stemming from a new global conflict, as well as other factors— allowed the European second generation to move steadily up the U.S. economic and social ladders. Their generally successful experiences were subsequently abstracted into academic theories, among them the concept of a linear process of assimilation. Children of Southern blacks and Puerto Rican migrants arriving later in the century were less fortunate. A different combination of circumstances, including widespread racial discrimination and a changing economy, blocked the mobility of these migrants' children and confined many of them to the same inferior jobs held by their parents. The perpetuation of these negative conditions eventually led to an interrelated set of urban pathologies. These experiences gave rise to a different set of academic theories, such as the concepts of a culture of poverty and the urban underclass (Moynihan 1969; Wilson 1987; Gans 1990; Jencks 1992).

The great diversity of contemporary immigration simultaneously conceals the fundamental economic determinants of its arrival and renders its long-term social consequences uncertain. The typology of modes of incorporation described previously represents an attempt to understand the relative advantages and disadvantages with which different groups of immigrants start their adaptation to U.S. society. So far the evidence leans strongly in the direction of what sociologists describe to as a process of cumulative causation, or self-reinforcing effects: early and apparently trivial differentials of advantage evolve into large differences in educational and occupational mobility (Becker 1963; Goffman 1963). In their study of the educational attainment of twenty-five religioethnic groups in the United States, Hirschman and Falcon (1985) found, for example, that generation or time in the country did not make much difference. In other words, children of highly educated immigrants were significantly better educated than fourth- or fifth-generation descendants of less-educated ancestors. The same process of cumulative causation of early modes of incorporation seems to be taking place today among second-generation children, as I discuss in the next section.

The reason why contemporary immigration is not generally discussed in the same context as U.S. domestic poverty should now be clear. Poverty is an attribute of native-born groups, usually descendants of earlier migrants whose upward mobility has been blocked. Immigration since 1965 is a relatively new phenomenon, and its diversity makes it difficult to reconcile with the notion of an impoverished underclass. The obvious next question is whether today's immigrants will follow the path of their European predecessors or that of subsequent black and Puerto Rican migrants. The proper focus for attempting to answer this central question is not the immigrant or first generation but the second. Indeed, most of the concerns pertaining to the social adaptation and economic impact of today's wave of immigration will not be elucidated by an exclusive concentration on first-generation immigrants.[6]

The New Second Generation[7]

As noted previously, first-generation immigrants are not generally regarded as poor, no matter what their objective situations are, because they are seen as somehow different from domestic minorities. The same is not true of their children who as citizens and full participants in U.S. society are unlikely to use a foreign country as a point of reference or view it as a place to return to. Instead, they will be evaluated and will evaluate themselves by the standards of their new country. Whether they manage to join society's mainstream, following the example of second-generation Europeans, or are blocked from it depends on two sets of forces. The first involves general processes in the U.S. society and economy; the second comprises specific characteristics linked to their parents' mode of incorporation.

Three features of the social contexts encountered by today's newcomers create vulnerability to downward assimilation. The first is prejudice, the second is location, and the third is the absence of mobility ladders. The majority of contemporary immigrants are nonwhite.[8] Although this feature may appear at first glance as an individual characteristic, in reality it is a trait belonging to the receiving society. Prejudice is not intrinsic to a particular skin color or racial type, and, indeed, many immigrants have never experienced it in their native lands. It is the move into a new social environment, marked by different values and prejudices, that causes physical features to become redefined as a handicap.

The available evidence indicates that children of immigrants are overconcentrated in urban areas and, within them, in central cities. According to census data, 95 percent of children in households with at least one foreign-born parent lived in metropolitan areas in 1990, as compared to 80 percent of children of native-born parents. According to a 1980 estimate, 40 percent of children of immigrants lived in central city areas, as compared to 17 percent of those of native parentage. This overconcentration in the inner city, which is a direct consequence of the lower economic resources of many recent immigrants, has an unexpected consequence: namely, it brings immigrants' offspring into close contact with downtrodden domestic minorities.

During the last third of a century or so, U.S. central cities have become the repository of the children and grandchildren of those earlier migrants who failed to move up the socioeconomic ladder. As seen previously, this failure was, to a large extent, the direct consequence of outside discrimination coupled with changing requirements in the U.S. labor market. But, regardless of the reasons, the end product was to foster an adversarial outlook toward the white mainstream among descendants of earlier immigrants and domestic migrants caught in underprivileged situations (Burgois 1991; Ogbu 1987; Rumbaut 1990). Holders of this outlook can exercise a powerful influence on newly arrived youth by virtue of their numbers and native-born status.

The aftermath of the blocked mobility of earlier migrant waves thus becomes part of the social milieu with which new immigrants and their children have to contend. The encounter between native minority youth and immigrant children mainly takes place in the urban public schools that both groups attend. The confrontation with the culture of the inner city places second-generation youth in a forced-choice dilemma: to remain loyal to their parents' outlook and mobility aspirations means to face social ostracism and attacks in school; to become "American" often means adopting the cultural outlook of the underclass and thus abandoning any hope for upward mobility based on individual achievement (Matute-Bianchi 1986; Suarez-Orozco 1987; Fernández-Kelly 1995).

The third source of structural vulnerability is changes in labor market opportunities. Fifty years ago, the United States was the premier industrial power in the world, and its diversified industrial labor requirements offered to second-generation youth the opportunity to move up gradually through skilled occupations while remaining part of the working class. Such opportunities have increasingly disappeared in recent years as a result of rapid global industrial restructuring. This process has left entrants to the U.S. labor force confronting a widening gap between the minimally paid jobs that immigrants commonly accept and the high-tech and professional occupations requiring college degrees that native elites occupy (Sassen 1991; Harrison and Bluestone 1988).

The new "hourglass" economy created by industrial downsizing and restructuring means that new labor force entrants, including second-generation youth, must negotiate a narrow bottleneck to occupations requiring advanced training if their careers are to keep pace with middle-class aspirations. This gives rise to a race between the acquisition of U.S. consumption expectations by children of immigrants and their ability to attain them.[9] Clearly, this third structural vulnerability interacts with the other two, as racial prejudice creates additional obstacles to traversing the narrow path to economic success and as the inner-city message that education does not pay for people of color discourages the effort even further.

The Construction of Transnational Communities[10]

There are, however, important exceptions to the confinement of immigrants to dead-end occupations and of their children to a growing "rainbow" underclass. One variant comes in the form of a set of grassroots economic initiatives that only recently have drawn the attention of social scientists. For example, there exist today in the Dominican Republic literally hundreds of small and medium enterprises founded and operated by former immigrants to the United States. They include small factories, commercial establishments of different types, and financial agencies. What makes these enterprises transnational is not only that they are created by former immigrants but that they depend for their existence on continuing ties to the United States. A study of 113 such firms that Luis Guarnizo and I conducted in the late 1980s found that their mean initial capital investment was only $12,000, but that approximately half continued to receive periodic capital transfers from abroad, averaging $5,400 each. Moneys were remitted by kin and friends who remained in the United States but were partners or co-owners of the firms. In addition to capital, many firms received transfers in kind, producer goods, or commodities for sale (Portes and Guarnizo 1991, 16).

In the course of fieldwork for this study, we found a second mechanism for capital replenishment: namely, owners' periodic trips abroad to encourage new potential immigrant investors. Such promotions may take place directly, through existing kin and friendship networks, or through the mediation of Dominican-owned financial and real estate agencies in New York City. These trips are also used by factory owners and managers to sell abroad part of their production. Proprietors of small garment firms, for example, regularly travel to Puerto Rico, Miami, and New York to sell their wares. On their way back to the Dominican Republic, the informal exporters fill their empty suitcases with inputs needed for business, such as garment designs, fabrics, and needles.

To the untrained eye, these loaded-down international travelers appear to be common migrants visiting and bearing gifts for their relatives back home. In reality, they are engaged in a growing form of transnational informal trade. The information requirements for this traffic are invariably transmitted through kin and friendship networks spanning the distance between places of origin and destination. By the same token, it is clear that the men and women who operate these firms are not return immigrants in the traditional sense of the term. Instead, they make use of their time abroad to build a base of property, bank accounts, and business contacts from which to organize their returns home. The result is not a final departure from the United States but rather a cyclical back-and-forth movement through which the transnational entrepreneur makes use of differential economic opportunities spread across both countries (Portes and Guarnizo 1991, 21–22).

A similar story, but with a unique cultural twist, is told by David Kyle (1994) in his study of the Otavalan indigenous community in the highlands of Ecuador. Traditionally, the region of Otavalo has specialized in the production and marketing of clothing, developing and adapting new production skills since the colonial period under Spain. During the last quarter of a century or so, Otavalans have taken to traveling abroad to market their colorful wares in major cities of Europe and North America. By so doing, they appropriate the exchange value pocketed elsewhere by middlemen between third world indigenous producers and final consumers. After years of traveling abroad, they have also brought home a wealth of novelties from the advanced countries, including foreign wives. In the streets of Otavalo, it is not uncommon to meet white European women attired in traditional indigenous dress, the spouses of transnational traders who brought them back from their long-distance journeys.

During the same period, semipermanent Otavalan enclaves began to appear abroad. Their distinct feature is that their members do not make their livings from wage labor or even local self-employment but from the sale of goods brought from Ecuador. They maintain constant communication with their home town in order to replenish supplies, monitor their *telares* (garment shops), and buy land. The back-and-forth movement required by this trade has turned Otavalans into a common sight, not only at the Quito airport but also in street fairs in New York, Paris, Amsterdam, and other large cities. According to Kyle, Otavalans have even discovered the commercial value of their folklore, and groups of performers have fanned throughout the streets of first world cities in recent years.

The sale of colorful ponchos and other woolens, accompanied by the plaintive notes of the *quena* flute, have been quite profitable. The economic success of these indigenous migrants is evident in their near-universal refusal to accept wage labor abroad and in the evident prosperity of their town. Otavalo is quite different in this respect from other regions in the Andean highlands. Its indigenous entrepreneurs and returned migrants form a good portion of the local upper stratum, reversing the traditional pattern of dominance by white and mestizo elites.

Another variant involves considerably greater economic power. The growth of Asian communities in several U.S. cities has created opportunities for moneyed entrepreneurs from Taiwan, Hong Kong, and South Korea to invest profitably in the United States and, in the process, become themselves part of the transnational community. Smith and Zhou (1995) explain, for example, how the rapid growth of Chinese home ownership in the New York suburb of Flushing has been largely financed by new Chinese banks established with Taiwanese and Hong Kong capital. The rapidly growing Chinese population in Flushing and adjacent cities in the borough of Queens is very motivated to acquire their own homes but lacks the knowledge of English and credentials to seek credit from mainstream institutions. To meet the burgeoning demand for housing loans processed in the immigrants' own language, local entrepreneurs went to Taiwan and Hong Kong to pool capital for new banks, and new investors came to the United States bearing the necessary resources. As a result, Chinese-owned banks in Flushing proliferated. Although small by conventional standards, they serve simultaneously the economic interests of the immigrant community and those of overseas investors.

Three thousand miles to the west, the city of Monterey Park, California, has been transformed into the "first suburban Chinatown" largely by the activities of well-heeled newcomers (Fong 1994). Many Taiwanese and Hong Kong entrepreneurs established businesses in the area less for immediate profit than as a hedge against political instability and the threat of a Chinese communist takeover. Opening a new business in the United States facilitates obtaining permanent residence permits, and many owners bring their families along to live in Monterey Park, while they themselves continue to commute across the Pacific.

The activities of these "astronauts," as the entrepreneurs are dubbed locally, adds a new layer of complexity to the transnational community. In this instance, returned immigrants do not invest U.S.-accumulated savings in enterprises at home; rather, immigrants bring new capital to invest in firms in the United States. The birth of a child on U.S. soil guarantees U.S. citizenship and anchors the family definitively in their new setting. As a result of the twin processes of successful investments and citizenship acquisition, Chinese immigrants have moved swiftly from the status of marginal newcomers in Monterey Park to the core of the city's business class (Fong 1994).

I have dwelt on these examples at some length to give credibility to a phenomenon that, when initially described, strains the imagination. A multitude of similar examples could have been used, as illustrated in the pioneering collection by Basch and her collaborators (1994). The central point that these examples illustrate is that, once started, the phenomenon of transnationalization can snowball, expanding not only in numbers but in the qualitative character of its activities. Hence, while the original wave of these activities is economic and their initiators can be properly labeled transnational entrepreneurs, subsequent activities encompass political, social, and cultural pursuits as well.

The end result of this cumulative process is the transformation of the original pioneering economic ventures into transnational communities, characterized by dense networks across space and an increasing number of people who lead dual lives. Members are at least bilingual, move easily between different cultures, frequently maintain homes in two countries, and pursue economic, political, and cultural interests that require a simultaneous presence in both. It bears emphasizing that the onset of this process and its development is nurtured by the forces underlying the process of capitalist globalization. Grassroots transnational entrepreneurship represents the popular underside of this process, allowing common immigrants to avail themselves of some of the technologies and distance-based opportunities for profit long utilized by transnational corporations. Simultaneously, access to such opportunities allows a growing number of immigrants to escape the fate of being trapped in a semipermanent low-wage manual labor force.

Conclusion: The Decade of Immigration[11]

Passage of the 1990 Immigration Act and the fading deterrent capacity of the 1986 IRCA indicate that the last decade of the century will surpass the first's record number of new immigrants. Despite restrictionist voices, heard with increasing persistence during the 1980s and 1990s, the sense of the U.S. Congress and administration until recently has been that the effects of immigration on society and the economy are mostly benign. In signing the inclusionary 1990 immigration bill, President Bush declared that it would be "good for families, good for business, good for crime fighting, and good for America."[12] Indeed, the bill appeared to respond to objections to immigration raised by different constituencies by *increasing* the number of immigrants said to be missing from the pre-1990 inflow without reducing earlier categories.

The 1990s will indeed be this century's decade of immigration. A number of cities are slated to repeat the experiences of the 1910s, when half or more of the urban population was foreign born or of foreign parentage. This massive inflow will be diverse, but not along the national lines explicitly promoted by the diversity provision of the 1990 act, which sought to stimulate anew European immigration. Despite it, Mexico, Asia, and the Caribbean will continue as the dominant sources of immigration. Diversity will lie in the modes of entry of new immigrants and their modes of incorporation in U.S. society. Based on this analysis, it is possible to project a growing number of communities of immigrant entrepreneurs prospering alongside a large number of poorly educated immigrants filling menial jobs and clustered in impoverished inner-city neighborhoods. Unauthorized immigrants from Mexico and Central America, as well as sizable groups of earlier refugees and would-be asylees will be in the latter category.

The social and economic adaptation of those immigrants at the bottom of the labor market will not follow the path commonly portrayed in descriptions of the assimilation process. Instead, it will be far more problematic. Fifty years ago, the dilemma of Italian-American youngsters, according to studies by Irving Child (1943), consisted of assimilating into the U.S.

mainstream, sacrificing along the way their parents' cultural heritage, or of taking refuge in the ethnic community against the challenges of the outside world. In the contemporary context, the options have become less clear. Children of nonwhite unskilled immigrants may not even have the option of gaining access to middle-class white society, no matter how acculturated they become. Joining those native circles to which they do have access may prove to be a ticket to permanent subordination and disadvantage. In this context, remaining ensconced in dense immigrant communities, especially those that have gone transnational in their strategy of economic adaptation, may not be a symptom of escapism but a rational strategy for capitalizing on the moral and material resources that only these communities can make available. This strategy is not, however, a universal option, and the extent to which it is possible depends on the history of each group and its specific profile of vulnerabilities and resources.

It is still too soon to tell what the long-term implications of the rise of transnational communities will be. While in some small peripheral countries such as El Salvador, the Dominican Republic, and Belize they have acquired great importance, in most cases they still represent primarily a channel to implement individual and household economic initiatives. Yet because the process is driven by the very forces promoting global capital accumulation, it may acquire new dimensions and political significance considerably beyond those of the present. The main basis for this expectation is that, when it occurs, transnationalization directly places everyday people, common immigrants, on the same plane as dominant actors engaged in global restructuring. Given sufficient time, those transnational communities that emerge may partially neutralize strategies of accumulation based on wage differentials, information asymmetries, and vast gaps in the power of capital and labor. Whether these dynamics eventuate in a new international solidarity opposite to the capitalist exploitation of these differences or create a new socioeconomic space where national differences become progressively irrelevant, it is clear that the process has the potential to become a central force shaping the future world order.

Notes

1. Based on Portes and Zhou 1995.
2. The apprehension figure in table 1 is for 1990, but the same distributional pattern has existed since the early 1970s. In every year, Mexico has consistently accounted for 90 percent or more of deportable aliens.
3. See Portes and Bach 1985 for a discussion of the historical process underlying this pattern of immigration.
4. Based on Portes and Bach 1985, ch. 2; and Portes 1994.
5. Based on Portes 1994; and Portes and Rumbaut 1990, ch. 3.
6. An obvious example, in addition to the key question of economic mobility, is language. The much-debated issue of the loss of English hegemony and the emergence of language enclaves in certain areas of the country will not be settled by today's immigrants. Loyalty to their home language among the foreign-born is a known and time-honored pattern; the key shift has taken place historically in the second generation, as U.S.-born children abandon parental languages in favor of English. Whether this pattern will reproduce itself today represents the strategic question in this area (Lieberson, Dalto, and Johnston 1975; Portes and Schauffler 1994).
7. Based on Portes and Zhou 1993; Portes and Zhou 1995; and Portes 1995.
8. An estimated 54 percent of post-1960 immigrants are either Asians, blacks, or nonwhite Hispanics. White Hispanics are excluded from this figure.
9. This picture is painted in stark terms for the sake of clarity. In reality, the middle of the labor market has not entirely disappeared. Skilled blue-collar jobs have declined in recent years but in 1980 still represented 13 percent of the experienced labor force, or 13.6 million workers. Clerical support occupations not requiring a college degree added another 16.9 percent, or 17.5 million jobs (U.S. Dept. of Commerce 1983a).
10. Based on Portes 1996.
11. Based on Portes and Zhou 1995.
12. *Interpreter Releases* 67 (3 Dec. 1990): 1359, quoted in Fix and Passel 1991, 10.

References

Bach, Robert L., and Howard Brill. 1991. *Impact of IRCA on the U.S. Labor Market and Economy*. Report to the U.S. Department of Labor, Institute for Research on International Labor. Binghamton: State University of New York.

Barrera, Mario. 1980. *Race and Class in the Southwest: A Theory of Racial Inequality*. Notre Dame, Ind.: Notre Dame University Press.

Basch, Linda G., Nina Glick Schiller, and Cristina Blanc-Szanton. 1994. *Nations Unbound: Transnational Projects, Post-colonial Predicaments, and De-territorialized Nation-States*. Langhorne, Pa.: Gordon and Breach.

Becker, Howard. 1963. *Outsiders: Studies in the Sociology of Deviance*. New York: Free Press.

Burgois, Philippe. 1991. "In Search of Respect: The New Service Economy and the Crack Alternative in Spanish Harlem." Paper presented at the conference on Poverty, Immigration, and Urban Marginality in Advanced Societies, Maison Suger, Paris, 10–11 May.

Child, Irving L. 1943. *Italian or American? The Second Generation in Conflict*. New Haven: Yale University Press.

Fernández-Kelly, Maria P. 1995. "Social and Cultural Capital in the Urban Ghetto: Implications for Economic Sociology." In *The Economic Sociology of Immigration, Essays in Networks, Ethnicity, and Entrepreneurship*, ed. A. Portes, 213–47. New York: Russell Sage Foundation.

Fix, Michael, and Jeffrey S. Passel. 1991. "The Door Remains Open: Recent Immigration to the United States and a Preliminary Analysis of the Immigration Act of 1990." Working paper, Urban Institute and the Rand Corporation, Washington, D.C.

Fong, Timothy P. 1994. *The First Suburban Chinatown: The Remaking of Monterey Park, California*. Philadelphia: Temple University Press.

Galarza, Ernesto. 1977. *Farm Workers and Agribusiness in California, 1947–1960*. Notre Dame, Ind.: Notre Dame University Press.

Gans, Herbert J. 1992. "Second Generation Decline: Scenarios for the Economic and Ethnic Futures of Post-1965 American Immigrants." *Ethnic and Racial Studies* 15 (Apr.): 173–92.

_____. 1990. "Deconstructing the Underclass." *APA Journal* 56 (summer): 1–7.

Goffman, Erving. 1963. *Stigma: Notes on the Management of Spoiled Identity*. Englewood Cliffs, N.J.: Prentice-Hall.

Harrison, Bennett, and Barry Bluestone. 1988. *The Great U-Turn*. New York: Basic Books.

Hirschman, Charles, and Luis Falcon. 1985. "The Educational Attainment of Religio-Ethnic Groups in the United States." *Research in Sociology of Education and Socialization* 5: 83–120.

Jencks, Christopher. 1992. *Rethinking Social Policy: Race, Poverty, and the Underclass*. Cambridge: Harvard University Press.

Kyle, David. 1994. "The Transnational Peasant: The Social Structures of Economic Migration from the Ecuadoran Andes." Ph.D. diss., Johns Hopkins University, Baltimore, Md.

Lebergott, Stanley. 1964. *Manpower in Economic Growth: The American Record since 1800*. New York: McGraw-Hill.

Lieberson, Stanley, Guy Dalto, and Mary Ellen Johnston. 1975. "The Course of Mother Tongue Diversity in Nations." *American Journal of Sociology* 81 (July): 34–61.

Margolis, Maxine L. 1994. *Little Brazil*. Princeton, N.J.: Princeton University Press.

Marks, Carole. 1991. "The Urban Underclass." *Annual Review of Sociology* 17: 445–66.

Matute-Bianchi, Maria Eugenia. 1986. "Ethnic Identities and Patterns of School Success and Failure among Mexican-Descent and Japanese-American Students in a California High School." *American Journal of Education* 95 (Nov.): 233–55.

Moynihan, Daniel P. 1969. *Maximum Feasible Misunderstanding*. New York: Random House.

Nieves-Falcón, Luis. 1990. "Migration and Development: The Case of Puerto Rico." Economic Development Working Paper no. 18, Woodrow Wilson Center, Washington, D.C.

North, David. 1990. "Looking Back: Five Aspects of the Legalization Program." Working paper, Program for Research on Immigration Policy, The Urban Institute and the Rand Corporation, Washington, D.C.

Ogbu, John U. 1987. "Variability in Minority School Performance: A Problem in Search of an Explanation." *Anthropology of Education Quarterly* 18 (Dec.): 312–34.

Papademetriou, Demetrios G., and Robert L. Bach. 1991. *Employer Sanctions and U.S. Labor Markets: First Report*. Washington, D.C.: Bureau of International Labor Affairs, U.S. Department of Labor.

Piore, Michael. 1979. *Birds of Passage*. New York: Cambridge University Press.

Portes, Alejandro. 1996. "Transnational Communities: Their Emergence and Significance in the Contemporary World-System." In *Latin America in the Word-Economy*, ed. W. A. Smith and R. P. Korzeniewicz, 151-68. Westport, Conn.: Greenwood Press.

_____. 1995. "Children of Immigrants: Segmented Assimilation and its Determinants." In *The Economic Sociology of Immigration: Essays on Networks, Ethnicity, and Entrepreneurship*, ed. A. Portes, 248–80. New York: Russell Sage Foundation.

_____. 1994. "Immigration and Its Aftermath." *International Migration Review* 28 (winter): 632–39.

_____. 1978. "Migration and Underdevelopment." *Politics and Society* 8: 1–48.

Portes, Alejandro, and Robert L. Bach. 1985. *Latin Journey: Cuban and Mexican Immigrants in the United States*. Berkeley: University of California Press.

Portes, Alejandro, and Ramon Grosfoguel. 1994. "Caribbean Diasporas: Migration and the Emergence of Ethnic Communities in the U.S. Mainland." *Annals of the American Academy of Political and Social Sciences*, no. 533: 48–69.

Portes, Alejandro, and Luis E. Guarnizo. 1991. "Tropical Capitalists: U.S.-Bound Immigration and Small Enterprise Development in the Dominican Republic." In *Migration, Remittances, and Small Business Development: Mexico and Caribbean Basin Countries*, ed. S. Díaz-Briquets and S. Weintraub, 101–31. Boulder, Colo.: Westview.

Portes, Alejandro, and Rubén G. Rumbaut. 1990. *Immigrant America: A Portrait*. Berkeley: University of California Press.

Portes, Alejandro, and Richard Schauffler. 1994. "Language and the Second Generation: Bilingualism Yesterday and Today." *International Migration Review* 28 (winter): 640–61.

Portes, Alejandro, and Min Zhou. 1995. "Divergent Destinies: Immigration, Poverty, and Entrepreneurship in the United States." In *Poverty, Inequality, and the Future of Social Policy*, ed. K. McFate, B. Lawson, and W. J. Wilson, 489–520. New York: Russell Sage Foundation.

_____. 1993. "The New Second Generation: Segmented Assimilation and Its Variants among Post-1965 Immigrant Youth." *Annals of the American Academy of Political and Social Sciences*, no. 530: 74–96.

Rosenblum, Gerald. 1973. *Immigrant Workers: Their Impact on American Radicalism*. New York: Basic.

Rumbaut, Rubén G. 1992. "The Americans: Latin American and Caribbean Peoples in the United States." In *The Americas: New Interpretive Essays*, ed. A. Stepan, 275–307. New York: Oxford University Press.

_____. 1990. "Immigrant Students in California Public Schools: A Summary of Current Knowledge." Report no. 11, Center for Research on Effective Schooling for Disadvantaged Children, Johns Hopkins University, Baltimore, Md., Aug.

Sassen, Saskia. 1991. *The Global City*. Princeton, N.J.: Princeton University Press.

_____. 1980. "Immigrant and Minority Workers in the Organization of the Labor Process." *Journal of Ethnic Studies* (spring): 1–34.

Smith, Christopher, and Min Zhou. 1995. "Flushing: Capital and Community in a Transnational Neighborhood." Russell Sage Foundation, New York. Photocopy.

Smith, Robert. 1992. "New York in Mixteca: Mixteca in New York." *NACLA Report on the Americas* 26, no. 1.

Suarez-Orozco, Marcelo M. 1987. "Towards a Psychosocial Understanding of Hispanic Adaptation to American Schooling." In *Success or Failure? Learning and the Languages of Minority Students*, ed. H. T. Trueba, 156–68. New York: Newbury House.

U.S. Department of Commerce, Bureau of the Census. 1983a. *Census of Population and Housing, 1980: Public Use Microdata Samples A (MRDF)*. Washington, D.C.: U.S. Department of Commerce.

_____. 1983b. *General Social and Economic Characteristics: Florida*. Washington, D.C.: U.S. Government Printing Office.

U.S. Immigration and Naturalization Service. 1994. *Statistical Yearbook of the Immigration and Naturalization Service*. Washington, D.C.: U.S. Government Printing Office.

_____. 1991. *Statistical Yearbook of the Immigration and Naturalization Service*. Washington, D.C.: U.S. Government Printing Office.

_____. 1987. *Statistical Yearbook of the Immigration and Naturalization Service*. Washington, D.C.: U.S. Government Printing Office.

Waters, Mary. 1994. "West Indian Immigrants, African Americans, and Whites in the Workplace: Different Perspectives on American Race Relations." Paper presented at the meetings of the American Sociological Association, Los Angeles, Aug.

Wilson, William J. 1987. *The Truly Disadvantaged: The Inner-City, the Underclass, and Public Policy*. Chicago: University of Chicago Press.

Zhou, Min. 1992. *New York's Chinatown: The Socioeconomic Potential of an Urban Enclave*. Philadelphia: Temple University Press.

Chapter 3

Governmental and Nongovernmental Roles in the Absorption of Immigrants in the United States

Nathan Glazer

The Overall Context of Immigrant Policy

U.S. policy regarding immigration and immigrants falls naturally into two parts: policies regarding who may enter the United States and policies regarding those who have entered. This paper deals with the latter category. Whereas the former is relatively easy to study, because one level of government—the federal—has full control of immigration policy, through Congress, the executive departments, and the federal courts, the latter is a more difficult matter to study. There is no centralized source for immigrant policy. Wendy Zimmermann and Michael Fix write, "While immigration policy is almost exclusively the responsibility of the federal government, immigrant policy has fallen largely to the states" (1994b, 287).

It is true the federal government plays a very small role in "immigrant policy," but that does not mean we can discover any common or coherent "immigrant policy" in the states and in the

---

Notes for this chapter begin on page 80.

other levels of government (city, county, school, etc.) that determine many of the conditions under which Americans live and work and study and under which immigrants adapt to life in the United States. Indeed, the settlement, adaptation, and progress, or lack of it, of immigrants is largely, in the U.S. context, up to them, the immigrants themselves. When we consider the course of immigrant adaptation in the United States and the degree to which immigrants assimilate to, or become absorbed into, the U.S. population, economy, society, and polity, we cannot resort to any coherent body of policy. There are more or less coherent attitudes, which have undergone change and development over time. To properly understand assimilation, absorption, and adaptation, we must deal with complex social processes, only partially determined by any state role.

Today there is a growing debate, which will affect immigration policy, about whom we shall welcome. There is also a debate, which will affect policy and attitudes at all levels, about how we shall welcome them. We are entering, it seems, a fourth major stage, still somewhat inchoate, in U.S. attitudes toward immigration and immigrants.

In the first stage, in which I will lump together for convenience most of the nineteenth century and the early twentieth century, white immigrants were welcome and expected to be assimilated into U.S. life. Concerning South and East Europeans, who became dominant in the immigrant stream at the end of the nineteenth century, there was much doubt as to their suitability to become Americans, compared to northwestern European (and mostly Protestant) immigrants. Thus their immigration was sharply restricted in the 1920s. As for nonwhites, policy was variable but over time became hostile. When immigration from an Asian country became substantial, sentiment against immigrants rose, and first Chinese and then Japanese immigration was sharply restricted, and all Asians were banned in the 1920s. (Blacks, though able to enter as immigrants, were considered by Americans to belong to a separate and subordinate category. Mexicans, who were not restricted at all, were nevertheless doubtfully considered suitable candidates for full Americanization. Both were for the most part considered inferior castes, at least through the first half of this century.)

In this first phase, immigrants, despite negative attitudes toward many groups—indeed all but northwestern European Protestants—were expected to become Americans and encouraged to do so. Many would argue that they were not only expected but forced to become Americans; some state measures, for example, restricted the use of foreign languages in public education. In World War I, there was suspicion of and restrictions on the foreign language press, fears about the disloyalty of immigrant groups, and a hysterical wave of anti-Germanism, followed by a hysterical wave of anti-Bolshevism, and rising restrictionist sentiment led to the sharp restriction of immigration after World War I.

Then ensued a period of forty years, from 1924 to 1965, of greatly reduced immigration, during which only those from northern and western Europe and the Western Hemisphere could enter easily. During World War II, in contrast to World War I, there was almost no fear over the unassimilability of immigrants. Despite the fact the United States was at war with Germany and Italy, Germans and Italians were considered full citizens and suffered no limitation. The only immigrant group that fell under suspicion on grounds of possible disloyalty was the Japanese. After World War II, the ethnic, national, and racial restrictions in immigration policy came under sharp attack. In the post-World War II United States, racist attitudes went into rapid decline. It was inevitable that U.S. attitudes toward South and East Europeans would change: after all, so many Americans were now South and East European immigrants, their children, or their grandchildren, and they were participating fully in U.S. politics.

In 1965 there followed a third phase, in part as a by-product of the civil rights revolution that was transforming the legal and social position of blacks. The United States opened up to the entire world, entering a period during which anyone, regardless of race, language, or national origin, was considered a possible candidate for entry and assimilation. Assimilation then seemed to be the universally accepted objective for immigrants.

It was not long before attitudes toward Americanization and assimilation began to change. These ideals rapidly lost their position as universally desirable objectives for immigrants, expected and hoped for by immigrants and natives alike. There were many reasons for this change. Many blacks turned against the color-blind and assimilationist objectives for which they had previously fought. This affected some intellectuals and political leaders among Mexican-Americans.

The immigration legislation of 1965 favored close relatives of citizens or permanent residents as immigrants. Its intention was to make it easier for the relatives of east European and southern European Americans to enter. But political and economic changes in Europe meant that people found it either difficult to emigrate from communist Eastern Europe or no longer wished to emigrate from an increasingly prosperous Italy or Greece, and that pool was rapidly exhausted. Instead, the legislation produced an unintended consequence, as small streams of Asian, Caribbean, and Latin American immigrants rapidly swelled under the family provision.

This change in the ethnic and racial composition of immigration also raised questions in U.S. minds about the likelihood of assimilation. A self-confident assumption that this was the best (and richest) of societies and that immigrants would of course want to assimilate to it in all respects began to change, undermined by the impact of the troubles of the previous thirty years: assassinations, a lost war, ever more effective foreign competition. For many, particularly among the intellectual elites, assimilation and Americanization no longer seemed self-evidently the best thing in the world.[1] These troubles, political, economic, and social, have affected our attitudes toward immigration, and we are now entering a fourth stage in immigration policy history, in which it is very likely there will be some substantial restriction on immigrant entry and some deterioration in law and social policy in the position of the immigrant, legal and illegal.

So in U.S. immigration policy, an early epoch of welcome (for whites) was followed by one of exclusion (of all but some whites) and then by one of welcome for anyone. This is now being succeeded by a new phase, whose outline is still indeterminate. Moreover, a long period during which assimilation and Americanization, hard or soft, were taken for granted as objectives for immigrants is being succeeded by one in which the nation is becoming multicultural, and what that will mean for immigrant absorption and assimilation is still unclear.

The Role of the States and Local Government

Policy refers to the state, or, as we more commonly say in the United States where *state* seems too grand a term (unless it refers to the states of the union), to *government*. When one speaks of "government" or "state" policy in the United States, one is of course aware that the term refers to the federal government, to the fifty state governments, to the innumerable city and county governments and school districts, all of which have independent taxing power and an independent ability to determine some kind of policy affecting immigrants.

It is easiest to study federal policies. There we find only one government, after all. Even so, it is divided into three quite independent branches, each of which might have its own policies in opposition to the others, not to mention the fact that each independent power has many subpowers—the various committees and the two houses of Congress often take different points of view, as do the various federal courts, and even the more unified executive branch has many agencies dealing in some measure with immigrants, such as Justice, Labor, Education, Health and Human Services, each of which might have its own distinctive policies. Beyond state and local government, and most importantly, one must also keep in mind the role of agencies quite independent of government altogether—religious, ethnic, social-service, educational, and many others— that also affect the course of immigrant absorption. But one cannot limit an examination of immigrant absorption to formal governmental and nongovernmental agencies. That would leave out the most important factors affecting immigrant absorption: the interaction of diverse immigrant groups, quite independent of any governmental role, whether encouraging or restrictive, with the U.S. environment, the capacities and attitudes of immigrant groups in dealing with that environment, and the resistance or welcome that various elements of U.S. society present to immigrant efforts.

This entire gamut of factors relevant to understanding immigrant absorption in the United States obviously cannot be addressed in any adequate detail in one paper. Thus, while I will have something to say about policies at the federal level, because on occasion the federal government has taken a role in immigrant settlement, most of my paper deals with policies at the other levels of government, state, city, and school and with some key factors independent of government that affect the fate of immigrants in the United States.

One final preliminary point about government in the United States: the population generally views its operations with a level of respect markedly below that found in Germany, or France, or England. Many factors contribute to this disrespect, in particular the nation's inability to create a civil service possessing the degree of independence from politics and the level of professionality in training and outlook that we find in the civil services in other developed countries. This is undoubtedly one reason that much in the United States takes place independently of government, and most Americans consider that a good thing. The United States, despite the outrage over taxes and the antigovernment mood now prevailing, still collects less in taxes as a percentage of gross domestic product than does any developed European nation. Americans apparently simply want government to do less, for many reasons, primarily their distinctive history. And they balance this on the whole by doing more that is independent of and outside government, including providing services to immigrants.

Nevertheless, governments and their roles are not unimportant, both in the practical measures affecting immigrants that they undertake and in the symbolic attitudes toward immigrants that these measures express. Anyone living in Cambridge, Massachusetts, cannot be unaware of the purely symbolic roles of certain city initiatives on immigration. For example, there the city, churches, and various local groups took measures in the 1980s to welcome illegal immigrants from El Salvador as political refugees, quite independently of (or in opposition to) federal determination of whether or not these individuals qualified for refugee status. (This was also state policy in the liberal Massachusetts of Governor Michael Dukakis, Democratic presidential candidate in 1988.) Today there commonly appears on the Cambridge city ballot a measure to give the right to vote to noncitizen immigrants. If it were to pass, it would perhaps be found to transgress state or federal law or the Constitution; still, its appearance signifies the welcoming posture of a liberal community. This is a purely local phenomenon. Local interventions in many other communities express hostility to immigrants, such as protests against the building of mosques or Hindu temples in suburban neighborhoods or against placing street signs in Korean in a community with many Koreans.

Cambridge's effort to permit noncitizen immigrants to vote may be considered the eccentricity of a university town. (One might find similar or even more distinctive eccentricities if one explored developments in Madison, Wisconsin, or Ann Arbor, Michigan, or Berkeley, California.) But one should not ignore this independent power of local government to facilitate, inhibit, or otherwise affect the quality of immigrant absorption or assimilation. The high school of the city of Cambridge displays scores of flags from different countries in its lobby. This is meant to serve as a welcome to the students of diverse backgrounds, many immigrant, a good number of whom are undoubtedly illegal immigrants, who are students at the school. This is the local policy, the policy of the high school and the school department of Cambridge and of the city of Cambridge, expressing the generally tolerant view of its inhabitants. Local or not, however, it reflects an orientation that one must consider in viewing the gamut of influences affecting immigrant absorption. What would it mean, for example, if the high school displayed instead only the American flag (which is undoubtedly what it did until the 1970s)? That, of course, presented a different image and reflected different policies. Similarly, the portraits on the walls of thousands of schools changed from depictions of Washington, Jefferson, and Lincoln to those of Martin Luther King and other heroes of minority groups. It was not the presence of immigrants or immigrant sentiment alone that led to this change but rather the civil rights revolution and all the other developments of the 1960s that changed the sentiments of Americans in general. This must have meant something to immigrant schoolgoers of nonwhite racial groups.

Nor are these new policies simply symbolic. What kind of classes are offered to those who do not know English? Are they courses of immersion in classes operating only in English? Is special help offered to aid children in learning English? Are there special classes for immigrant children? Are these offered by teachers speaking the children's native languages? Do these classes send the message that the children must learn English as soon as possible and forget their native tongues or that they must maintain and respect their native languages? Until the 1960s, the first message predominated; more recently, the latter message has become more prominent. It is well known that the very largest immigrant group, the Mexican, was educated in schools that until perhaps the 1970s often forbade the use of Spanish in classrooms and schools. Today the right to education in Spanish and in other foreign languages, for some time and to some degree, is protected by law in many states, required by some federal courts, and funded through a federal appropriation with specific regulations giving a limited right to education in one's native language.

City and school policies are thus important, both in what they communicate and in their practical consequences. The city of New York, for example, had during most of the ages of mass immigration substantial adult education programs to facilitate the learning of English.[2] These public programs have withered over the years, even as mass immigration has swelled, because of the perpetual financial crisis that has affected New York City and New York City public schools. It is not easy to give any overview of just what kind of city programs operate, and with what effect, in the major cities of immigration, although such information may be present in detailed city studies of which I am not aware. The point is simply that such variations exist.

Texas and Massachusetts: The Immigrant Welcome

It is easier to characterize state policies. One interesting study, by Wendy Zimmermann and Michael Fix (1994b, esp. 294–301), demonstrates the variety of state approaches by contrasting immigrant policies in Texas, a major immigrant state, and Massachusetts, which takes in many fewer immigrants but offers a striking contrast to Texas in that it has been the most liberal state in the union for some decades. The differences between the two states are great, in population (17 million in Texas, 6 million in Massachusetts); in the proportion of immigrants, in the categories of immigrants by status, race, and ethnicity; and, perhaps most significant for this comparison, in political culture. Texas is notorious for being one of the least generous states in welfare benefits; Massachusetts is one of the most generous. In foreign policy, Texas is militant and conservative; Massachusetts pacifist and liberal. Texas is stingy in funding public programs; Massachusetts generous. Zimmermann and Fix report that Texas spends $3,242 per capita; Massachusetts 44 percent more, $4,598. Massachusetts's debt per capita is much higher, and its taxes per capita are 41 percent higher (290). Its social services are more extensive and more expensive, as is true generally of the Northeast as compared to the South. The racial and ethnic composition of the two states is very different: Massachusetts is 5 percent black, as against Texas's 12 percent, only 5 percent Hispanic, against 25.5 percent in Texas, and both have only small but rapidly rising populations of Asians, about 2 percent in 1990. Texas, of course, was also a segregated southern state and fought desegregation; Massachusetts was in the forefront of civil rights liberalism. (The differences go all the way back: Massachusetts was also a leader in the movement for the abolition of slavery.) Zimmermann and Fix characterize the "newcomer" populations of the two states, a term they favor in preference to the more inclusive term *immigrant,* as very different. "Newcomers" is a useful category: unlike "immigrants," it excludes most of the older and naturalized immigrant population, who date back to the period when immigration was dominantly European, and includes primarily immigrants of recent decades. A mix of aging Italians, Jews, Greeks, Irishmen, Germans, on the one hand, and younger Latinos, Caribbean blacks, and Asians on the other, while all equally "immigrant" from the point of view of the census, makes for a very heterogeneous category indeed.

Newcomers make up 5 percent of the population of Massachusetts and 8 percent of the population of Texas. But their immigrant statuses are very different: far more of the Massachusetts newcomers are refugees (13 percent, in contrast to 4 percent in Texas); far fewer are undocumented or illegal (12 percent, as against 21 percent); far fewer are in the process of becoming legalized under the provisions of the Immigration Reform and Control Act of 1986 (5 and 27 percent, respectively); and far more are legal permanent residents (70 percent, in comparison to 48 percent) (293). The dominant difference, however, reflected in these differences in immigrant status, is that the Massachusetts newcomers are ethnically and racially diverse—Irish, Russian, Haitian, Jamaican, Dominican, Cambodian, Vietnamese, Latin American from various countries—while the newcomers of Texas are dominantly of one nationality, Mexican, reflecting the presence of the long border with Mexico and the long relations with that country, of which Texas was once a part.

The two states' policies regarding immigrants expressly and affecting immigrants as part of the general population are very different. Governor Michael Dukakis signed an executive order in 1985 that forbade denial of state benefits to any state resident because of citizenship or immigration status, unless this was required by federal law. The undocumented were made eligible for all state programs, including the state's generous General Relief program. Each state agency was required to develop a plan for refugees. For the purpose of conferring benefits, state agencies defined "refugees" more expansively than did federal law: Haitians, Salvadorans, and Guatemalans, who were not refugees under federal law, because they were not deemed to be escaping political or religious persecution, became refugees under Massachusetts regulations. The state and local police were prohibited from cooperating with the Immigration and Naturalization Service. This also reflected Massachusetts's disagreement with the Reagan administration's strong anticommunist policies in Central America, under which those fleeing communist governments gained refugee status much more easily than did those fleeing authoritarian right-wing governments. Some of these policies have become moot in recent years, first, because of the changing international circumstances that brought peace to El Salvador and Nicaragua and, second, because a Republican governor, William Weld, succeeded Michael Dukakis in 1991. Even so, Massachusetts must still be reckoned an immigration-friendly state.

Massachusetts also passed an immigrant impact aid bill that distributed state funds to school districts, community-based organizations, and legal assistance groups to assist them in helping the undocumented prepare asylum applications, as well as in other ways. "Massachusetts had seven special units in its state welfare offices staffed with bilingual/bicultural workers and specifically designed to serve refugees. Texas ... had only one such unit, although it did place individual bilingual/bicultural workers in the welfare offices across the state. In Massachusetts, the Department of Mental health has two offices serving refugees, ... fully funded by the state" (296). Texas has none. Massachusetts provided much more education and training for employment for refugees. Texas emphasized rapid job placement.

Because Massachusetts has higher payment levels and participation rates for welfare programs, including both cash assistance and medical assistance, it received much more federal reimbursement for costs of assistance to refugees: $3,168 per refugee in 1990, against $909 per refugee in Texas. Massachusetts's generous welcome reflected its economic prosperity in the 1980s, as well as its long-standing political liberalism. In 1990, however, it had to respond to the serious economic downturn that it faced in the late 1980s and elected a Republican governor. Many of its welfare programs were cut; simultaneously, the federal government was sharply reducing its refugee aid reimbursements to states, and the period of what Zimmermann and Fix call "extraordinary and visible activism on behalf of immigrants and refugees" began to draw to an end (298–99).

One final difference between the two states: Massachusetts was the first state, in 1971, to require local school districts to provide bilingual education for those who did not speak English. Many other states followed with similar legislation. Legislation that requires some degree of education in the child's native language is generally called "bilingual education," but the Massachusetts law specifically provided that the entire school program be given in the child's native language, as well as "instruction ... in the history and culture of ... the native land of the parents of children of limited English-speaking ability." The law also required some teaching in English but expected children with limited English to spend three years in a program in which they were taught at least in part in their native language (Commonwealth of Massachusetts 1994, 10–11). Texas, too, has a bilingual education law, though not as far-reaching as Massachusetts's. It was also the state in which the question of denying public schooling to undocumented immigrant children arose, leading to a case that reached the Supreme Court. The landmark case of *Plyler v. Doe* did not allow Texas to deny these benefits.

States do differ, but we should not make the distinction too sharp. Nor should we jump to the conclusion that prejudice is the reason for certain anti-immigrant policies. The issue of educating undocumented children did not arise in Texas, as one might think, because prejudiced redneck school boards wanted to punish Mexican children; rather, it arose in school districts that were themselves almost entirely populated by Mexican-Americans and governed by Mexican-Americans, and the amendment to a school finance bill to eliminate state funding for undocumented children was proposed by a Mexican-American legislator who had served as a school superintendent in this almost totally Mexican and Mexican-American area (Guerrero 1984).

If Texas is less welcoming to immigrants than Massachusetts, one should note that in 1995 it seems more welcoming than California, which has passed a state proposition eliminating state benefits to illegal immigrants and sued the federal government for reimbursement for some of the costs of illegal immigration. Its governor campaigned briefly for the Republican nomination for president, and one of the bases for his appeal was his hard line on illegal immigrants.[3] California's resentment of illegal immigration undoubtedly has something to do with its poor economic condition in recent years, as well as the fact that it is the largest recipient of immigrants, legal and illegal. But independently of any forces affecting particular states, a rising national tide of criticism of the scale of immigration, and of the inability to control illegal immigration, may reduce state and regional differences in attitudes to immigration.

As Zimmermann and Fix report, there was some convergence in the early nineties in the immigrant policies of Texas and Massachusetts. In the early nineties, Texas had a liberal Democratic governor while Massachusetts had a fiscally conservative (but otherwise liberal) Republican governor. (Texas in 1994 elected a conservative Republican governor, but he is liberal on immigration.) But the differences from area to area, state to state, will not disappear. While the governor of California, Pete

Wilson, supported a proposition to deny various public benefits to illegal or undocumented immigrants, the governor of New York, Mario Cuomo, praised immigrants: "I love immigrants. Legal, illegal, they are not to be despised" (quoted in Rosenthal 1995, A19). The difference between California and New York is likely to remain even under the Republican governor that succeeded Cuomo in 1994. Differences in political culture have long staying power.

Differences in Adaptation

How much do these differences matter? Do the generous welfare policies of New York and Massachusetts mean that more immigrants flock to these states? Do more extensive social services lead to more rapid adaptation of immigrants, or, alternatively, do they lead to greater dependency? There is much argument about these matters, but a cautious conclusion would be that, yes, substantial welfare benefits do play a role in where immigrants choose to live, even if not a determinative one (jobs and relatives play the principal role), and they may play a role in immigrant dependency.

The rate of welfare dependency among refugees in California, a state with relatively high welfare benefits, has been remarkably high, though other factors must also be involved. "Even after being in the country for five years, about two-thirds of Laotian and Cambodian households in California, as well as over one-third of Vietnamese households, receive public assistance" (Borjas 1993, 42). This high rate of welfare dependency is accompanied by what seem to be, according to other measures (family stability, educational attainment, creation of immigrant business areas), a good level of adaptation.

The issue of refugee dependency in Massachusetts was raised by President John Silber of Boston University, when he was running for governor of Massachusetts against William Weld in 1990. He asserted that Massachusetts had become a "welfare magnet" (Zimmermann and Fix 1994b, 296). He asked rhetorically why there were Cambodian refugees in Massachusetts, of all places. This outburst may have gained him a few votes, but in Massachusetts it probably cost him more. (He lost the election.)

On the question of welfare levels and immigrant settlement, Zimmermann and Fix write: "One would ... expect that variations in benefit levels might promote secondary migration of refugees to states, leading to additional burdens on those states. In fact, throughout the 1980's, substantial internal migration of refugees (from the states in which they settled) to high welfare states took place. In 1986, Massachusetts had a net secondary in-migration of 1,170 refugees, and California had a net secondary migration of 7,886. Texas, with its lower welfare payments, had a net in-migration of 982" (298).

These are small numbers, and they may well understate the welfare effect. But there are, as noted, many other factors that affect movement of refugees from state to state or influence the initial decisions of refugees and other immigrants as to where to settle: the presence of family, opportunities for work, quality of educational opportunities, climate, and the existence of a community of others of the same language and culture are all important. Refugees may also have little capacity to determine where to settle initially. Voluntary agencies selected by the U.S. government arrange for the initial settlement of many if they have no connections in this country.

Cuban refugees initially flocked to Miami and continue to do so, as the rapid creation of a very large Cuban community in Miami provided family and community support for later arrivals, even the poorly qualified Mariel refugees of 1980. (There are also large Cuban settlements in New Jersey, New York, and Massachusetts.) Russian Jewish refugees concentrated in New York and other cities with large Jewish communities, and they were assisted by well-established Jewish agencies. Vietnamese, Cambodian, and Laotian refugees, with no ties initially to any area of the United States and no preexisting ethnic community to relate to, were resettled by voluntary agencies operating with federal funds throughout the nation.[4] Dispersion seemed a good idea at the time, but many left first areas of settlement to concentrate in areas where the climate was more congenial, principally California. The creation of a substantial Vietnamese community in southern California made that the obvious place for later refugees to go. Other refugees from Southeast Asia—namely, Cambodians and Laotians— equally deprived of preexisting ties, found themselves in such

unsuitable areas as the declining industrial towns of Massachusetts. Refugees are least able to choose, and the situation of
Cambodians and Laotians has been among the worst.

Yet even immigrant communities without initial connections
in the United States may be able quite rapidly to establish immigrant niches in the economy, in occupations or businesses in
which they specialize and assist each other and that serve as a
base for economic mobility. For the Koreans, it was initially wigs
and fruit stores, from which they have graduated to upscale groceries (Kim 1981). For the Gujarati Patels of India, it was low-
cost motels. And even so recent a group as the Cambodians,
coming with all the handicaps of refugees, has established a substantial foothold in doughnut shops in California.[5] (How to reconcile a high rate of entry into a retail niche with the high rate
of dependency previously noted is not easy, and I will not
attempt to do so here.)

Explaining Differences in Adaptation

Some of our leading analysts of immigration and immigrants,
Michael Fix, Jeffrey Passel, and Barry Edmonston, emphasize a
tripartite division of immigrants in explaining differences in
adaptation in the United States. The distinction they find significant is that among legal immigrants, illegal or undocumented immigrants, and refugees, "these groups have different
social and economic characteristics, dissimilar countries of origins, and different starting points in their adjustment to the
United States" (Edmonston and Passel 1994, 12). Dividing the
10 million immigrants of the decade of the 1980s into 6 million
legal, 3 million illegal (of whom 2 million were legalized under
IRCA), and 900,000 refugees, they did indeed find many differences among the three groups.

Legal immigrants adapt with the least difficulty and are the
best off by various measures. They come through choice and are
supported by relative or employer sponsorship or by distinctive skills. They are also the best educated of the three groups.
The undocumented, on the other hand, even though they come
through choice, have less support and less opportunity for

unhampered choices in education and work. Refugees, in theory, come without choice, having been forced to leave their countries of residence (although some who formally have refugee status, such as Russian Jews, obviously chose to come, and their situation is closer to that of nonrefugee legal immigrants). It would stand to reason that the adaptation of the three groups would be different. Thus, concerning the apparent decline in the education and income levels of recent immigrants as compared to earlier immigrants, a point that has been emphasized by George Borjas (1990, 1993), Fix and Passel write that such arguments "fail to take into account the fact that U.S. Census data do not differentiate by immigration status. Legal immigrants, refugees and illegal immigrants are all included in U.S. Censuses. But refugees and illegal immigrants have tended to be poorer and less educated on average than other immigrants" (1994).

The overall pattern of immigration to the United States for the past thirty years has shown a bifurcation between groups with relatively low education and few professional skills and groups with relatively high education and substantial occupational and professional skills. The distribution of immigrants by educational attainment is U-shaped, compared to a more bell-shaped distribution of native Americans by education (see Zimmermann and Fix 1994a, 275 [table]). The lesser-educated, the left hook of the U, are predominantly found among Mexican and other Latin groups, though some Latin-American groups are favored with greater educational attainment and more advanced occupational skills, particularly the Cubans. The better educated, the right hook of the U, are to be found primarily among the Asian immigrants, though they, too, include groups with low education and poor occupational skills. (This is true of the tribal Hmong and of the Vietnamese Amerasians, the children of U.S. servicemen and Vietnamese women, raised in Vietnam).

Yet even more significant than the differences among legal, illegal, and refugee immigrants are those among the varied national groups of which the immigrants are a part. Legal, illegal, and refugee immigrants of a given ethnic group will have more in common than do illegals in general or legals in general. That is, the Irish illegal immigrant of Boston has more in common, from the point of view of adaptation and assimilability, with the legal Irish immigrant than with the illegal Mexican or Guatemalan immigrant. Legal immigrants will generally do better, because there are fewer restraints on them, but level of educational attainment and professional qualification will be decisive in affecting adaptation, and these are not very different among the legal and illegal immigrants of the same group. The illegal Irish immigrant in Boston is not very different, in education and job skills, from the legal one, just as the legal Mexican immigrant of California is not very different, in terms of education and job skills, from the illegal one.

Adaptation in the United States seems to be dependent on two factors, aside from and more important than legal, illegal, or refugee status. The first is educational attainment, one of the statistics on immigrants it is relatively easy to get. It seems that education even in a very different country permits one to connect with education in this country for further qualification or to enter, in time, a professional job (nursing, engineering, and the like), and even if language barriers make this difficult, education will give immigrants an advantage in an occupation that seems to need little, such as retail business or fast-food services.[6]

The second factor is harder to specify. Immigrants differ in qualities that are significant for adaptation but difficult to capture or measure. For example, there are great differences among groups in the degree to which they enter small business. The principal reason for entering into small business, which is risky and demands long hours and great commitment, is because other, better, jobs are not available, because of discrimination, language handicaps, and the like: Korean college graduates who open groceries in black neighborhoods would much prefer to do something else in line with their education if they could. But discrimination and language handicaps are not the whole story. We cannot explain the differences in the degree to which groups establish small business simply by the amount of discrimination they meet in the host society and its refusal to credit immigrants' skills or educational qualifications. One must also take into account such factors as a preexisting taste for and experience in business and the presence of means of group support through loans and assistance from relatives.[7] For some groups, such as the Koreans, no easy explanation is available. Koreans are not a group noted for having a taste for small business. It seems that once a niche has been pioneered, others of the group will flow into it, often with experience provided by the pioneers.

A study of self-employment among racial and ethnic groups documents the enormous range of difference in this regard.[8] Against a self-employment rate for all Americans of 11 percent for men and 6 percent for women in 1990, Koreans have the highest self-employment rates: 28 percent for men and 19 percent for women. Chinese and Japanese also show very high rates of self-employment, while Filipinos are low among Asian groups (5 percent for men, 3 percent for women). Hispanic groups have relatively low rates, except for Cubans. The lowest rates for self-employment are among Puerto Ricans (3.6 and 2.3 percent) and African-Americans (4 and 2 percent). These differences hold up even after adjustments "for differences in individual characteristics, such as age, education, and the number of years living in the United States" ("Ethnic Patterns in Self-Employment" 1994, summarizing Fairlie and Meyer 1994).

Immigrant groups differ in a host of qualities, which spread them across the spectrum of possibilities for successful adaptation to U.S. life. What they come with in the form of educational and professional attainment and in the form of something we may call "cultural characteristics," a term we invoke to explain such matters as the great differences in self-employment, are important. At least as important—and undoubtedly related—is how well they and their children do in U.S. schools. Here, as obvious to the naked eye as, say, Korean prominence in small business, is the substantially greater educational achievement of Asian children (again, with variations from group to group and within each group), the substantially poorer record of Hispanic children (again, with the obvious differences across groups, with Cubans markedly more advanced than Mexicans).

We have become accustomed from newspaper accounts to the astonishingly large number of Asian children—and they include refugees as well as the children of legal immigrants— who become school valedictorians only a few years after learning English,[9] win science prizes, flood the specialized high schools, such as New York City's Stuyvesant (more than 50 percent Asian, in an overall school population that is less than

10 percent Asian), and who are disproportionately to be found in the elite and selective colleges. The U.S. school system is regularly and fiercely criticized as failing, but it does not fail with all groups. It manages well enough, it appears, with those who come from families with a strong commitment to education who motivate their children, by whatever means (and, for Asians, this seems to include a great measure of guilt, shame, and obligation), to take advantage of the educational opportunities provided.

Of course, the Asians come with the advantage of higher-than-average levels of education among parents, and this must influence the educational achievement of the children. But when one looks at the scale of Asian children's success in education and the enormous difficulties many must overcome, such as harrowing experiences as refugees, it seems as though something more than that must be involved, just as, in the 1920s and 1930s, factors beyond what one could enter into a regression equation explained the academic success of East European Jewish children.

When we consider Hispanic and Caribbean immigrants, however, the story is quite different. Educational background, or the lack of it, and a pattern of family breakup and out-of-wedlock birth explain a good deal. Recently, sociologists have begun to notice something surprising that calls into question our ordinary assumptions about adaptation to life in the USA. We tend to take it for granted that coming closer to the values and practices of the host society is a good thing for adaptation and remaining distant is a bad thing. In some respects, this is undoubtedly true. It is good for immigrants to learn English, good for their successful adaptation in school and work, good for the society. It is good for them to become citizens and participate in politics. But we have also created in this country circumstances, particularly marked in some communities, such as high rates of family breakup, out-of-wedlock births, and crime, that are best not adapted to. We would hope that immigrant norms would not shift to native levels in these areas and would prefer less Americanization when it comes to them.

To what, then, do new immigrants assimilate? To those aspects of U.S. life where we want assimilation or to those from which we hope they will be protected? Alejandro Portes and

Min Zhou (1993), examining assimilation of various groups in Miami, find a danger that Haitian immigrants may be assimilating to the conditions they find in poor black areas. Haitians insist they are not like the native African Americans they encounter in the poor areas in which they have settled, whom they despise as shiftless and welfare dependent. But their children, alas, may find attractive the street life and culture of their African-American neighbors and so may assimilate to a form of U.S. life that would be disastrous for them. Mary Waters (1994), studying Caribbean immigrants in New York City, who have characteristically done better educationally and occupationally than native African Americans, finds a similar danger for their children.[10]

Here the issue is not, as so much discussion today has it, the dangers immigrants bring but the dangers they confront in creating a sound life for themselves in the United States and in contributing to their new country. There is bound to be increasing discussion of the potential dangers, economic, social, and cultural, brought by a large volume of immigration. These dangers could well be ameliorated by changing our immigration policies to admit more of the highly educated and qualified, fewer of the less educated and the less qualified. (There are moral and ethical issues to be considered in such a policy, but little argument that, from a national interest point of view, it would benefit the country.) Perhaps one danger that we have not sufficiently considered is that we have created in our large immigrant-receiving cities a culture among the low-income population that provides a very poor environment for new immigrants, one that we would not want them to adapt to but to escape.

The argument over immigrant assimilation and adaptation in the United States is framed by two very different orientations: One is shaped by the common history of most immigrant groups in the United States, which has shown over time, one or two or three generations, assimilation to what may be conceived of as a U.S. norm in language, in customs and habits, in educational achievement, and in occupation and income. This general pattern, however, covers a great range of variation. Whether this adaptation took place in two generations or four may not seem so crucial when one looks back over a history of 100 or 150 years of immigration, but it means much to the individual group and to the harmoniousness of its relations with other Americans. This orientation conflicts with the second, which concentrates on the difficulties of adaptation and assimilation, emphasizes differences in language, culture, religion, race, and education between an existing average U.S. norm (a rather mythical construct, itself created out of the different patterns of many groups and classes) and one or another group of immigrants, and raises an alarm as to whether this or that group can be assimilated and should be welcomed. The first orientation has prevailed for thirty years, since the immigration liberalization of 1965 but is now challenged by rising public support for the second (see, e.g., Brimelow 1995; Beck 1996).

The conflict between the two orientations cannot be settled by resorting to history, by insisting that what has happened in the past will happen again, that groups once considered unassimilable have become part of U.S. society and culture and polity and have contributed to making the nation and so new groups, no matter how distant and different, will do the same. Not only do the groups change, but the United States changes, too, and what it accomplished in the past it may not be able to accomplish today: its economic circumstances are different, its culture is different, its politics are different. Concerns and fears arising from these differences are what drive restrictionism today and make it quite different from the restrictionism of the 1920s, which was fuelled by ethnic and religious prejudice. Today the chief fears guiding immigrant restriction are concern over the shaky state and future of the U.S. economy, fears over welfare dependency, and concerns over our new multiculturalism, abetted by the general feeling—evident among many environmentalists—that the country has enough people and more will only lower the quality of life. These current fears may be misguided and may be temporary. But they cannot be dissipated by rewriting U.S. history into a pleasing myth in which all the difficulties and problems involved in creating an immigrant society are obscured and by insisting immigration is not a problem but rather our destiny and our salvation. These matters will have to be debated, and that is what is happening now.

Notes

1. On the fate of assimilation, see Glazer 1993.
2. See, for example, the classic comic account in Rosten 1937.
3. He maintains this hard line as of this writing, in July 1996. See Wilson 1996, where he argues for a disputed provision of immigration legislation that has been under consideration for many months that would allow states to deny education to illegal immigrant children and criticizes Texas's senators (Republicans, as he is) who oppose this provision. Wilson asserts that California spends $1.8 billion a year educating 355,000 illegal immigrant children.
4. One hundred sixty-four agencies assist in the resettlement in the United States of Amerasians (children of U.S. servicemen in Vietnam and Vietnamese women), about 75,000 of whom (this figure includes other family members) have immigrated since 1989 under the provisions of the *Amerasian Homecoming Act* (see U.S. General Accounting Office 1994). After various stages of processing and preparation, in Vietnam and the Philippines, the refugees are placed by the Refugee Data Center "with one of the national resettlement agencies. These nonprofit agencies have cooperative agreements with the Department of State to resettle and assist various refugee groups. Those Amerasians with relatives in the United States are resettled near their relatives with the help of a local affiliate agency. The majority, who do not have relatives in this country, are ... distributed to local affiliate agencies throughout the United States. About two-thirds of the cases are resettled in designated cluster sites across the country. These cluster sites, which total about 55, have been designated by the Department of Health and Human Services as areas that have a sufficient social service network and a core of previously resettled Amerasians. Both of these conditions are viewed as important for the successful resettlement of newly arrived Amerasian families." (4) This has been the pattern for refugee resettlement, insofar as they come in large numbers with no infrastructure in the United States to assist them.
5. See Kaufman 1995. The story notes that there are 69,000 Cambodians in California, and they run at least 2,450 doughnut shops, 80 percent of the total. These shops also provide a market for Cambodians who have moved up to provide equipment, mixes, coffee, and other supplies. Cambodians did not begin to come to the United States until the late 1970s.
6. Many of the Koreans who open small businesses have had higher education in Korea, which is not common among small businessmen and may well give them an advantage over competitors. See Waldinger 1989.
7. For an older and important analysis of these differences among groups see Light 1972. There are many more recent studies, among them Light and Bonacich 1988.
8. Self-employment includes retail business and occupations as independent professionals, so these statistics are not measures of entry into business alone but also reflect the concentration of professional qualifications in some groups, a result of their greater educational attainment. The study also covers native-born as well as immigrants of each ethnic and racial

group, but for the Asian and Hispanic groups immigrants and their children form the larger part of the group.

9. The *Boston Globe* regularly reports on the valedictorians of Boston high schools, public primarily, but including some private ones. Seven of twenty-one valedictorians in 1995 were Vietnamese, Chinese, and Korean. All were born abroad: one had been in the United States three years, one three and a half years, another five years. Three other valedictorians were born abroad, two in the West Indies and one in Greece. See *Boston Globe*, 16 June, 1995, "City" section, 11.

10. Waters's article is reprinted, along with others on second-generation adaptation, in Portes 1996.

References

Beck, Roy. 1996. *The Case Against Immigration*. New York: Norton.

Borjas, George. 1993. "Tired, Poor, on Welfare." *National Review*, 13 Dec., 40–42.

_____. 1990. *Friends or Strangers: The Impact of Immigrants on the U.S. Economy*. New York: Basic.

Brimelow, Peter. 1995. *Alien Nation: Common Sense About America's Immigration Disaster*. New York, Random House.

Commonwealth of Massachusetts. 1994. *Striving for Success: The Education of Bilingual Pupils*. Boston: Commonwealth of Massachusetts, Dec.

Edmonston, Barry, and Jeffrey S. Passel. 1994. "Ethnic Demography: U.S. Immigration and Ethnic Variations." In *Immigration and Ethnicity: The Integration of America's Newest Arrivals*, ed. Barry Edmonston and Jeffrey S. Passel, 1–30. Washington, D.C., Urban Institute Press.

"Ethnic Patterns in Self-Employment." 1994. *The NEBR Digest*, Nov.: 3–4.

Fairlie, Robert, and Bruce Meyer. 1994. "The Ethnic and Racial Character of Self-Employment." NEBR Working Paper No. 4791. Boston: NEBR.

Fix, Michael, and Jeffrey S. Passel. 1994. *Immigration and Immigrants: Setting the Record Straight*. Washington, D.C.: Urban Institute.

Glazer, Nathan. 1993. "Is Assimilation Dead?" *The Annals* 530 (Nov.): 122–36.

Guerrero, Andre L. 1984. "The Presence of Undocumented Mexican Children in Texas: A Challenge to the Public School System." Unpublished student paper, Harvard Graduate School of Education; available in Gutman Library, Harvard Graduate School of Education.

Kaufman, Jonathan. 1995. "How Cambodians Came to Control California Doughnuts." *Wall Street Journal*, 22 Feb., A1, A14.

Kim, Illsoo. 1981. *New Urban Immigrants: The Korean Community in New York*. Princeton, N.J.: Princeton University Press.

Light, Ivan. 1972. *Ethnic Enterprise in America*. Berkeley: University of California Press.

Light, Ivan, and Edna Bonacich. 1988. *Immigrant Entrepreneurs: Koreans in Los Angeles, 1965–1982*. Berkeley: University of California Press.

Portes, Alejandro, ed., 1996. *The New Second Generation*. New York: Russell Sage Foundation.

Portes, Alejandro, and Min Zhou. 1993. "The New Second Generation: Segmented Assimilation and Its Variants." *The Annals* 530 (Nov.): 74–96.

Rosenthal, Abe. 1995. "Working in Tijuana." *New York Times*, 21 Feb., A19.

Rosten, Leo. 1937. *The Education of Hyman Kaplan by Leonard Q. Ross*. New York: Harcourt, Brace.

U.S. General Accounting Office. 1994. *Vietnamese Amerasian Resettlement: Education, Employment, and Family Outcomes in the United States*. Washington, D.C.: U.S. Government Printing Office, Mar.

Waldinger, Roger. 1989. "Structural Opportunity or Ethnic Advantage? Immigrant Business Development in New York." *International Migration Review* 23, no. 1 (spring): 48–73.

Waters, Mary. 1994. "Ethnic and Racial Identities of Second Generation Black Immigrants in New York City." *International Migration Review* 28, no. 4 (winter): 795–820.

Wilson, Pete. 1996. "Piety, But No Help, On Illegal Aliens," *New York Times*, 11 July, A23.

Zimmermann, Wendy, and Michael Fix. 1994a. "After Arrival: An Overview of Federal Immigrant Policy in the United States." In *Immigration and Ethnicity: The Integration of America's Newest Arrivals*, ed. Barry Edmonston and Jeffrey S. Passel, 251–85. Washington, D.C., Urban Institute Press.

_____. 1994b. "Immigrant Policy in the States: A Wavering Welcome." In *Immigration and Ethnicity: The Integration of America's Newest Arrivals*, ed. Barry Edmonston and Jeffrey S. Passel, 287–316. Washington, D.C.: Urban Institute Press.

Chapter 4

Social and Economic Integration of Foreigners in Germany*

Wolfgang Seifert

Introduction[1]

Since World War II, Germany has had one of the highest immigration rates among the industrialized nations, yet it has never been officially regarded as a country of immigration. The nation has used two main strategies in order to maintain the illusion of its being a country without permanent immigration. First, the influx of ethnic Germans (*Aussiedler*) from East European countries has never been regarded as immigration. This reflects an institutionalized preference for immigrants of German origin. The second strategy is reflected in the guest-worker system. The employment of foreign workers was considered to be a short-term solution to bridge periods of extreme labor scarcity. Foreign workers received contracts only for limited periods of time. This was intended to keep workers rotating, thus preventing them from settling permanently (Seifert 1995). For eco-

* I would like to thank Rainer Münz and Klaus J. Bade for their helpful comments.

Notes for this chapter begin on page 109.

nomic and humanitarian reasons it was not possible to maintain such rotation arrangements and the guest-worker system was abandoned; however, the ideology of temporary migration survived (Hollifield 1992). This had enormous consequences for the position of migrants in German society.

In the decade after World War II, expellees from former German territories and repatriated soldiers filled the labor market. In addition, German industry's demand for labor was easily met by refugees from the GDR (see Rainer Münz and Ralf Ulrich, "Changing Patterns of Immigration to Germany, 1945–1995," ch. 3 in vol. 1 of this series). While the first contract for the recruitment of foreign workers had been signed with Italy in 1955, such recruitment on a large scale did not begin until 1961, with the end of the supply of labor from the GDR (Bade 1992). In cooperation with industry, the German government began to recruit foreign workers from southern Europe. The granting of work permission only for limited periods of time was intended to prevent foreign workers from settling permanently in Germany and to keep the foreign labor force flexible and adaptable to the demands of the labor market. During the economic recession of 1966–67 the guest-worker system produced the desired effects: the number of foreign workers employed decreased sharply and then quickly increased again during the subsequent economic recovery. After the oil price shock of 1973, the recruitment of foreign labor was halted, although the number of foreigners in Germany remained at a high level. Rotation slowed in the late sixties and early seventies because industry wanted to avoid having continually to train new workers. Additionally, foreign workers had an employment profile different from that of the German labor force and thus could not be replaced by German workers. Even in economically weak phases, there were insufficient German workers, especially for jobs with low wages and stressful working conditions. Industrial jobs with minimal qualifications had become the domain of foreign employment.

In the eighties and nineties, the German government took measures intended to prevent further immigration. But strict prevention of immigration was impossible. Citizens of the European Community had the right to settle and work in Germany, and ethnic German immigrants and citizens of the GDR also had access to the German labor market. After the fall of the Iron

Curtain, a limit of 220,000 ethnic German immigrants annually was fixed by administrative measures (Vogel 1994, 141). When immigration pressure from the East European countries increased, the German government reacted by intensifying border controls and establishing legal processes for entry into the German labor market, particularly for the neighboring countries of Poland and the Czech Republic (Sandbrink 1996; Werner 1996; Rudolph 1994). For many would-be immigrants to Germany, asylum was the only remaining gate of entry.

In the remainder of this paper, I will examine how access to the labor market varies among immigrants from the recruiting countries and for the new immigrants. I differentiate three status groups: East Germans working in West Germany; ethnic Germans from East European countries; and immigrants from other states. (Members of this last group belong to various status groups; they range from EU citizens, who have easy access to the labor market, to asylum seekers, who have only limited rights.) I also show in which sectors new immigrant groups work. I also provide some background information on the different functions immigrants fill in the German economic system and the immigration processes that new immigrant groups face.

Economic Development and Labor Market Integration of Immigrants

The first oil crisis of 1973 was considered to be a turning point in worldwide economic development. In the period after World War II, production was concentrated in the most highly developed industrial countries. Expanding production drew migrants into the industrial centers from the European periphery (Gordon 1989) and largely reduced overseas migration. Starting with the oil price shock, however, labor-intensive production shifted for cost reasons from the highly developed centers to less developed countries. At the same time, the demand for manual workers has been reduced as a result of the increased use of microelectronics (Castles and Miller 1993, 65ff.). Branches with a high share of migrant workers have been hit especially hard by this structural transformation. Technological changes also "lead to a recomposition of the working class, involving a new segmentation of the labor market along lines of gender, ethnicity and age. New growth regions in the world economy attract large flows of labor while other regions are marginalized and become exporters of labor" (Overbeek 1995, 21). Modern technology has no need for unskilled workers; the demand is for multiskilled and autonomous workers capable of flexible work (Esping-Andersen 1990, 1993). At the same time, however, it fosters the creation of new jobs in the service sector. Thus the stratification of the society changes from a Fordist to a postindustrial hierarchy with professionals and scientists at the top, technicians and semiprofessionals in the next stratum, skilled service workers under that stratum, and unskilled service workers or a service proletariat at the bottom of the hierarchy (Esping-Andersen 1993, 24f).

Because of this restructuring unemployment among immigrants soon rose above that of the German labor force (Werner 1994). In periods of increasing competition immigrants often fail to find jobs because they lack the required qualifications and supporting networks. The disadvantaged position of immigrants can be seen in many societal areas: e.g., children of immigrants have fewer chances in the educational system than German children do (Richard D. Alba, Johann Handl, and Walter Müller, "Ethnic Inequalities in the German School System," ch. 5 in this volume; Bommes and Radtke 1993; Faist 1993; Herrmann 1993; Boos-Nünning 1990; Seifert 1992, 1995).

The most important factor governing integration into the labor market is an immigrant's legal status: both the possibility of direct access to the labor market and the availability of special integration measures depend highly on legal status. The overall economic situation in the year of entry also influences the immigrant's chances of gaining access to the labor market and career opportunities. The new immigrant first of all needs a residence permit. If such a permit is granted the immigrant must next apply for a work permit. This will be granted depending on the economic situation and only for jobs for which no German or other EU applicants are available (Velling 1995). A large proportion of the immigrants currently arriving in Germany do not need a work permit, either because they are ethnic Germans or because they are citizens of other

EU member states. As a result, the power of the work permit to regulate new immigrants' access to the labor market according to economic need is limited.

In this paper, I analyze only immigration to West Germany, so for my purposes East Germans coming to West Germany can also be considered immigrants. From the legal point of view, migration between East Germany and West Germany must be regarded as domestic migration, but East Germans in West Germany can form a control group for transnational migrants. The experience of East German immigrants exemplifies the effects of job changing and moving to a distant city in general, as well as effects specific to the different status groups. But when comparing East German immigrants with other immigrant groups one must recall that East Germans benefit from special conditions not enjoyed by other immigrant groups: They may begin searching for work from their places of residence in East Germany. If they are successful, they can then commute between their residences and their jobs. For the majority, commuting is the first step to a permanent settlement in West Germany (Schupp and Wagner 1992), but a substantial number continue commuting for years (Sandbrink and Wagner 1995). East German immigrants also have an advantage over other immigrants in that the access to skilled positions in Germany is strictly linked to educational certification (Esping-Andersen 1993), and their certificates are recognized.

Compared to other immigrants, ethnic Germans are in a privileged position. They are allowed to immigrate to Germany, acquire citizenship, and have free access to the labor market. They benefit from special integration measures such as language courses and occupational training programs. Within ten years (from 1985 to 1995) 2.2 million ethnic Germans entered Germany. On average, they had high levels of education; indeed, the share of those with a university degree has been above the average of the West German population (Velling 1994, 283). Compared to other immigrant groups, a higher share of elderly people can be observed among ethnic German immigrants, but overall their mean age is still lower than that of the native German population. The most important countries of origin were Kazakhstan, Russia, Poland, and Romania (Koller 1993).

Given the privileges granted to ethnic Germans settling in Germany, good integration into the labor market is to be expected. But most of the studies dealing with the labor market integration of this group reveal that ethnic German immigrants have substantial problems in finding jobs, because their knowledge and skills often do not meet the current requirements of the labor market. As a consequence, they are affected by unemployment (Puskeppeleit 1995; Koller 1993) or dequalification, that is, forced to take positions for which they are overqualified (Heinelt and Lohmann 1992). Labor market opportunities differ substantially according to immigrants' occupations. Generally blue-collar workers have better chances on the labor market than do ethnic Germans with white-collar occupations (Leciejewski 1990; Bundesministerium für Raumordnung, Bauwesen und Städtebau 1993).

The third important group of new immigrants comprises foreign migrants. Foreign migrants can be subdivided into various status groups with differing chances of gaining access to the labor market. For example, citizens of the European Union gain easy access to the labor market; however, immigration from EU countries is relatively slight.

For a small elite, access to the labor market is unrestricted. The internationalization of labor markets has opened up the possibility, especially for highly qualified individuals, to choose work irrespective of national borders (Münz 1995). Such individuals are often associated with international corporations or work in the field of science.

Seasonal and contract workers, mostly from east-central Europe, have only limited access to the labor market. In 1994 150,000 east-central European seasonal workers and 80,000 contract workers were employed in Germany (SOPEMI 1995). A fixed number of guest workers (5,500 in 1994) from east and east-central European countries were permitted to stay, but only for limited periods and within particular segments of the labor market (Werner 1996).

Despite the existence of legal paths of entry into the German labor market, there are signs of increasing numbers of illegal immigrants. The number of illegal entrants increased from 7,200 in 1990 to 31,000 in 1994 and reached a peak in 1993, when 54,300 illegal entrants were apprehended at the borders

(Vogel 1996, 6). The number of illegal entrants is no clear indicator of the levels of illegal immigration, however. Higher figures can be the result of intensified border controls, while decreasing figures might indicate a less effective control system. But other indicators also show an increasing number of illegal workers. For example, in 1990 there were 28,800 indictments for illegal employment, while in 1994 the figure had risen to 71,600 (Vogel 1996, 6). Even if some of this increase is attributable to intensified controls, there remains sufficient evidence of increasing numbers of illegal immigrants. In any case, compared with the USA, the problem of illegal employment is of minor importance in Germany. The highly regulated German labor market offers fewer opportunities for illegal employment than does its more liberal counterpart in the United States.

For asylum seekers and refugees, the access to the labor market is restricted. Political asylum has been an emotional issue in Germany in recent years. During the cold war refugees from the communist countries were warmly welcomed. But a change in the composition of asylum seekers (a higher proportion now being immigrants from the third world) and the increasing numbers of refugees during recent years have led to a growing demand for the number of the asylum seekers to be reduced. However, for asylum seekers, refugees, and dependent family members access to the labor market is not the primary incentive for migration. Thus the qualifications of these groups and the requirements of the labor market often do not match. Given this, and recalling the legal restrictions valid for these groups, the smooth integration of these groups into the labor market cannot be expected.

The preceding summary shows that the most important immigrant groups in Germany are not homogeneous in nature but rather characterized by different migration incentives and legal statuses and therefore by different preconditions for successful integration into the labor market.

....

Table 4.1 Socioeconomic Status and Mobility of Germans and Immigrants, 1984–1994 (percentages)

Type of worker	first longitudinal cohort				second longitudinal cohort			
	Immigrants		Germans[1]		Immigrants		Germans[1]	
	1984	1989	1984	1989	1990	1994	1990	1994
Number of cases ("N")	1,086	1,141	2,565	2,755	1,106	1,148	2,833	2,867
total								
unskilled	25	20	4	4	20	16	4	3
semiskilled	45	44	12	12	44	44	11	9
skilled	19	23	18	17	24	22	19	17
white-collar low-level	4	3	10	9	4	6	10	12
white-collar mid- & higher-level	3	6	33	37	4	6	35	39
self-employed	4	4	12	11	3	6	11	10
second-generation[2]								
unskilled	22	15	9	3	13	7	4	2
semiskilled	25	35	11	14	29	27	9	4
skilled	32	28	21	24	37	28	31	28
white-collar low-level	14	7	18	11	13	20	16	16
white-collar mid- & higher-level	5	15	29	37	9	16	31	37
self-employed	2	2	3	6	0	2	3	4
women								
unskilled	35	33	6	7	38	25	8	5
semiskilled	48	44	12	14	35	39	13	11
skilled	3	5	3	4	9	5	5	4
white-collar low-level	8	7	21	18	10	17	19	24
white-collar mid- & higher-level	3	8	39	42	7	11	43	41
self-employed	4	4	13	9	2	3	7	9
Turkish immigrants								
unskilled	36	27			26	19		
semiskilled	42	42			37	40		
skilled workers	14	22			24	21		
white-collar low-level	5	2			3	7		
white-collar mid- & higher-level	2	6			3	5		
self-employed	2	1			6	8		

1. The columns do not add up to 100 percent for the German population, because civil servants ("Beamte," an occupation closed to immigrants by law) were excluded.
2. The same age cohort (16 to 25 years) was used for Germans and representatives of the second generation.
Source: German Socioeconomic Panel, longitudinal samples, 1984–1989 and 1990–1994.

Occupational, Economic, and Social Mobility of Labor Migrants in Germany[2]

Occupational Mobility

In 1984 70 percent of the foreign labor force was employed in unskilled or semiskilled work;[3] among German workers this share was only 16 percent (see table 4.1). A certain degree of mobility, especially from semiskilled to skilled work, was observed in the period from 1984 to 1989. Although the share of white-collar middle- and higher-level employees among foreigners doubled, it was still far below the share of Germans similarly employed. Between 1990 and 1994 the share of unskilled workers decreased. Nevertheless, more than 60 percent of immigrants still performed unskilled and semiskilled work in 1994.

A somewhat more favorable picture is characteristic for children of immigrants, the so-called second generation. About half of them still worked as unskilled or semiskilled workers in 1984, but 32 percent were involved in skilled labor. The share of unskilled workers declined between 1984 and 1989. In 1990 the starting conditions of the second cohort of the second generation were somewhat better than were the conditions for the 1984 cohort, and in 1994 the picture was still more favorable. Sixteen percent of the second generation were now in middle- and higher-level white-collar positions. But this share is low in comparison to the corresponding German age group, where 37 percent had attained such positions. Great differences between the second generation and the corresponding German age group can also be observed with regard to the share of those performing semiskilled work.

Foreign women were still almost exclusively employed as unskilled or semiskilled workers in 1984. In the period up to 1994 the dominance of the blue-collar professions receded, but two-thirds of female foreign employees were still employed in these kinds of positions. They were, however, also found to a much greater extent in white-collar middle-level and higher-level positions. In comparison to German women (41 percent), though, the share for foreign women is still very low (11 percent).

Table 4.2 Foreign and German Wage and Salaries Earners by Sector (percentages)

Type of worker	first longitudinal cohort				second longitudinal cohort			
	Immigrants		Germans[1]		Immigrants		Germans[1]	
	1984	1989	1984	1989	1990	1994	1990	1994
total								
manufacturing	63	64	33	35	62	53	34	34
construction	13	13	8	6	12	11	6	6
distributive services	8	6	16	16	8	11	16	17
production-oriented services	2	3	7	8	3	5	10	8
consumer-oriented services	6	6	3	3	8	7	4	3
public admin./ social services	6	5	28	29	8	11	28	31
second generation[2]								
manufacturing	43	55	35	40	68	50	32	31
construction	10	7	8	9	2	6	11	9
distributive services	23	12	20	15	16	16	22	16
production-oriented services	1	4	6	8	2	4	8	8
consumer-oriented services	15	9	4	4	5	4	3	3
public admin./ social services	6	12	24	23	6	20	24	32
women								
manufacturing	63	57	22	24	54	42	22	21
construction	0	1	2	2	1	0	2	1
distributive services	9	7	21	20	9	14	21	22
production-oriented services	2	6	9	10	4	3	10	8
consumer-oriented services	13	13	6	5	18	15	6	3
public admin./ social services	12	17	36	38	14	27	39	43
Turkish immigrants								
manufacturing	71	69			61	53		
construction	11	12			11	9		
distributive services	6	5			8	11		
production-oriented services	2	3			3	8		
consumer-oriented services	4	3			5	7		
public admin./ social services	5	7			12	13		

Notes from Table 4.2:

1. The columns do not add up to 100 percent for the German population; self-employed farmers were excluded from the calculation.
2 The same age cohort (16 to 25 years) was used for Germans and representatives of the second generation.
Source: German Socioeconomic Panel, longitudinal samples, 1984–1989 and 1990–1994.

The occupational structure of Turkish wage and salary earners, which was characterized by a higher share of unskilled workers in 1984, had reached the average of other immigrants by 1994. Their mobility in this period was somewhat greater than that of the other nationalities.

As a whole it can be concluded that the employment profile of foreign workers clearly differs from that of German workers and is characterized by jobs with low qualification requirements. Between 1984 and 1994, however, a slow rise into higher-paying positions can be observed. The second generation in particular showed a more favorable structure. Even competition on the labor market, which increased after German unification, has not resulted in a displacement of foreign workers. Unemployment among foreigners has increased since German unification, but so has the rate of those gainfully employed, so that, all in all, immigrants have not been ousted from the labor market.

I now turn to the question of whether foreign employees can make their way into attractive branches of the service sector or whether they are largely tied to industrial jobs. Manufacturing is still the dominant employment sector for foreign workers, whereas German employees are primarily employed in the service sector (see table 4.2). It is interesting to note, however, that the number of foreigners employed in manufacturing declined substantially between 1990 and 1994. At the same time, immigrants gained access to all branches of the service sector.

For the second generation, the number of those working in manufacturing declined substantially between 1990 and 1994, whereas increases were visible elsewhere, especially the areas of public administration and the social services. Even so, half of the second generation was still employed in manufacturing in 1994.

Among foreign women, the share of those employed in manufacturing in 1984 corresponded exactly to the average of all foreign employees. By 1994, however, a strong shift toward the service sector can be noted. In particular, public administration and the social services had become more important. German women are, however, employed to a much greater extent in the service sector, above all in public administration and the social services. An occupational improvement for foreign women based solely on the change from the secondary sector to the service sector cannot be assumed. It is also conceivable that foreign women have been ousted from manufacturing by the introduction of shift work and thus forced to switch to less favorable employment positions in the service sector.

Table 4.3 Average Gross Earnings of Wage and Salary Earners (in Deutschmarks per month)

	first longitudinal cohort				second longitudinal cohort			
	Immigrants		Germans[1]		Immigrants		Germans[1]	
	1984	1989	1984	1989	1990	1994	1990	1994
total	2,400	2,870	2,760	3,200	2,810	3,330	3,270	4,160
second generation[1]	1,970	2,700	1,960	2,710	2,320	3,310	2,240	3210
women	1,820	2,040	1,960	2,300	2,010	2,570	2,360	2,940
Turkish immigrants	2,300	2800			2,770	3,360		
occupational status								
unskilled	2,100	2,340	1,710	1,670	2,240	2,700	1,500	1,940
semiskilled	2,360	2,860	2,230	2,530	2,790	3,230	2,510	2,920
skilled	2,850	3,240	2,830	3,270	3,240	3,870	3,440	3,960
white-collar low-level	1,760	2,250	1,840	2,070	2,330	2,630	2,010	2,520
white-collar mid/high-level	3,490	3,710	3,240	3,810	3,160	3,930	3,720	4,960
sector								
manufacturing	2,450	2,930	3,040	3,590	2,930	3,470	3,630	4,810
construction	2,720	3,170	2,880	3,320	3,080	3,910	3,270	4,210
distributive services	2,340	2,730	2,160	2,630	2,660	3,040	2,630	3,480
production-oriented services	*	*	3,130	3,490	2,040	3,490	3,560	4,580
consumer-oriented svc	1,500	1,850	1,760	2,180	1,430	2,290	1,790	2,390
public admin./social services	2,460	2,970	2,590	2,870	2,480	3,000	3,340	3,990

1. The same age cohort (16 to 25 years) was used for Germans and representatives of the second generation.
*Number of cases below thirty.
Source: German Socioeconomic Panel, longitudinal samples, 1984–1989 and 1990–1994.

Between 1984 and 1989 the share of Turkish immigrants in manufacturing was above average. This share decreased to 53 percent by 1994, thus equaling the share of all foreigners in this sector. Turkish employees now work to a greater extent in public administration and social services.

In general, the importance of manufacturing for foreign workers declined between 1984 and 1994. The increase in the share of those employed in the service sector was most noticeable for foreign women and the second generation.

Distribution of Income and Income Dynamics

As a whole, the average earnings of foreign employees are below those of German employees. This is to be expected in view of the large share of unskilled and semiskilled workers (see table 4.3). Income development in the second generation is clearly more favorable. Earnings reached the levels characteristic for the respective German age group in 1984 and 1989, and between 1990 and 1994 the income of the second generation was even somewhat higher than that of the comparable German age group. This can be explained by both occupational mobility and the entry of better-qualified people into gainful employment; however, the differentiation of income according to qualification is relatively unpronounced in the occupational entry phase.

Foreign and German women draw below-average incomes. While the high rate of part-time employment is an important reason for the lower earnings of German women, the lower earnings of foreign woman are above all explained by their employment in jobs with no or low qualification requirements. The increase in foreign women employed in the service sector did not cause above-average increases in income: their entrance into the service sector was not linked to the attainment of greater qualifications.

In 1984 the earnings of Turkish wage and salary earners were still below the average of all foreigners, but in 1994 they were somewhat above average. This reflects an increase in the number of Turks employed in qualified positions.

If the income situation of foreign and German employees is examined according to their occupational positions, it becomes obvious that foreigners who work as unskilled and semiskilled

Table 4.4 Language Proficiency, Interethnic Friendships, Permanent Settlement National Identification (percentages)

	first longitudinal cohort		second longitudinal cohort	
	1984	1989	1990	1994
good verbal knowledge of German				
total	42	46	55	58
second generation	86	89	87	94
women	35	40	49	51
Turkish immigrants	30	31	45	47
no German friends[1]				
total		52	54	57
second generation		40	31	43
women		54	61	61
Turkish immigrants		65	67	71
intention for permanent settlement				
total	30	39	41	46
second generation	34	54	52	56
women	27	38	39	45
Turkish immigrants	26	35	43	47
identification as a German[2]				
total	10	11	14	16
second generation	15	19	31	26
women	10	10	12	14
Turkish immigrants	6	4	9	8

1. Question not asked in 1984. The values for 1989 relate to 1988.
2. The values for 1984 relate to 1985.
Source: German Socioeconomic Panel, longitudinal samples, 1984–1989 and 1990–1994.

laborers on average clearly earn more than their German counterparts. This can be explained by the large share of part-time employees, predominantly women, among German unskilled workers. The main reason for the differences in income is thus due to the smaller number of hours worked by German employees. From 1989 on, the earnings of foreigners who work as lower-level white-collar employees are also clearly higher than the average for the respective German group. Again, German women working part-time are overrepresented in these positions. Another clear income differential between foreign and German employees appears among middle-level and higher-salaried employees. Foreign salaried employees in these positions earn substantially less, indicating that they have not been able to advance into higher positions.

Differentiated by branches it can be seen that foreign workers in the employment sector most important for them—i.e., manufacturing—earn considerably less than do Germans. This reveals again that German workers hold the higher positions. Up to 1990 foreign workers earned less in the service sector than in the manufacturing and construction sector. This situation had changed in 1994. The small numbers of immigrants employed in the production-oriented services now gain on average a slightly higher income than do those employed in manufacturing. Below-average incomes are found above all in the consumer-oriented services. In 1994 in each branch the income of foreign employees was lower than that of German employees in the same branch. There are large wage differences in the production-related sector as well as in public administration and the social services, where foreign employees hold low-paying positions.

All in all, the income data indicate that the income development of foreign wage and salary earners is comparable to that of their German colleagues with the same qualifications. Indications of wage discrimination cannot be established. A favorable income development is apparent above all in manufacturing. In the service sector, however, the incomes of foreign employees are considerably lower than those of German employees.

Social Integration of Immigrants

According to their self-assessment, more than half of all immigrants had a good knowledge of German in 1994 (see table 4.4). This share increased noticeably between 1984 and 1994. It is considerably higher in the second generation, of which 94 percent indicated in 1994 that they had a good verbal proficiency in the German language. It can be assumed that hardly any language barriers exist for the second generation. A below-average language competence was found among foreign women and among Turkish immigrants in general. The language skills of Turkish immigrants improved noticeably, however.

Increased possibilities for interaction and longer durations of stay could lead one to expect an increase in intensive social relations between migrants and the local population. This is not the case, however; indeed, segregation increased between 1990 and

1994. When foreigners were asked to name their three most important friends, the people with whom they most often spent time, more than half did not name a single German. For the second generation, the share of those who did not name a German among their three most important friends was clearly below average, despite their better knowledge of German: in 1990 31 percent did not name any Germans as friends. This share increased, surprisingly, to 43 percent in 1994. The sharp decline in interethnic friendships must be viewed as indicating an increasing distance between the foreign and German population. This is especially true for Turkish immigrants. The share of those without German friends reached nearly three-quarters in 1994.

The majority of the foreigners from Mediterranean countries have been living in Germany for a long time or were even born there. Nevertheless, it is worth asking whether migrants have decided to settle permanently in Germany. In 1984 relatively few—i.e., less than one-third—intended to settle permanently in Germany. In 1994 that share rose to almost one-half. A clear increase can also be found among the second generation. Those who do not want to stay permanently are not planning to return to their countries of origin immediately; most intend to settle for longer periods of time in Germany.

Even though nearly half of the immigrants and their children have already decided to settle permanently in Germany, they hardly identify themselves as Germans. In 1994 only 16 percent of all immigrants saw themselves as Germans, and among the Turkish immigrants that share was only 8 percent. The second generation is an exception, especially the second cohort that was analyzed here. The distance from the country of origin is apparently greatest for younger people. One-fourth of the second generation saw themselves as Germans in 1994, and this share was higher in 1990.

All in all, the situation of the foreign population is characterized by increasing segregation, although the foreign population has prepared itself for permanent or at least long-lasting stays in Germany. Most of them see themselves primarily as members of their ethnic community and not as Germans.

The Integration of New Immigrant Groups in the Labor Market

Demographic Structure and Migration Incentives of New Immigrant Groups

Most of the immigrants who entered Germany between 1984 and 1995 came immediately after the fall of the Iron Curtain in 1989 and 1990, when migration pressure was greater than at any time since 1947. East Germans and ethnic Germans from Poland, Romania, and the former Soviet Union made particular use of their newly acquired freedom of movement. The unification boom had created a favorable economic situation in West Germany, but despite this the unemployment rate remained high in West Germany, and competition in the labor market increased as a result of immigration pressures. In the subsequent slowdown of economic activity, competition on the labor market increased again. It can therefore be expected that the conditions for integration into the labor market became less promising for immigrants who came later.

The arrival of new immigrant groups is due to a large degree to the phenomenon of chain migration. More than half of the immigrants arriving in Germany between 1984 and 1995 already had a family member in Germany (see table 4.5). Two-thirds of ethnic Germans migrated within a family network. For East Germans, family ties were less important: only one-third entered West Germany to join a family already established there. Immigrants who did not have relatives in Germany had at least friends or acquaintances whom they knew before moving to West Germany. Only 19 percent were pioneer migrants, i.e., immigrants with neither relatives nor friends in Germany before they arrived.

Judging from the high proportion of immigrants with relatives in Germany, the most important migration incentive during this period was family unification. This is especially relevant for ethnic German and foreign immigrants. Economic factors were not important: Having a better life, better housing, and more consumption possibilities were reasons to migrate for only a fifth of foreign immigrants, a fourth of the East Germans, and more than a third of the ethnic Germans. Earning money for to support one's family and to save was rarely a motive for migration. About a fifth of the ethnic German and foreign immigrants were driven to migrate by poverty in their countries of origin. But nonmaterial reasons were more important. Living in freedom was important for 46 percent of the East German and 41 percent of the ethnic German immigrants. Other groups had different reasons, however, most notably the desire to be safe from war and persecution in the country of origin, which was an important reason for a third of foreign immigrants. To sum up, the change to live with one's own family is the most important migration incentive for the new immigrant groups, nonmaterial motives have some relevance, but economic reasons are not very important.

Table 4.5 Networks and Migration Incentives of New Immigrant Groups by Status and Period of Entrance (percentages)

	Legal Status			Period of Entrance		
	East Germans	ethnic Germans	foreign immigrants	1984-1988	1989-1990	1991-1995
networks						
family members in West Germany	36	65	48	55	52	57
no family members	64	35	52	45	48	43
no friends in West Germany[1]	63	75	40	54	67	60
neither family nor friends in West Germany	27	10	33	22	18	19
migration incentives						
having a better life	27	37	19	24	34	28
earning money for the family	11	16	12	13	15	12
to live in freedom	46	41	17	35	40	31
to live with the family	29	45	41	41	38	40
poverty in the country of origin	1	22	21	14	14	21
to be safe from persecution	5	18	32	15	13	24
to live in West Germany	24	41	12	24	34	27
intention to return to country of origin	15	1	40	12	10	20

1. Percentage of those who did not have family members in Germany.
Source: Immigration survey of the German Socioeconomic Panel (1994/1995).

A large proportion of immigrants have decided to stay permanently in Germany. Ethnic Germans in particular feel strongly about this matter. Only 1 percent of them plan to return to Romania, Poland, or the successor states of the USSR. The majority of East German immigrants have also decided to remain permanently in West Germany; only 15 percent are thinking of returning to East Germany. The majority of foreign immigrants also want to stay forever, but at least 40 percent have some intention of returning to their countries of origin.

Entry into the Labor Market

Generally good conditions for the integration of new immigrant groups can be expected because of their high levels of education and their low mean ages. Only 5 percent are above the retirement age, and on average they are younger than the German population. Compared to the labor migrants of the sixties and seventies new immigrant groups have substantially higher levels of education. One would thus anticipate new immigrant groups to distribute more evenly over all levels of the occupational hierarchy than did the labor migrants of the sixties.

Table 4.6 Labor Force Participation and Unemployment by Status and Entry Period (percentages)

	Legal Status			Period of Entrance		
	East Germans	ethnic Germans	foreign immigrants	1984-1988	1989-1990	1991-1995
labor force participation rate	67	46	40	56	54	40
registered unemployed[1]	12	26	27	13	18	35
seeking a job[2]	11	19	24	12	16	27

1. Based on the working population (employed and registered unemployed).
2. Based on all people of working age (defined as 16 to 64 years of age).
Source: Immigration survey of the German Socioeconomic Panel (1994/1995).

Immigrants from East Germany more often find access to the labor market than do ethnic German or foreign immigrants (see table 4.6). The unemployment rates also differ substantially among these groups. While only 12 percent of the East Germans who moved to West Germany were unemployed in 1995, the share of ethnic German and foreign immigrants without work was twice as high.

Differentiated by period of entrance, substantial differences in the percentages of employment and unemployment can be seen. Fifty-six percent of those who settled in Germany between 1984 and 1988 were gainfully employed in 1995. The employment rate of those coming to West Germany in 1989 and 1990 was only slightly lower. But out of those who entered Germany in 1991 and later only 40 percent were in gainful employment. Sharp differences can also be seen in the unemployment rates. The latest arrivals experience unemployment at rates almost three times higher than those of the group arriving between 1984 and 1988.

But which groups gained access to the labor market, and which did not? Differentiating between people who are in gainful employment and those who are seeking employment, one-tenth of East German immigrants of working age in 1995 were seeking jobs. The share was considerably higher for ethnic German and foreign immigrants. One in five ethnic Germans and one in four foreign immigrants were seeking work. This suggests that legal status and citizenship are crucial factors governing access to and success on the labor market. But another important differentiating factor is the historical period during which the immigrant entered Germany. Of those who came to Germany between 1984 and 1988 only 12 percent were looking for a job in 1995, in contrast to 27 percent of those who came after 1991. Clearly, in periods characterized by an unfavorable economic climate, access to the labor market is more restricted for immigrants than it is during boom periods.

Bivariate analyses have shown that both legal status and the period of entrance are relevant for getting a job, but it is difficult to determine which of these is the more important. I therefore used a multivariate model, i.e., a logistic regression analysis.[4] First, I analyzed which factors are relevant for entering employment during the year after immigration. Aside from the correlation between access to the labor market and legal status, I included in the model the entrance period, education, gender, age, and the presence of networks. Because the information on previous employment is based on calendar data surveyed retrospectively, no information is available as to whether an immigrant had the intention of seeking a job. For this reason, a second model analyzes the characteristics of those seeking work and those already in employment.

In the first model, the dichotomous dependent variable has the categories 0 ("not employed in the year after immigration") and 1 ("employed in the year after immigration"). The B-coeffi-

Table 4.7 Factors of the Labor Market Integration: Logistic Regression (B-values).

	in the year after entrance employed/not employed	1995 employed/seeking work
legal status[1]		
ethnic Germans	–1.38*	–1.09*
foreign immigrants	–1.05*	–1.52*
period of entry[2]		
1989–1990	0.08	–0.38
1991–1995	–0.31	–1.00*
gender[3]		
female	–0.88*	–1.35*
age at arrival	–0.01	0.03
education[4]		
without education	–0.18	–0.14
primary school	0.26	–0.23
networks		
no contacts before arrival	0.09	–0.09
no assistance from family members in seeking a job	–0.60*	–0.61*
constant	1.40	1.93
Pseudo r^2	0.13	0.15
–2 Log likelihood (zero model)	1,114.95	896.50
–2 Log likelihood (model)	970.06	765.28
significance	0.0000	0.0000
N	806	739

*significant at 1 percent level.
1. Reference category: East Germans.
2. Reference category: 1984–1988.
3. Reference category: male.
4. Reference category: secondary school.
5. Reference category: family members or friends before arrival in Germany.
6. Reference category: support in seeking employment by family members or friends

Source: Immigration survey of the German Socioeconomic Panel (1994/1995)

cients show the positive or negative correlation for each singular category.[5] Even when controlling for all other variables, the legal status of an immigrant has considerable explanatory power (see table 4.7). The negative result for ethnic Germans is caused by the duration of the integration measures. For this reason, ethnic Germans come later into employment. The effects of the period of entrance are not significant, but the probability of coming into employment is lower in the group of those who immigrated after 1991. The effects of the period of entrance and the economic situation during this time are minor. Effects of the duration of stay are more important. This means that an occupational integration of immigrants is also possible in periods of recession. For women, it is considerably more difficult to gain access to the labor market. A positive effect of networks can be observed in the group of those who had friends or relatives who helped them to find jobs. The degree of education influences the chances of coming into employment only to a minor degree. Altogether the model has only an explained variance of 13 percent (r^2, McFadden method), but it was not possible to control whether the immigrants were seeking work in the year after immigration. The second model controls for this.

In the second model, the dichotomous dependent variable has the categories 0 ("seeking for a job in 1995") and 1 ("employed in 1995"). Again, different chances of access to the labor market according immigrants' legal status can be observed. East Germans more often find access to the West German labor market than ethnic Germans do, but compared to the first model the chances of coming into employment clearly improved for ethnic Germans. A lower probability of gaining access to the labor market is given for those who entered after 1991. This might be explained by the economic conditions as well as by the short duration of stay. For women, the chances of gaining access to the labor market are again lower. The presence of friends and relatives who help in the job search has a positive effect; education and age have only minor effects.

Both models show that the legal status of an immigrant is the most important factor in gaining access to the labor market. For ethnic German and foreign immigrants, it is more difficult to find work. Important, too, is the period of entrance. A longer duration of stay seems to have a positive effect. The level of education has no significant influence, so it can be assumed that immigrants have found access to the labor market at all levels of the occupational hierarchy.

New Immigrant Groups in the Labor Market

The share of new immigrants working in blue-collar jobs is above average (see table 4.8). More than half of East German and foreign immigrants and even two-thirds of ethnic Germans are employed in blue-collar jobs. A quarter of the East German and ethnic German immigrants are employed in skilled positions, in contrast to foreign immigrants, who more often work in unskilled and semiskilled positions. But at least 21 percent of foreign immigrants have gained middle- and higher-level white collar positions. A third of the East German immigrants can also be found in these kinds of jobs, but obviously it is easier for immigrants to gain access to blue-collar work than to white-collar positions. Two factors might be relevant here. First, because the blue-collar sector is less attractive to the West German labor force, the competition in this sector is lower. In addition, qualification certificates issued by non-West German institutions tend to be recognized more often in blue-collar occupations than in white-collar professions, which either require more country-specific qualifications or have well-established lobbies (e.g., in medicine) restricting access. In the German dual system of vocational education and training, certificates are generally of great importance, and lacking one is a crucial disadvantage, especially during periods of slow or no economic growth.

But immigrants are not generally excluded from positions with high qualifications. Sixty percent of East German immigrants were employed in jobs with high qualification requirements. For ethnic German and foreign immigrants the share was above 40 percent. Of those who immigrated between 1984 and 1988 a substantially higher share had reached positions with high qualification requirements in 1995 than had those who entered Germany after 1991. This suggests that immigrants do not gain qualified positions immediately. Instead, they often start in positions with lower qualification requirements and get opportunities for advancement later.

Table 4.8 Labor Market Positions of Immigrants by Legal Status and Period of Entrance (percentages)

	Legal Status			Period of Entrance		
	East Germans	ethnic Germans	foreign immigrants	1984-1988	1989-1990	1991-1995
unskilled workers	6	11	23	11	10	22
semiskilled workers	17	35	23	21	27	27
skilled workers	28	26	13	21	26	19
white-collar low-level	11	11	10	12	11	10
white-collar middle- and higher-level	33	16	21	27	22	17
self-employed	5	1	8	8	4	4
position with high-qualification requirement	60	43	44	58	50	38
gross income (mean values)	3,630	3,280	3,600	3,760	3,470	3,210

Source: Immigration survey of the German Socioeconomic Panel (1994/1995).

The gross income of immigrants does not reflect precisely the differences between the different status groups. East German and foreign immigrants have comparable gross incomes in West Germany, whereas the income level of ethnic Germans is lower. Clear differences by the period of entrance can be seen. While those who immigrated in 1991 and later have an average gross income of DM 3,210 per month, those who entered Germany between 1984 and 1988 have a significantly higher gross income of DM 3,760 per month on the average. All in all, the income level of new immigrant groups is somewhere between that of the old immigrant groups and that of the native German labor force.

Conclusion

Immigrants from Turkey, Italy, Spain, Greece, and former Yugoslavia largely hold the lower positions in the German labor market. Minor improvements in the occupational positions of the first generation since their immigration in the 1960s and 1970s can be observed. Unskilled and semiskilled jobs in industry are still dominant. In contrast to the first generation of immigrants, the situation of the second generation has clearly improved. In small proportions they have even found access to attractive jobs in the service sector. But the second generation performs work with low qualification requirements to a greater degree than does the corresponding German age group. Higher mobility can be observed among Turkish immigrants, who were especially disadvantaged compared to other groups of immigrants in 1984. An increase in the number of those working in the service sector can be seen among foreign women, with a simultaneous decline in the importance of manufacturing. Even after German unification, when the competition in the labor market increased, foreign workers and employees as a whole could not only retain their positions but also improve them slightly.

For new immigrant groups, access to the labor market and career patterns are shaped decisively by legal status. In West Germany, East German immigrants had the best chances for successful integration into the labor market. Ethnic Germans were less successful, but it can be assumed that the integration measures offered to ethnic Germans, such as occupational- and language-training programs, had a positive effect on the labor market performance of this group.

Another important factor is the period of entrance: integration opportunities are more favorable for those who immigrated earlier. For women of all status groups integration into the labor market is more difficult than it is for men. The minor differences attributable to education that could be observed suggest that access to the labor market was possible for all educational groups. But the concentration of immigrants in blue-collar jobs points up difficulties in the access to white-collar jobs. But despite these problems it cannot be assumed that there exists a labor market segmentation that systematically excludes immigrants from positions with a higher qualification requirements.

Old immigrant groups fill in gaps that cannot be filled by the domestic labor force. Therefore competition between Mediterranean immigrants and the domestic labor force is not evident. The on-average high educational level of the new immigrant groups is a positive factor in the integration of new immigrant groups. Thus the integration of new immigrant groups is more successful than is that of the Mediterranean immigrants of the sixties.

It can be assumed that in the third generation of Mediterranean immigrants the disparities between migrants and the host population will be reduced. But there is no evidence pointing to an "assimilation" of the foreign population; at least, the increase in ethnic segregation makes this unlikely. Germany has become a "multicultural society" in the sense that "non-Germans" have become a major element in the German employment structure, but in the urban centers where they are concentrated they organize their lives primarily within their own ethnic structures.

Appendix: Methods and Database

In the first part of the analysis, I showed how the living conditions of immigrants from Turkey, Italy, Greece, Spain, and former Yugoslavia changed between 1984 and 1994. These analyses are based on the German Socioeconomic Panel, which is a representative longitudinal survey with a total sample of 12,000 individuals, 3,000 of them immigrants. Five separate samples were drawn for each immigrant group. The questionnaires were translated into the respective languages. Because of the concentration of immigrants in West Germany, only the West German population forms the reference group for the immigrants. Based on the data of the German Socioeconomic Panel two cohorts were formed for the years 1984 to 1989 and 1990 to 1994. In this way, the examined span is subdivided into periods before and after unification. The analyses thus focus on how German unification has influenced immigrant's career opportunities.

For the second generation, an upper age limit of twenty-five was set for the longitudinal samples of 1984 and 1990 in order to permit comparisons with the German control group, which ranged from sixteen to twenty-five years of age. Therefore the phase of the first entry into the labor market is the focal point of the study of the second generation. Special attention is also paid to Turkish immigrants and foreign women, as they are generally considered to be especially disadvantaged.

The analyses of new immigrant groups are based on the immigration sample of the German Socioeconomic Panel. This sample, compiled in 1995, covers 1,001 immigrants that entered Germany after 1984, 964 of whom were of working age. Of these, 27 percent were East Germans, and 51 percent were ethnic Germans.

Interviewing immigrants poses some problems that may affect the representative selection, especially for groups with no or poor proficiency in German. For the labor migrants of the sixties and seventies this problem was solved by translating the questionnaire into the languages of the five major sending countries. But new immigrant groups are far more heterogeneous, so translation of the questionnaire was not possible. For this reason, new immigrants with poor command of German are probably underrepresented in this sample. This is especially important in the case of foreign immigrants. Ethnic German immigrants generally attend a language course in Germany, so language problems are negligible for this group.

Because only people living in a private household were surveyed, asylum seekers were underrepresented in the sample. In general, then, the sample of new immigrant groups represents that part of the foreign population that had settled permanently in a private household and had sufficient knowledge of German to answer the questionnaire.

Notes

1. This article provides only basic information on the different types of migration and the history of migration. For detailed information on these topics, see Klaus J. Bade, "From Emigration to Immigration: The German Experience in the Nineteenth and Twentieth Centuries," and Rainer Münz and Ralf Ulrich, "Changing Patterns of Immigration to Germany, 1945–1995," chs. 1 and 3, respectively, in vol. 1 of this series. Further interesting literature in these fields includes Bade 1994a, 1994b, 1996; Beauftragte für die Belange der Ausländer 1995; Blanke 1993; Esser 1980; Heckmann 1981; Münz and Ulrich 1996; and Thränhardt 1995.
2. A description of the database and the methods is given in Appendix 1.
3. The values given are for immigrants from Turkey, Italy, Greece, Spain, and former Yugoslavia who pursue at least a regular part-time employment.

4. In the logistic regression model, a dichotomous dependent variable is predicted by one or more independent variables. The independent variables can be categorical. My purpose was to examine which factors are decisive with regard to access to the labor market.
5. For the independent variables, the subgroups for which the most positive assumptions regarding access to the labor market had been made were always chosen as the reference category.

References

Alba, Richard D., Johann Handl, and Walter Müller. 1994. "Ethnische Ungleichheit im Bildungssystem." *Kölner Zeitschrift für Soziologie und Sozialpsychologie* 46, no. 2: 209–37.

Bade, Klaus J. 1994a. *Ausländer—Aussiedler—Asyl: Eine Bestandsaufnahme.* Munich: Beck.

_____. 1992. "Paradoxon Bundesrepublik: Einwanderungssituation ohne Einwanderungsland." In *Deutsch im Ausland, Fremde in Deutschland. Migration in Geschichte und Gegenwart,* ed. Klaus J. Bade, 391–410. Munich: Beck.

_____, ed. 1996. *Migration—Ethnizität—Konflikt: Systemfragen und Fallstudien.* Osnabrück: Universitätsverlag Rasch.

_____, ed. 1994b. *Das Manifest der 60: Deutschland und die Einwanderung.* Munich: Beck.

Beauftragte der Bundesregierung für die Belange der Ausländer. 1995. *Bericht der Beauftragten der Bundesregierung für die Belange der Ausländer über die Lage der Ausländer in der Bundesrepublik Deutschland.* Bonn: Beauftragte der Bundesregierung für die Belange der Ausländer.

Blanke, Bernhard, ed. 1993. *Zuwanderung und Asyl in der Konkurrenzgesellschaft.* Opladen: Leske and Buderich.

Bommes, Michael, and Frank-Olaf Radtke. 1993. "Institutionalisierte Diskriminierung von Migrantenkindern: Die Herstellung ethnischer Differenz in der Schule." *Zeitschrift für Pädagogik* 39, no. 3: 483–97.

Boos-Nünning, Ursula. 1990. "Einwanderung ohne Einwanderungsentscheidung: Ausländische Familien in der Bundesrepublik Deutschland." *Aus Politik und Zeitgeschichte: Beilage zur Wochenzeitung Das Parlament* B23–24: 16–31.

Bundesministerium für Raumordnung, Bauwesen und Städtebau. 1993. *Integration von Aussiedlern und anderen Zuwanderern in den deutschen Wohnungsmarkt*. Bonn: Bundesministerium für Raumordnung, Bauwesen und Städtebau.

Castles, Stephen, and Mark J. Miller. 1993. *The Age of Migration: International Population Movements in the Modern World*. Houndmills: Macmillan.

Esping-Andersen, Gœsta. 1993. "Post-industrial Class Structures: An Analytical Framework." In *Changing Classes. Stratification and Mobility in Post-Industrial Society*, ed. Gœsta Esping-Andersen, 7–31. London: Sage.

————. 1990. *The Three Worlds of Welfare Capitalism*. Princeton, N.J.: Princeton University Press.

Esser, Hartmut. 1980. *Aspekte der Wanderungssoziologie: Assimilation und Integration von Wanderern, ethnischen Gruppen und Minderheiten*. Darmstadt: Luchterhand.

Faist, Thomas. 1993. "Ein- und Ausgliederung von Immigranten: Türken in Deutschland und mexikanische Amerikaner in den USA in den achtziger Jahren." *Soziale Welt* 44, no. 2: 275–99.

Gordon, Ian. 1989. "The Role of International Migration in the Changing European Labor Market." In *European Factor Mobility. Trends and Consequences*, ed. Ian Gordon and A. P. Thirlwall, 13–29. Houndmills: Macmillan Press.

Heckmann, Friedrich. 1981. *Die Bundesrepublik ein Einwanderungsland? Zur Soziogenese der Gastarbeiterbevölkerung als Einwandererminorität*. Stuttgart: Klett.

Heinelt, Hubert, and Anne Lohmann. 1992. *Immigranten im Wohlfahrtsstaat am Beispiel der Rechtspositionen und Lebensverhältnisse von Aussiedlern*. Opladen: Leske and Buderich.

Herrmann, Helga. 1993. "Ausländische Jugendliche in Schule, Ausbildung und Beruf." Beiträge zur Gesellschafts- und Bildungspolitik no. 184 (Mar.), Institut der deutschen Wirtschaft, Cologne.

Hollifield, James F. 1992. *Immigrants, Markets, and States: The Political Economy of Postwar Europe*. Cambridge: Harvard University Press.

Koller, Barbara. 1993. "Aussiedler nach dem Deutschkurs: Welche Gruppen kommen rasch in Arbeit?" *Mitteilungen aus der Arbeitsmarkt- und Berufsforschung*, no. 3: 207–21.

Leciejewski, Klaus. 1990. "Zur wirtschaftlichen Eingliederung der Aussiedler." In *Aus Politik und Zeitgeschichte: Beilage zur Wochenzeitung das Parlament* B3: 52–62.

Münz, Rainer. 1995. "Where Did They All Come From? Typologie and Geography of European Mass Migration in the Twentieth

Century." Demographie aktuell no. 7, Humboldt Universität zu Berlin, Lehrstuhl Bevölkerungswissenschaft.

Münz, Rainer, and Ralf Ulrich. 1996. "Internationale Wanderungen von und nach Deutschland, 1945–1994: Demographische, politische und gesellschaftliche Aspekte räumlicher Mobilität." *Allgemeines Statistisches Archiv* 80, no. 1: 5–35.

Overbeek, Henk. 1995. "Towards a New International Migration Regime: Globalization, Migration and the Internationalization of the State." In *Migration and European Integration: The Dynamics of Inclusion and Exclusion*, ed. Robert Miles and Dietrich Thränhardt, 15–36. London: Pinter.

Puskeppeleit, Jürgen. 1995. "Die Minderheit der (Spät)Aussiedler und (Spät)Aussiedlerinnen." In *Ethnische Minderheiten in der Bundesrepublik Deutschland*, ed. Cornelia Schmalz-Jacobsen and Georg Hansen, 75–89. Munich: Beck.

Rudolph, Hedwig. 1994. "Grenzgängerinnen und Grenzgänger aus Tschechien in Bayern." In *Wanderungsraum Europa: Menschen und Grenzen in Bewegung*, ed. Mirjana Morokvasic and Hedwig Rudolph, 225–49. Berlin: Edition Sigma.

Sandbrink, Stefan. 1996. "Die Beschäftigung von osteuropäischen Werkvertrags-Arbeitnehmern in der BRD: Vorstellung des Forschungsprojekts." In "Neue Migrationsprozesse: Politisch-institutionelle Regulierung und Wechselbeziehungen zum Arbeitsmarkt," ed. Thomas Faist, Felicitas Hillmann, and Klaus Zühlke-Robinet, 94–105. Working paper no. 6/96, Zentrum für Sozialpolitik, Bremen.

Sandbrink, Stefan, and Gert Wagner. 1995. "Arbeitskräftemobilität und Lebensqualität—Das Beispiel der 'Westpendler' und ihrer Lebenspartner in Ostdeutschland." Diskussionspapier no. 95–09, Fakultät für Sozialwissenschaft, Ruhruniversität Bochum.

Schupp, Jürgen, and Gert Wagner. 1992. "Arbeitsmarktentwicklungen und individuelle Erwartungen. In *Datenreport 1992: Zahlen und Fakten über die Bundesrepublik Deutschland*, ed. Statistisches Bundesamt, 546–55. Bonn: Bundeszentrale für politische Bildung.

Seifert, Wolfgang. 1995. *Die Mobilität der Migranten: Die berufliche, Ökonomische und soziale Stellung ausländischer Arbeitnehmer in der Bundesrepublik*. Berlin: Edition Sigma.

_____. 1992. "Die zweite Ausländergeneration in der Bundesrepublik: Längsschnittbeobachtungen in der Berufseinstiegsphase." *Kölner Zeitschrift für Soziologie und Sozialpsychologie* 44: 677–96.

SOPEMI. 1995. *Trends in International Migration: Annual Report, 1994*. Paris: OECD.

Thränhardt, Dietrich. 1995. "Keine Unterschichtung aber politische Herausforderugen: Bericht über die Lebenslage der Einwanderer aus Anwerbeländern in Nordrhein-Westfalen." In "Wie Migranten leben: Lebensbedingungen und soziale Lage der ausländischen Bevölkerung in der Bundesrepublik," ed. Wolfgang Seifert, 93–102. Arbeitspapier FSIII 95–401, Wissenschaftszentrum Berlin für Sozialforschung.

Velling Johannes. 1995. *Immigration und Arbeitsmarkt: Eine empirische Analyse für die Bundesrepublik Deutschland.* Baden-Baden: Nomos.

_____. 1994. "Zuwanderer auf dem Arbeitsmarkt: Sind die neuen Migranten die 'Gastarbeiter' der neunziger Jahre?" *ZEW Wirtschaftsanalysen* 2, no. 3: 261–95.

Vogel, Dita. 1996. "Illegale Zuwanderung und soziales Sicherungssystem: Eine Analyse Ökonomischer und sozialpolitischer Aspekte." ZeS-Arbeitspapier no. 2/96. Zentrum für Sozialpolitik, Universität Bremen.

_____. 1994. "Sozialpolitische Integration als zuwanderungspolitisches Steuerungsinstrument." *Forum Demographie und Politik*, no. 5: 132–55.

Werner, Heinz. 1996. "Befristete Zuwanderung von ausländischen Arbeitnehmern." *Mitteilungen aus der Arbeitsmarkt- und Berufsforschung* 29, no. 1: 36–53.

_____. 1994. "Integration ausländischer Arbeitnehmer in den Arbeitsmarkt—Deutschland, Frankreich, Niederlande, Schweden." In Heinz Werner and Wolfgang Seifert, *Die Integration ausländischer Arbeitnehmer in den Arbeitsmarkt*, 85–186. Beträge zur Arbeitsmarkt und Berufsforschung no. 178. Nuremberg: Institut für Arbeitsmarkt- und Berufsforschung.

Chapter 5

Ethnic Inequalities in the German School System*

Richard D. Alba, Johann Handl, and Walter Müller

Nearly all minorities arising from immigration initially face some degree of disadvantage. Speaking the tongue of the host society imperfectly if at all, distinguished from natives by physical appearance and culture, and frequently lacking full-fledged legal equality, immigrants and their children generally lag behind natives in educational accomplishment, occupational position, income, residential situation, and other consequential ways. Even when they come with unusually high levels of human capital, as is the case with some Asian immigrants to the United States today, they generally find that their socioeconomic payoff is less than that obtained by comparable natives. But

*We are grateful to Bernhard Schimpl-Neimanns and Achim Wackerow of ZUMA (the Zentrum für Umfragen Methoden und Analysen) for making the Microcensus data available to us. The analyses of these data, which were conducted at ZUMA, are based on an anonymized 70 percent subfile made available to ZUMA by the Federal Statistical Office in Wiesbaden. Bernhard Schimpl-Neimanns also gave us excellent counsel about the analysis and interpretation of educational inequality. The research represented by this paper was supported by a Fulbright grant to the first author and conducted while he was in residence at the Zentrum für Europäische Sozialforschung in Mannheim. A previous version of this paper was published in German in the *Kölner Zeitschrift für Soziologie und Sozialpsychologie.*

Notes for this chapter begin on page 150.

despite the near universality of such inequalities at the outset, the degree and permanence of disadvantages borne by immigrant groups vary considerably. Some groups in some contexts rapidly overcome any disadvantage to achieve parity with, and occasionally superiority to, natives. The inferior status of other groups persists more or less across generations, thus transforming what originally were immigrant disadvantages into ethnic ones. Characteristics of the immigrants—e.g., their human capital and their intentions to stay or to return home—of the communities they enter—e.g., economic and social infrastructures —and of the surrounding society—e.g., the legal positions of immigrants and subsequent generations—all play significant roles in determining the outcome (Portes and Rumbaut 1990).

For the Federal Republic of Germany, the long-run significance of the disadvantages faced by immigrant minorities remains uncertain. What makes these disadvantages especially worthy of investigation is the unusual degree of variation in the initial circumstances and legal situations of immigrant groups. As Rainer Münz and Ralf Ulrich describe ("Changing Patterns of Immigration to Germany, 1945–1995," in vol. 1 of this series), Germany has received a number of distinct migration waves since the end of World War II. Following Bade (1994a), these can be grouped into three broad categories:

1. So-called guest workers and their families, who came especially from the countries ringing the Mediterranean. The workers were recruited in large numbers starting in the late 1950s, and their families came later, many after the formal period of recruitment was brought to an end (in other European countries as well as in Germany) by the oil-price rise and the resultant economic shock of the early 1970s.
2. Ethnic Germans (known as *Aussiedler*, literally "out-settlers"), whose first wave corresponds with the huge inflow of refugees (known as the *Vertriebenen*, the expellees) created by the expulsions at war's end from the dismantled eastern regions of the former German Reich and East European nations. Further migration was encouraged by postwar German law, which incorporated an assumption derived from the expulsions that ethnic Germans faced discrimination throughout Eastern Europe and the Soviet Union; new waves thus followed the collapse of the Iron Curtain.

3. Asylum seekers, who come in larger numbers to Germany than to other European nations because of the liberal asylum provision in the German Constitution. The flow of asylum seekers, many coming from the third world, was especially heavy in the late 1980s and early 1990s, until legislation in 1992 effectively restricted access to the right to asylum.

The legal handicaps faced by these groups are as varied as the circumstances of their migration. Given the jus sanguinis principle at the root of German citizenship law, the German-born offspring of some groups remain legally as foreign as their immigrant parents (Brubaker 1992; for a comprehensive review of the legal situation of foreigners in Germany, see Kugler 1993; Gerald L. Neuman, "Nationality Law in the United States and the Federal Republic of Germany: Structure and Current Problems," ch. 8 in this volume). For nationals of other European Union states, however, the legal distinction between natives and foreigners is presumed to be neutralized in many respects by the provisions of EU treaties and law. For East Europeans who can demonstrate German ethnic origin, this distinction is even eliminated, because they have an automatic right to German citizenship (which makes research about their situation difficult as they are not tracked in census and other national data sets).

One domain of uncertainty is the labor market, for which two rather opposing positions concerning ethnic disadvantage have been put forward in the recent empirical literature. On the one hand, Baker and Lenhardt (1991), in a study based largely on aggregate employment data, argue against the commonly encountered thesis that non-Germans are subject to discrimination and labor-market segmentation or to concentration in disadvantaged tiers of the workforce (*Unterschichtung*); they claim instead that ethnic disadvantages are quite modest, once the lower qualifications of ethnic workers are taken into account. On the other hand, Seifert (1992, 1996; see also Deutsches Institut für Wirtschaftsforschung 1994a; Heckmann 1992), in a study of the early work careers of the second generation in the Socioeconomic Panel data (a longitudinal database collected since 1984 that is widely used to study immigrant minorities), paints a decidedly more negative picture. He maintains that members of the second generation show a number of substantial disadvantages in comparison to native Germans of comparable age, ranging from much less vocational training to greater unemployment and employment in un- and semiskilled jobs. Seifert (1996), however, also finds evidence that the labor market position of the second generation represents a substantial improvement over that of its immigrant parents, and he, too, argues against the thesis that minorities are increasingly subject to segmentation. Both sides agree that the labor-market situations of foreigners and Germans are not the same but differ in their emphases and, to some extent, their interpretations.

Similarly opposing positions could be argued in the sphere of educational attainment. It is well known that the educational accomplishments of foreign children in the German school system do not match those of their German age peers (Boos-Nünning 1994; Boos-Nünning et al. 1990; Deutsches Institut für Wirtschaftsforschung 1994b; Esser 1990; Faist 1993b; Geiersbach 1989; Köhler 1992; Seifert 1992; Zentrum für Türkeistudien 1994). Nevertheless, Baker and Lenhardt (1988; see also Baker et al. 1985) have argued that the school system is functioning as an agent of integration for foreign children and that, from an institutional perspective, German and foreign children are subject to the same regime of standards and opportunities. This position, of course, does not exclude the possibility of rather different educational outcomes for the two groups. Yet much that is necessary to interpret ethnic differences in education remains unknown. Many studies employ regional rather than national data, focus on a single ethnic group (especially the Turks), or do not make ethnic differentiations within the non-German population. Additional problems concern the adequacy with which other important factors, such as socioeconomic background or length of residence in the Germany, are taken into account.

In this paper we seek to redress some of these gaps. Like most of the research on Germany, our paper focuses on groups that are legally defined as foreign; these are mainly the groups arising from the guest-worker immigration that reached its zenith in the 1960s.[1] We review what is known about the educational achievement of the children of these groups and ask whether there is substantial improvement for the second generation, i.e., those born in Germany or arriving before the age of schooling.

Our own analysis of two major national data sets permits us to go beyond previous research in some respects. The 1989 Microcensus allowed us to establish the precise extent of ethnic disadvantage in the German school system (more precisely, in the West German states, where the vast majority of non-Germans reside). The Socioeconomic Panel allowed us to investigate possible explanations for the ethnic differences we found, since it provides a wide range of potential explanatory variables, from the cultural climate in the home, to the parents' intention to return to the homeland, to the ethnic composition of the residential neighborhood.

The Roots of Ethnic Educational Disadvantage

Ethnic inequalities in such spheres as the educational system and the labor market have received more attention than any other topic in the vast, worldwide literature on ethnicity. Nowhere has this attention been more intense than in the United States (among the many that could be cited, see, e.g., such diverse works as Wilson 1987, Perlmann 1988, and Portes and Rumbaut 1990). For this reason, our discussion draws initially on the U.S. literature, where virtually the full range of interpretive variability is on display. Of course, there are very important differences between the United States and Germany in terms of the legal, institutional, and national-cultural contexts for receiving immigrant children, and we must also consider how well conclusions drawn from the U.S. experience can be applied to German minorities.

Certain dominant threads run through the highly varied explanations for ethnic inequalities. Some scholars tend to emphasize differences in the socioeconomic, or social class, origins of majority and minority populations. Particularly in the discussion of labor migrations, it is argued that immigrants, who often come from rural areas in less industrialized societies, tend to enter the labor force of the receiving society on its lower rungs (Piore 1979; Portes and Rumbaut 1990). Their children, even when raised in the receiving society and exposed to its opportunities, tend to attain less than do the average members of the majority, because of the impact of socioeconomic disadvantages. This sort of argument has been applied to quite diverse groups in the United States, such as second-generation Italian Americans (Gans 1982) and even African Americans, a nonimmigrant group (Wilson 1978, 1987). It is also commonly raised in relation to various immigrant groups in Germany, such as the southern Italians and Turks (Schiffauer 1991).

Another explanatory strategy sees the source of a minority's disadvantage (or, in some cases, advantage) in its cultural distinctiveness—its worldview, in other words—which can hinder (or help) its members in competing on equal terms with members of the majority group. A wide range of traits have been drawn on to construct cultural explanations. Rosen (1959), for instance, provides a classic illustration in the U.S. context, arguing that the limited socioeconomic success of some ethnic groups is explainable in terms of their cultural distance from the middle-class values and beliefs (e.g., future orientation) of an "achievement syndrome." This line of explanation has sometimes been associated with the highly controversial notion of a "subculture of poverty" (Lewis 1965) and discredited as a consequence. Steinberg (1989) has provided a classic rebuttal, claiming that the traits relevant to the achievement syndrome are in turn the consequence of the typical social class origins of different groups and thereby folding cultural explanations into the socioeconomic one. (A further objection is that cultural explanations tend to be ex post facto rather than predictive.) But the appeal of the cultural argument is sufficiently strong and the repertoire of traits that can be pressed into its service sufficiently varied that the argument recurs in new forms. One contemporary expression lies in analyses of entrepreneurial minorities, such as the Cubans and Koreans in some U.S. cities, that find some of the roots of business success in cultural capital, which is often described in terms of traits reminiscent of Weber's Protestant Ethic (Light 1984); obviously, then, groups that lack these traits are handicapped when it comes to small-business success and consequently exposed to ethnic disadvantage in the open labor market.

A different type of argument, which, like the preceding ones, still relies primarily on characteristics of the minority group itself, focuses on minority intentions with respect to the host society. Here, minorities are seen to be disadvantaged when they define themselves as "sojourners," i.e., temporary residents in the receiving society, because their sights remain set on their societies of origin, and they thus are hampered in conceiving or implementing long-term plans based on a permanent stay. Sojourner status may lead them, for instance, to withdraw their children from school as early as possible in order to send them into the labor market to contribute to the family income, in the hope (often illusory) of speeding the return home, or to school their children partly in the homeland, in the belief that they must be prepared for a life there (the back-and-forth migration of immigrant children is common enough in Germany to merit a German word, *pendeln*). For the European migration to the United States, this argument has been made most forcefully in the case of the Italians (see Alba 1985; Perlmann 1988).

The sojourner orientation may have particular relevance for explaining immigrant disadvantage in Germany. It is often encountered in relation to the Turks (see, e.g., Geiersbach 1982; Korte 1990; Schiffauer 1991), but it has a broader application. The labor migrations of the 1950s and 1960s that gave rise to the largest non-German immigrant groups were conceived at the time, by both Germans and probably most of the immigrants, as involving short-term stays. Initially, most of the immigrants were men who left their families at home; only after the cessation of immigrant recruitment in the early 1970s (the so-called *Anwerbestopp*) did women and children put in an appearance in large numbers, thus giving the immigration a more long-term, but not necessarily permanent, character. Though the probability of a successful return home is no doubt declining over time for many immigrants and especially for their children, who have spent most of their lives in the Federal Republic, the intention to remain is hedged with uncertainties because of the legalities and cultural meanings of citizenship (see the revealing data in Seifert 1996). Only small fractions of immigrants and the second generation have naturalized, and many perceive their right to stay permanently as uncertain (despite current law). Thus a common feeling among immigrant families is that they must be prepared for the possibility of return, and accordingly a sojourner orientation is relevant.

In application to Germany, the sojourner orientation obviously expands the explanatory focus beyond the characteristics of immigrant minorities exclusively to include features of the receiving society, such as its citizenship laws. Other explanations of inequality focus more narrowly on the natives of the receiving society. The simplest and most influential is to see minority disadvantage as the product of majority exclusion, or discrimination. In this view, the majority excludes minorities, either through individual acts of discrimination or through institutionalized, discriminatory mechanisms, in order to defend its privileges (Blauner 1972). In the United States, this type of explanation generally takes center stage when, for instance, the high degree of ethnic and racial residential segregation is under scrutiny (Massey and Denton 1993). However, the empirical verification of explanations relying on discrimination is more problematic than is the case for most other explanations of inequality because discrimination is usually not directly measured. Its presence must thus be inferred from ethnic differences that exist after all other relevant factors are controlled. Since one can rarely be certain that all such factors have been taken into account, discrimination as an explanation tends to remain a hypothesis.

Finally, the characteristics of minority communities have also been scrutinized in the search for an explanation. Here, too, a variety of characteristics has come under the magnifying glass. For instance, the institutional and economic impoverishment of some inner-city minority communities in the United States is featured in the well-known if controversial underclass theory (Wilson 1987). In the study of U.S. immigrant minorities, a great deal of attention is currently being paid to their ability to establish ethnic subeconomies consisting of minority-owned firms that employ group members (Light 1984; Portes and Bach 1985). It is argued that, where such subeconomies exist, ethnic workers are able to avoid the disadvantages that would face them in the mainstream economy and instead take advantage of special routes of mobility, i.e., rising to supervisory or even ownership positions in ethnic firms. Examples are the Cubans of Miami and the Koreans of Los Angeles. The conditions under which such subeconomies arise are not yet fully clarified, and the existence of advantages for ethnic workers in them is disputed (e.g., Sanders and Nee 1987). Still, given the enormous educational success of the children of participants in a previous ethnic subeconomy, that of East European Jews in New York City, the phenomenon is worthy of attention.

Beyond explaining the extent of existing ethnic disadvantage, other important questions concern the evolution of disadvantages over time. Here, the most significant body of theory is still assimilation theory (Gordon 1964; Esser 1980; Hirschman 1983), despite all the challenges flung at it in recent decades. It leads to the expectation that, in many cases, especially where immigrant minorities are involved, inequalities should diminish over time and, in particular, across different generations of the same ethnic group (see, for the United States, Neidert and Farley, 1985; for Germany, see Esser and Friedrichs 1990). The reasons for this expectation are not difficult to derive from the explanations given above. Thus, insofar as inequality is culturally rooted, it should diminish as a minority assimilates culturally to the receiving society (see, for example, Nauck and Özel 1986). Insofar as it derives from socioeconomic differentials between minority and majority, it may be eroded by the intergenerational social mobility of a minority, even if this is modest. If discrimination lies behind inequality, it may be affected by assimilation, since discrimination requires minority-group membership to be visible, and many (but not all) forms of visibility—e.g., language, dress—are reduced by assimilatory processes.

In any event, in the case of immigrant minorities, all these considerations indicate that one must take generational position into account in the measurement of ethnic inequalities. The first generation, composed of immigrants, is too shaped by socialization in the society of origin and by the disadvantages associated with migration itself to take full advantage of the opportunities in the new society. Thus it is with the second generation, raised in the receiving society, that inequalities rooted in ethnic, as opposed to immigrant-native, differences begin to manifest themselves clearly. Yet the assimilation process is rarely completed in the second generation. Hence, since the third and fourth generations of the guest-worker groups in Germany are still small, one has to be careful in assessing the long-run implications of contemporary ethnic differences, which may be altered by intergenerational changes.

This review, based principally on frameworks derived from the U.S. experience, has turned up little that would not in principle have potential application to immigrant minorities in Germany, despite the obvious differences between the United States and Germany as immigration societies. Socioeconomic and cultural differences, sojourner orientations, exclusion by the majority, and ethnic community characteristics can all potentially have an impact on the educational and socioeconomic trajectories of immigrant groups in Germany, though perhaps not in ways that precisely parallel those in the United States. With this conceptual background in mind, it is now appropriate to turn to the educational context in which ethnic disadvantages manifest themselves in specific ways.

Ethnic Differences in Educational Placement

The German educational system, like most European ones, is formally more stratified than the U.S. system is. As a result of the legacy of the hierarchical society of the nineteenth century in which it originated, the German system is characterized by a tripartite structure at the secondary level, as shown in figure 5.1 (for discussion, see Allmendinger 1989; Max Planck Institute 1979; Müller, Steinmann, and Eli forthcoming). In most states (*Bundesländer*) of the Federal Republic, the secondary level begins after four years of primary education and is divided among three tracks: *Hauptschule, Realschule,* and *Gymnasium.* (The system is not entirely uniform, however, because jurisdiction over education is assigned constitutionally to the states.) Despite the challenges to this rigid structure in the post-World War II era—reforms include some convergence in curriculum (e.g., introduction of foreign languages in the lowest, or *Hauptschule,* track) and the introduction of "comprehensive" secondary schools, *Gesamtschulen*—it has not changed fundamentally (Müller, Steinmann, and Eli forthcoming). The *Gesamtschulen,* for instance, remain of marginal significance within the total system.

The three main tracks are clearly ranked in terms of their prospects for subsequent education and occupations. The most direct route to a university or other institution of higher education runs through the *Gymnasium* and requires eight or nine years of study there, followed by the successful completion of final examinations (the *Abitur*). An alternative route, which leads to a more limited range of possibilities, in the *Fachhochschulen* (which offer, for example, training in civil engineering and social work), can be pursued after study at a *Realschule*, followed by the achievement of the required credential, the *Fachhochschulreife*; *Gymnasium* students can also earn this credential and attend *Fachhochschulen*, if they choose. Otherwise, successful completion of six years at the *Realschule* and of an examination leads to the *Mittlere Reife* certificate (a certificate of intermediate secondary education). This certificate has been considered to be the key credential for entry into many white-collar occupations, the traditional province for children of the middle classes. While a transition to a *Gymnasium* is possible from the *Realschule* (and occurs in a limited number of cases), it is extremely rare in the case of the *Hauptschule*. The last is clearly the least prestigious track. It offers the least demanding curriculum and has more and more become the track for educationally disadvantaged children and foreigners. The *Gesamtschule*, the fourth kind of school, provides the option to combine more and less demanding courses. But this type, which has not successfully established itself as an alternative to the main tracks, enrolls only a small percentage of all secondary school students.

The linkage of the German educational system to the labor market is more institutionalized than is the case in the United States. This linkage is manifested in the central role played by vocational apprenticeships (*Lehren*), which typically combine on-the-job training with some classroom instruction and are thus generally described as a dual system (see Faist 1993a, 1993b). They can be entered following any of the tracks of secondary education, but the higher the track, the better are the opportunities to obtain apprenticeship places in occupations with good income, security, and social prestige. Currently, high percentages of the relevant age groups participate in the apprenticeship system: the figure was close to 70 percent during the 1980s, a substantial rise from the half or so who obtained apprenticeships in the 1950s. Apprenticeships have become attractive even to students in higher tracks who are eventually going on to the university or some other form of postsecondary education. Apprenticeships are a virtual necessity for students coming from the *Hauptschule* track, who are otherwise qualified only for jobs on the lowest rungs of the labor market.

Figure 5.1 The German Educational System

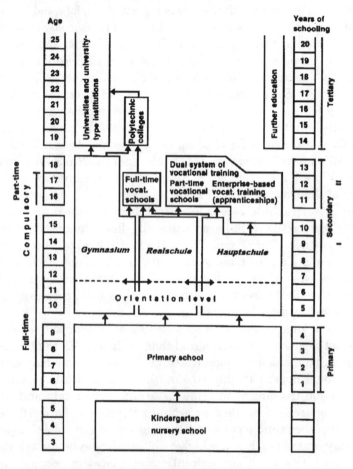

Source: Max Planck Institute 1979, 68.

A salient feature of this system is the fatefulness of an early decision point. At the end of the fourth grade, children are shunted into one of the three main branches, with relatively little chance to change (especially to a higher track) should the decision prove premature. This decision point is especially momentous for immigrant children, who may have only recently arrived in Germany and are confronted by a decision whose implications they and their parents may not fully comprehend. The decision is based not just on the academic abilities of a child, which in any event are hard to assess in the case of immigrant children because of language and other cultural differences. Proficiency in the German language, teacher evaluations, and parental aspirations for children all play consequential roles. The role of teacher evaluations suggests the possibility that culturally skewed perceptions of children's abilities work in some cases to the disadvantage of immigrant children. The parental role indicates that the acculturation of parents is as important as that of their children in opening up the full range of educational opportunity: parents may not correctly perceive the complexity of the system and the near finality of its linkages to different tiers of the labor market. Indeed, there is evidence to this effect (Boos-Nünning et al. 1990). Further, the intention of parents to return to their homeland or, perhaps better put, their unwillingness to surrender the possibility of return may undermine their children's prospects for optimal educational placement; parents may see little point in allowing their children to invest in a form of education, such as the *Gymnasium*, that may be interrupted by a return home and is unlikely to provide any economic payoff in the homeland in any event.

This reasoning makes more understandable a well-known aspect of the immigrant experience in German schools: the concentration of immigrant children in the lowest track of the German school system, the *Hauptschulen* (see, e.g., Deutsches Institut für Wirtschaftsforschung 1994b; Zentrum für Türkeistudien 1994).[2] In table 5.1, we present some relevant data from the 1989 Microcensus, which represents a 1 percent sample of the resident population of the Federal Republic before reunification (the omission of the five eastern states of the current Federal Republic has little practical consequence, because only a tiny fraction of immigrant children are found in the east). The Microcensus is superior to most of the other data sets that we could have used to examine educational differences because of the completeness of its population coverage (with the notable exception of the eastern *Länder*); the size of its sample, which

Table 5.1 Educational Placement and/or Outcome by Ethnic Group and Age (13- to 21-year-olds)

	Hauptschule without apprenticeship	Hauptschule with apprenticeship	Realschule without apprenticeship	Realschule with apprenticeship	Gymnasium	Abitur (Gymnasium completed)	Vocational education	No educational certificate/ no answer	N
13- to 15-year-olds									
German	34.1	1.3	32.7		31.4		0.5		9521
Turkish	66.7	2.9	22.3		7.1		0.9		645
Yugoslav	54.9	1.9	27.7		14.6		1.0		206
Italian	66.7	3.2	23.0		6.3		0.8		126
Greek	56.3	0.0	19.8		24.0		0.0		96
Other nationalities	46.1	0.7	29.2		23.6		0.4		267
16- to 18-year-olds									
German	8.7	23.5	15.7	18.3	28.8	0.8	4.0	0.3	12,298
Turkish	31.8	29.5	17.4	5.9	7.0	0.3	7.1	1.1	661
Yugoslav	24.0	26.9	12.6	12.0	16.8	0.0	7.8	0.0	167
Italian	33.6	32.9	11.9	7.0	7.7	0.0	5.6	1.4	143
Greek	15.8	14.9	15.8	4.0	35.6	7.9	5.9	0.0	101
Other nationalities	24.4	18.2	14.1	9.3	24.7	1.3	6.2	1.7	291
19- to 21-year-olds									
German	9.3	24.9	6.7	30.2	17.5	9.7	1.0	0.7	16,139
Turkish	47.2	25.9	7.3	7.0	3.7	4.3	1.0	3.6	618
Yugoslav	24.2	34.7	6.3	18.9	7.4	3.2	2.1	3.2	95
Italian	38.1	24.9	12.2	12.2	6.1	3.4	2.2	1.1	181
Greek	28.8	23.1	11.5	11.5	13.5	10.6	1.0	0.0	104
Other nationalities	19.5	18.0	9.6	14.2	17.0	15.5	2.8	3.4	323

allows us to examine educational outcomes for the four largest immigrant groups, Greeks, Italians, Turks, and immigrants from the former Yugoslavia (called "Yugoslavs" below); and the inclusion of data about the family backgrounds of schoolchildren, which we subsequently use to investigate some possible explanations for educational differences. (U.S. readers may find odd the definition of national origin: unlike the United States, where some measure of ethnic ancestry is standard, in Germany such definitions are based on citizenship, and immigrants and their children who naturalize cease to be foreign and become simply German, at least in data. Given the low rate of naturalization in Germany, the error created by the omission of naturalized members of immigrant groups is presumably small.)

The panel for thirteen- to fifteen-year-olds in table 5.1 offers a snapshot of ethnic differences at a point when children have completed elementary school but, with rare exceptions, are too young to have entered vocational training programs (Köhler 1992). This age stratum thus offers a very clear picture of school placement inequalities. It is readily apparent that foreign children of all groups are considerably more likely than German children of the same ages to attend *Hauptschulen*.[3] The order of magnitude of these differences is quite large, approaching 2 to 1 in some cases; thus, while approximately one-third of German children are found in *Hauptschulen*, two-thirds of Turkish and Italian children are in this track. Germans, by contrast, are more likely than foreign children to attend the *Gymnasien* (the plural form of *Gymnasium*). Again, the order of magnitude of the differences between Germans and most groups is quite substantial, and is largest (4 or 5 to 1) in relation to the Turks and Italians. But differences among the ethnic groups are also noteworthy. Aside from the residual category, in which children from such countries as France and the United States figure importantly, Greek and, to a lesser extent, Yugoslav children are more likely than Turks and Italians to be in the *Gymnasium* track. The Greek case is quite singular, however, because of the existence in some parts of Germany of a separate *Gymnasium* system for Greek students, with instruction in their mother tongue (this system is briefly described by Hopf 1987; see also Zentrum für Türkeistudien 1994). Obviously, this gives many Greek children an advantage that other immigrant children lack.

The data for sixteen- to eighteen-year-olds add the possibility of entry to an apprenticeship or other vocational training, primarily for those who have attended *Hauptschulen* or *Realschulen* (in this age group, a small percentage of children has already left the school system; they are allocated in the table according to their diploma and further training). In terms of the three-way division among the *Hauptschule*, *Realschule*, and *Gymnasium* tracks, not much has changed between the previous age group and this one. The percentages of the various groups who have attended *Hauptschulen* are somewhat lower, but in general these differences are closely matched by the percentages in the "vocational training" category (for whose members the type of general education is not recorded), suggesting that many of these students were originally in *Hauptschulen*. Also noteworthy difference is that, among sixteen- to eighteen-year-olds, Greek students have caught up with, and even exceeded, German children in terms of *Gymnasium* attendance, underscoring the singularity of their situation.

But it is in terms of entry to an apprenticeship, especially after attending a *Hauptschule*, that the results for sixteen- to eighteen-year-olds appear most interesting. Among German students, to take one extreme, *Hauptschule* students who enter an apprenticeship outnumber those who do not by a large margin, nearly 3 to 1. (This margin is somewhat reduced by the presence of sixteen-year-olds, some of whom are still in the general school system.) Only a small fraction of Germans in this age group, about 9 percent at worst, appear to be destined to leave the school system with a *Hauptschule* diploma but no apprenticeship. Among foreign *Hauptschule* students, those who have entered an apprenticeship are about equal in number to those who have not. The result among the groups that have large fractions in the *Hauptschule* track, the Turks and Italians, is that a substantial proportion of students, about a third, have at this point only their *Hauptschule* experience. Most of them appear destined to leave the school system with the most minimal of credentials or perhaps no credentials whatsoever (see also Faist 1993b). (Other data, from the early 1990s, appear to indicate that one-sixth of foreign students leave the school system without a diploma [Zentrum für Türkeistudien 1994, 219; Herrmann 1995].) Similar differences, but not as striking in magnitude, appear among *Realschule* students.

Not only do foreign children have less chance than do Germans to enter apprenticeships, but, when they do, they cluster in those preparatory for a limited range of jobs. Beautician and pharmacist's assistant apprenticeships for girls, metal worker, mechanic, and electrician slots for boys—these typify the choices most open to foreign children (Zentrum für Türkeistudien 1994, 242). Some immigrant parents may prefer such apprenticeships for their children because the occupations to which they lead permit self-employment and may also be practiced in the country of origin in the event of return. But, as Faist (1993b) points out, the apprenticeships where immigrant youth are concentrated tend also to be in industries where apprenticeships are used as a major source of low-wage labor and there are relatively few full-time jobs. Hence a relatively high risk of unemployment is associated with these apprenticeships. Higher-status white-collar apprenticeships—in banks, for instance—are largely closed to immigrant youth because of the knowledge of language and cultural norms that they require and also because they are more and more usurped by youth coming from higher educational tracks.

However, a glance in table 5.1 at the next older age group, nineteen- to twenty-one-year-olds, suggests that the present picture for foreign children nevertheless represents an improvement over the recent past. In this age group, where education is complete for most students (aside from those attending technical colleges or universities), even larger fractions of foreign children completed their schooling with no more than a *Hauptschule* diploma (at best). For the Turks, this was true for about half; for the Italians, for about 40 percent. Greeks, too, show a large concentration in this category. The conclusion that some improvement in the placement of immigrant children has taken place is also supported by data over time, which show between 1985 and 1991 a shift in the direction of *Gymnasien* and *Realschulen* and away from the *Hauptschulen* (Zentrum für Türkeistudien 1994, 213).

One of the frequently encountered explanations for the lower placement and attainment of foreign children in German schools is that many of them come to Germany after the age of school entry and after already having attended schools in their home countries (see, e.g., Herrmann 1995, 24). The problem is familiar enough to be described by a special designation in German, *Seiteneinsteiger* (literally, a "lateral entrant"). But the data in figure 5.2 suggest that late arrival in Germany can explain only a limited amount of the ethnic inequality in school placement. The figure displays the percentages of the different ethnic groups that belong to the second generation, which, by the definition we use, encompasses those who were either born in Germany or immigrated before the age of school entry (at five years of age). Large fractions of the three age categories presented in table 5.1 are already in the second generation. In the thirteen- to fifteen-year-old age group, for example, three-quarters or more of children from the four main immigrant groups belong to the second generation, yet these children still lag demonstrably behind their German peers. Nevertheless, the generational distribution of these groups is shifting, and rather dramatically so. In general, the proportions belonging to the second generation are lower among sixteen- to eighteen-year-olds. To take the extreme case, barely half of Turkish children belong to it, although otherwise clear majorities of the remaining groups (aside from the residual category) do. The size of the second generation is further reduced in the nineteen- to twenty-one-year-old group, where it makes up barely a third of Turks and slightly more than half of the remaining groups (of course, some of the youths in this age group may have arrived in Germany after their schooling was complete). This pattern indicates that the fraction constituted by the second generation is increasing over time among foreign school-age children.

The conclusion that immigration after the age of school entry cannot explain by itself the profound differences in educational placement and outcome between German and non-German children can be demonstrated by restricting the comparison of school placement to native Germans and second-generation immigrant children (for the data, see Alba, Handl, and Müller 1994, 221). Among the thirteen- to fifteen-year-olds, the percentages in the *Hauptschulen* are quite similar to those in table 5.1. Some reductions, quite modest, seem noticeable among the sixteen- to eighteen-year-olds, and somewhat more substantial ones are found among the nineteen- to twenty-one-year-olds. However, the generational distribution does appear to explain the differences noted earlier between the oldest age group and the younger ones. Thus the improvements in educational placement noticeable in table 5.1 are due less to any change in the educational system, i.e., a lowering of barriers for immigrant children, than to changes in the immigrant groups themselves: a rising proportion of children belonging to the second generation who presumably have better command of the German language and are acclimated in other ways that enhance their prospects in schools. But, obviously, a great disparity remains between Germans and non-Germans in the school system.

Figure 5.2 Second Generation among Immigrant Children

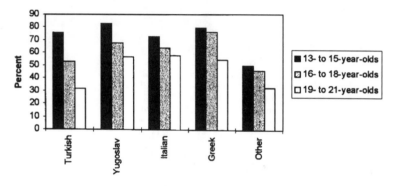

Note: The second generation as defined here is constituted of immigrant children who were either born in Germany or immigrated before the age of five.

Influences on the School Success of Immigrant Children

To consider the extent to which background factors such as socioeconomic origins can explain the very substantial differences between foreign and German students, we take advantage of one of the strengths of the Microcensus: namely, for children who live with their parents (the vast majority of children in the two younger age groups we are considering), we are able to take into account various characteristics of their families, such as their parents' occupations. In particular, we control statistically for the effects of socioeconomic background as measured by the educa-

Table 5.2 Effects of Ethnic and Social Background on Placement in a *Hauptschule* for Thirteen- to Fifteen-Year-Olds

Ethnicity

German**	—
Turkish	+12.4*
Yugoslav	+7.4*
Italian	+18.0*
Greek	+0.0
Other nationalities	-0.2

Generation/age at arrival

German— second generation**	—
5-9 years old	+12.7*
10-14 years old	+18.5*
Unknown	+5.4

Household head's education

No diploma (or no information)	+49.5*
Hauptschule without apprenticeship	+50.2*
Hauptschule with apprenticeship	+43.9*
Realschule without apprenticeship	+34.3*
Realschule with apprenticeship	+29.2*
Abitur (*Gymnasium*)	+17.9*
Technical college	+14.8*
College or university**	—

Household head's occupation

Agricultural	+21.0*
Simple manual	+30.8*
Qualified manual	+24.3*
Technical	+3.0
Engineering	+2.2
Simple service	+28.8*
Qualified service	+13.1
Semiprofessional	+11.7
Professional**	—
Clerical/simple administrative	+12.2
Qualified administrative	+4.2
Managerial	+3.6
Unemployed/Social welfare	+43.1*
Other employment	+23.3*
Unknown	+26.1*
Self-employed	-2.6

Family size, gender

Number of children in household	+3.9*
Male	+8.4*

Residence

In state with high proportion of foreigners	-0.9
Small city**	—
Medium-sized city	-2.4
Large city	-11.0*

p <.05
** indicates reference category.

tional attainment and occupational position of the head of the child's household. We also take note of the head's self-employment, which, in light of the U.S. experience, might be thought to confer an educational advantage. Family size is another likely influence on educational attainment, since parents of large families are less able to invest in the educations of individual children. Finally, our analysis takes into account geographic variables that may impact on educational attainment, because the complexity of a school system and the relative availability of certain tracks depend on location. Two such variables are community size (the opportunity to enter higher tracks may be curtailed in smaller communities) and the proportion of foreigners in a state's (*Bundesland*) population (immigrant children who reside where there are few other foreigners may be at some advantage because they are less likely to be segregated in separate classes [Baker and Lenhardt 1988]). The discussion that follows is based on the results of a multivariate logistic regression analysis, in which these factors are included, along with ethnic group and generation. Thus the ethnic differences that remain are net of the other variables included in the equations; in others words, they reveal educational differences between immigrant and German children who are statistically made equal in terms of socioeconomic origins, family size, and geographic location. Further, the generational variable is specified in such a way that the ethnic differences are estimated for immigrant children of the second generation.

For the most part, the background factors have the effects one would anticipate. The most pronounced effects are associated with the educational attainment of the household head (in the vast majority of cases, a parent), as shown in table 5.2. For instance, the chance of placement outside the lowest, or *Hauptschule*, track increases quite substantially with each step

upward in the head's education. The discrepancy in track placement associated with the extreme categories of parental educational attainment is great: 50 percentage points in placement
probability.[4] That is, the child of a university graduate is about
50 percentage points less likely to be in the lowest school track
than the child of a parent who completed only the *Hauptschule*
(or its non-German equivalent) him- or herself. Compared to
this impact, the effects of other socioeconomic background characteristics are more modest. To be sure, the occupation of the
household head also contributes to determining a child's educational track. Compared to the children of parents with professional occupations, those whose parents perform simple manual
or service occupations are the most likely to be in *Hauptschulen*.
The difference associated with these parental occupational categories is 60 percent of the magnitude of that associated with
the extreme categories of parental education. Also having
markedly lower chances to escape the *Hauptschulen* are the
children of parents with manual occupations requiring few
qualifications or agricultural occupations. Even more disadvantaged are the children of parents whose main income comes
from unemployment compensation or social welfare payments.
Children who come from large families are also more likely to
be found in the *Hauptschulen*. The children of the self-employed are, however, not different from the children of parents
employed by others.

Geography plays a role, too. In particular, children who grow
up in substantial-sized cities (with populations of 100,000 or
more) have an advantage compared to other children when it
comes to attending a *Realschule* or *Gymnasium*. Presumably,
this advantage occurs because places in these tracks are more
available in larger cities than elsewhere. However, location in a
state with a large foreign population does not seem to affect the
kind of school a child attends. Possibly, this effect is absent here
because our analysis assumes that it is similar for both German
and non-German students. But some evidence indicates a more
complex interaction with ethnic origin that results from what is
effectively an ethnic queue within school systems (Baker et al.
1985; Baker and Lenhardt 1988; for a general discussion of such
queues, see Lieberson 1980): namely, that German students are
in a variety of ways preferred in school. Therefore, in areas with

relatively many foreign schoolchildren—or, alternatively put, relatively few German children—the *Hauptschule* track is more completely occupied by foreign students, and the relative chance of the average German student to enter one of the more desirable tracks is enhanced. Of course, in such areas, there may also be more spillover of the numerous foreign students into higher tracks, creating a more distinct non-German presence in *Realschulen* and *Gymnasien*, so that indeed the effects of geography are not simple in this respect.

After the more straightforward socioeconomic and geographic differences have been taken into account, immigrant children of the second generation are still better situated in the school system than are those of the first: they are more likely to be placed in favored tracks than are children who came to Germany after their fifth birthday. There is also an observable tendency, though it is not entirely uniform, for the disadvantage of the first-generation children to rise with their age at arrival (this is clearer when all the models in our analysis are considered, not just the one presented in table 5.2). The older children are when they first come to Germany, in other words, the more likely they are to wind up in the *Hauptschulen*.

With statistical controls in place, what is left of ethnic differences? A substantial portion, it appears, though a considerable part is also explained, thus narrowing the apparent extent of ethnic disadvantage (see figure 5.3). The most salient aspect of that disadvantage, according to table 5.1, lies in the concentration of the children from non-German groups in the *Hauptschulen*. When socioeconomic and other background factors are controlled, Italian and Turkish children of the second generation still stand out in the degree of their concentration in the *Hauptschulen*. For second-generation Greek children, there is no difference from German children, while for Yugoslavs the degree of disadvantage is modest. The same cannot be said for the Turkish and Italian children, however, who in the thirteen- to fifteen-year-old group have a 12 to 18 percentage point greater probability of attending *Hauptschulen* than do German children who are comparable in socioeconomic background, family size, and geographic location. To be sure, this margin of disadvantage is substantially less than the more than thirty point differential in table 5.1.

Figure 5.3 Ethnic Differences Net of Background

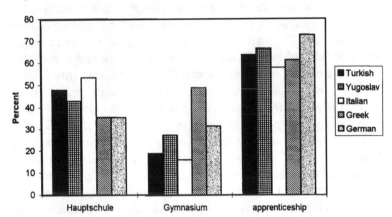

Note: The percentages shown are approximations derived from the coefficients in logistic regression analyses in which socioeconomic background, geographic location, generation, and other factors have been controlled. In each
case, a reference percentage has been attributed to the German group based
on its educational distribution in table 5.1, and other percentages have been
computed accordingly. The percentages in apprenticeships are for
Hauptschule students only.

Concentration in *Hauptschulen*, the least advantaged track of
the system, implies underrepresentation in the *Gymnasien*, the
most advantaged. To some extent, there is a mirror-image quality to representation in the lowest and highest tracks, but the
reversals—overrepresentation in one, underrepresentation in
the other—do not coincide exactly. This is true, in particular, for
second-generation Greek and Yugoslav children, once other
background factors are controlled. In terms of placement in the
Gymnasium track, Yugoslav children are not significantly disadvantaged compared to Germans, and Greek children even
appear to be advantaged, for the reason we have already suggested. Once again, though, the second-generation children of
Italian and Turkish parents are disadvantaged. Our analyses
imply that their chances of attending a *Gymnasium* are 13 to 16
percentage points lower than those for German children of comparable family background and geographic location. Nevertheless, this is smaller than the magnitudes in table 5.1
(twenty-four to twenty-five points in this age group); in this

sense, some of the original difference has been explained. But much remains.

The fork to the three main branches of the educational system is one with great and long-term consequences. But, as we have seen, a second fork is potentially consequential for older children, sixteen- to eighteen-year-olds: entry into an apprenticeship rather than immediate entry into the labor market. Though students from any of the tracks may enter apprenticeships, this fork has its most serious impact for children in *Hauptschulen*. The multivariate analysis suggests that children of all foreign groups have relatively low access to this typically German educational outcome. Unquestionably disadvantaged once again are second-generation Italian and Turkish children; that is, they are less likely to obtain apprenticeships than are comparable German children who also attended *Hauptschulen*. For second-generation Greek and Yugoslav children, the estimated differences from German children are not statistically significant, but they are nevertheless in the direction indicating disadvantage (because of this consistency, we hold open the possibility that there are real differences).

The disadvantages of Turkish and Italian children in gaining entry to apprenticeships are all the more noteworthy, of course, because these are the very groups that are most highly concentrated in the *Hauptschulen* in the first place. If both kinds of disadvantages, in track placement and in apprenticeship entry, are considered simultaneously, the cumulative effect of various educational selection processes manifests itself clearly. From this perspective, second-generation Yugoslav children also appear to be disadvantaged. They, the children of Turkish parents, and those of Italian origins leave, with increasingly greater frequency from first to last, the school system with only a *Hauptschule* education, no more in other words than the legally required minimum of schooling (which, for many foreign children, also entails no formal credential). The magnitude of the differences is considerable. For the Yugoslavs and Turks, the probability of leaving school with the minimum education is 1.5 to 1.6 times that for comparable Germans; for the Italians, it is 2.2 times.

In sum, a rather consistent picture has emerged. The recent arrival of many foreign families and their lower socioeconomic origins do not appear capable of fully explaining the substantial disadvantages borne by the children of some ethnic groups in the German educational system. Disadvantages are narrowed by time, but persist into the second generation. The most consistently disadvantaged groups are the Italians and the Turks, who are considerably less likely than their German peers to attend *Gymnasien* and consistently more likely to be found in *Hauptschulen* and to emerge from them without apprenticeship training. There is some evidence that Yugoslav youths are also more likely to be allocated to the *Hauptschule* track and not to be admitted to apprenticeships. But not all foreign groups are disadvantaged: Greek students are more likely than Germans and other groups to enter the *Gymnasium* track. Nevertheless, the heterogeneity of the disadvantaged groups indicates that one commonsense explanation fails. The groups include, on the one hand, one with origins outside the European Union, salient religious and cultural differences from the German population, and a relatively brief presence in Germany (the Turks) but, on the other, the EU group with the longest history of migration to the Federal Republic (the Italians).

It is worth noting at this juncture that a recent analysis of similar data concerning the French system demonstrates that immigrant children are not everywhere disadvantaged in school systems. Vallet and Caille (1995) find that, once socioeconomic origins are taken into account, the apparent disadvantage of immigrant children in French schools largely disappears and, in a few respects, they even have more favorable educational outcomes than do French children coming from similar socioeconomic milieus. A point made by Vallet and Caille also deserves to be introduced here: equating the low educational attainment of immigrant parents who come from societies where the majority receives the same amount of education (e.g., rural Turkey) with the low education of natives in societies like France and Germany where the majority completes at least secondary school understates the expectations for school success on the part of immigrant children (in effect, the socioeconomic peers of these children are set too far down in the social structure of the host society). As a consequence, an analysis that controls for parental education, such as the one above, may also understate the net educational differences between the children of natives and those of immigrants. In short, the substantial differences we have found are most likely a minimum estimate.

Ethnic Home Contexts and Educational Disadvantage

Perhaps features of the situations of immigrant groups in the Federal Republic other than generation and socioeconomic position can explain the remaining portion of educational disadvantage. To look at this possibility, we must go beyond the Microcensus, because, like U.S. census data, it contains little more than standard demographic and labor-market variables. We turn therefore to another important body of data, the Socioeconomic Panel, a long-running longitudinal survey of a representative set of German households supplemented by samples of the five largest immigrant groups (Spaniards, not included in our analysis, make up the fifth group; for an English-language discussion of the data set, see Wagner, Schupp, and Rendtel 1993). These data allow us to probe the educational impact of three major dimensions related to our earlier conceptual discussion: (1) immersion in an ethnic cultural and social world, which is measured in the panel data by the German-speaking ability of a student's parents, an index of the cultural climate in the home (based on the food, music, and newspapers it contains), and a count of the coethnic friends of the parent who is named as household head; (2) intentions to return home, measured by remittances to the homeland (often a form of investment), the desire to return as expressed by the household head, the self-identification (as German or non-German) of the household head, and whether the child has been educated at least partly in the homeland (which we take as a reflection of the desire to prepare the child for return); and (3) discrimination, measured as the ethnic composition of the neighborhood, which arguably correlates with such forms of institutional discrimination as separate classes for foreign students (this measure is the most debatable in terms of conceptual significance, and we grant that it could also be placed with the first dimension).

Figure 5.4 shows the distributions of these ethnic indicators across the four major immigrant groups. One sees, first of all, that the differences among the groups in terms of the indicators only partly correspond with their ranking in educational disadvantage. In general, the Turks appear to be the most ethnic in all dimensions and the Yugoslavs the least, though both patterns are not consistent across every indicator. Italians and Greeks occupy the middle ground, which therefore includes the least disadvantaged group (the Greeks) and one of the two most disadvantaged (the Italians).

Turkish distinctiveness is reasonably clear. Consider, for example, the language likely to be spoken at home: in two-thirds of Turkish students' families, at least one parent speaks German poorly; this is true for no more than one-third of the families of students from other groups. Turks are equally distinctive when it comes to the food, music, and newspapers at home. Further, Turkish parents are the most likely to have educated their children partly in the homeland. In some cases, the Turks are roughly tied with one of the other groups for ethnic distinctiveness. For instance, Turkish and Greek household heads are least likely to express a wish to remain indefinitely in Germany, and they are also the least likely to identify, even partially, as Germans.

Figure 5.4 Ethnic Characteristics of Immigrant Children

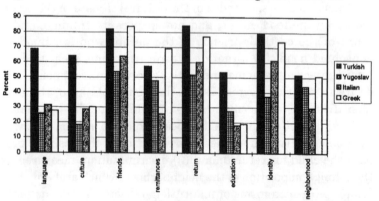

Note: "Language" is based on the German-speaking ability of parents; specifically, it is the percentage of children with a parent who speaks German poorly or not at all. "Culture" is a measure of the cultural climate at home, as reflected in cuisine, newspapers, and music; the bars present the

percentages of homes where at least two of these three are mainly non-German. "Friends" refers to the ethnicity of the three best friends of the household head and is reported as the percentage who name at least two coethnic friends. "Remittances" indicates that the household head has sent money to the home country. "Return" is the self-declared intention of the household head to return eventually to the home country. "Education" presents the percentages of children who have been partly educated in the home country. "Identity" reports the percentages of household heads who define themselves largely or exclusively in terms of homeland (i.e., non-German) identities. "Neighborhood" indicates the percentage of children residing in mainly non-German neighborhoods.

The distinctiveness of the Yugoslav groups, who anchor the other end of the spectrum, is not quite so sharply defined. On the one hand, they have the most German cultural climate at home (at least as measured by cooking, listening, and reading), and Yugoslav parents are the most likely, and by a good margin, to identify with Germans. In a similar vein, Yugoslav parents are the least likely to have only coethnic friends. On the other hand, when it comes to the parents' ability to speak German, Yugoslavs are just slightly ahead of Italians. They are also not much ahead of the Italians in terms of the household head's desire to remain in Germany. Further, Yugoslavs are more likely than Italians to send remittances to the homeland, while they are less likely to reside in a neighborhood dominated by Germans.

These indicators seems consistent with the Turkish disadvantage in the school system but not with the Italian disadvantage or the Greek advantage. Of course, to assess the explanatory usefulness of these indicators, we must also look to their association with placement in the *Hauptschulen*. (Because of the more limited size of the Socioeconomic Panel, we must streamline the analysis to focus solely on placement in a *Hauptschule* versus one of the other tracks; this is undoubtedly the most critical decision point.) This issue is addressed by table 5.3. It demonstrates that only some of the indicators are potentially of value in explaining ethnic disadvantage. The most consistently positive findings are for the measures of ethnic immersion, which mainly tap into cultural affiliations and secondarily into ethnic social ones. For each of these indicators, students who come from more ethnic homes are more likely to be found in the *Hauptschulen*. For instance, three-quarters of students from homes where at least one parent speaks German badly are in the *Hauptschulen*, compared to half of those whose parents both speak German well. Likewise, two-thirds of students from homes where the household head has mainly coethnic friends are in the *Hauptschulen*, compared to one-third from homes where the head has mainly friends of other backgrounds (usually Germans). Though this is not shown in the table, which simplifies matters by not presenting ethnic detail, these patterns also hold separately within three of the four groups; the exception is the Greek group, where none of the cultural indicators bears any relationship to placement in a *Hauptschule*. The exception underscores our consistent finding that a different set of forces is at work in Greek school placement.

Table 5.3 Ethnic Characteristics in Relation to *Hauptschule* Placement among Immigrant Children

	Percentage in *Hauptschule*
German-speaking ability of parents	
good or very good	47.0
fairly good	61.5
poor or not at all	77.1
Cultural climate at home (1-3 scale)	
mainly German (0-1)	50.0
mainly ethnic (2-3)	68.8
Number of coethnic friends of household head	
0-1	35.0
2-3	66.0
Remittances to homeland	
no	69.1
yes	63.9
Intention of household head to return to homeland	
no	63.4
yes	67.6
Continuity of education in Germany	
educated only in Germany	57.8
partly in homeland	77.5

Self-identification of household head

mainly/only German	60.5
mainly/only foreign	69.2

Ethnic composition of neighborhood

mostly German	65.7
mostly non-German	66.2

In general, the other indicators do not show much relationship to *Hauptschule* attendance. This absence is especially striking for the multiple indicators of the intention to return. Neither money sent to the homeland nor the expressed desire to return there has a statistically meaningful relationship to *Hauptschule* placement. There is only a modest relationship in the case of the head's self-identification, and while this relationship seems more pronounced for the Italians and Yugoslavs, it is missing for the Turks (and even reversed among the Greeks). The neighborhood composition measure, included as an indicator of the potential for institutional discrimination, also displays no relationship to school placement.

The one nonimmersion measure with possible explanatory value derives from the child's school career and expresses whether this has been solely in German schools or partly (or, though this is much less likely, wholly) in schools in the homeland. Although, according to the Socioeconomic Panel data, the great majority of children from all groups but the Turks have attended only German schools, the measure is still relevant because it reflects a contingency that is quite likely to influence school placement. As the figure shows, those children who received at least some of their education in their homelands are considerably more likely than others to have been placed in *Hauptschulen* (or their country-of-origin equivalents). Only the Greeks deviate from this pattern.

Even when socioeconomic background and other factors are taken into account in a multivariate analysis, it still appears that the culture in the parental home, as reflected in, say, the German-speaking ability of parents, along with the degree to which school careers take place solely in Germany play independent roles in determining school placement for the children of immigrants. The conclusion is drawn from analyses that parallel those described in the previous section as much as possible within the limits of the data set (the precise results are presented in Alba, Handl, and Müller 1994, 232). Because the number of cases in the Socioeconomic Panel is much less than in the Microcensus, it is necessary both to simplify the detail in which variables such as parental occupation are represented and to ignore the nationality distinctions among foreign children. Further, because of the high degree of correlation among the different indicators of the cultural atmosphere in the parental home, it is also necessary to select one of them to represent this important dimension. For largely technical reasons, we have selected the German-speaking ability of parents to serve in this role.

The evidence of an effect on school placement is strong for parental language, where the critical distinction lies between those whose parents speak German poorly or not at all and everyone else. Stated in probability terms, children who come from such backgrounds have, ceteris paribus, a probability of placement in the *Hauptschule* track that is 14 percentage points higher than that of foreign children whose parents speak German well. The potential impact of this sort of cultural immersion is further underscored by the fact that a quarter to a third of the children from most immigrant groups come from such homes and, in the case of Turkish children, the proportion rises to two-thirds. The evidence for an effect of homeland school attendance is weaker but still sufficient to give it credibility. Such an effect is not likely to be merely the consequence of late immigration to Germany after the onset of schooling, given that our analysis takes into account generation and age at immigration. We believe that it reflects also the school placement of children who migrate between Germany and their home countries (*pendeln*), which has been reported as a pattern for some of these groups (for the Turks, see Schiffauer 1991). When the two effects—of parental language and homeland school career—are taken into account, there is no longer any statistically significant difference between foreign and German children.

In general, we regard the findings of this section as very suggestive that the cultural atmosphere in the family, along with the continuity of the school career in Germany, contribute important elements to the explanation of ethnic disadvantage in German schools. We are nevertheless cognizant of the limitations of our analysis, and accordingly these results should not be viewed as definitive (nevertheless, they are largely confirmed and also extended in the recent analysis of the Socioeconomic Panel data in Büchel and Wagner 1996). Of the two types of variables that appear to be influential, the cultural one is probably the more important. In most of the major foreign groups, the majority of children attend only German schools (at least insofar as we can track their careers in the Socioeconomic Panel data). But the cultural atmosphere is more variable, and if it is associated with disadvantages, these are presumably quite pervasive.

Conclusion

Our analysis has demonstrated unambiguously that some of the largest non-German groups in Germany are disadvantaged in its school system: their children are more likely to be placed in the lowest track of that system, the *Hauptschulen*, and to leave it with its least valuable credential, a *Hauptschule* diploma without an apprenticeship, if they achieve any credential at all. The analysis further demonstrates that these disadvantages are not just by-products of the lower socioeconomic origins of foreign children or the recency of their arrival. When these factors, along with others, are taken into account, substantial disadvantage persists for at least two groups, the Italians and Turks (and, arguably for a third: children of parents from the former Yugoslavia). Disadvantages persist, then, into the second generation at least. Increasingly, these disadvantages have taken on an ethnic character, as opposed to an immigrant one.

The differing social acceptability and legal situations of the two most disadvantaged groups suggest that no simple explanation of disadvantage can be fashioned from these factors alone. One of these groups, the Turks, meets the criteria for a highly visible, socially stigmatized, and legally disadvantaged group. Studies of the Turkish group alone (e.g., Geiersbach 1989; Schiffauer 1991) often seem to suggest that such factors contribute heavily to disadvantage in school because, for instance, parents, reluctant to make a permanent commitment in an uncertain situation, must plan their children's school careers with the possibility of return ever in mind. But the same factors do not apply to the same degree to the second group, the Italians. Not only are they the longest residing guest-worker group (Spaich 1991), but they hold legal privileges associated with EU status and are socially accepted by Germans to a much greater degree than are Turks (this is indicated, incidentally, by a comparatively high rate of intermarriage with Germans, which is also revealed in the Microcensus data).

The fact that Greek children are advantaged, even by comparison with Germans when it comes to *Gymnasium* attendance, would seem to suggest that group-specific explanations for school disadvantage must be sought. But the Greek case is ambiguous in its implications for larger ethnic patterns. On the one hand, it could be, as one analyst has argued (Hopf 1987), that Greek school success is attributable to the selective character of Greek immigration. On the other, however, the Greek advantage is at least partly due to a peculiar aspect of Greek ethnic institutions in Germany: as already mentioned, Greek students can attend a separate *Gymnasium* system, with instruction in Greek. Although we cannot identify in the Microcensus or Socioeconomic Panel data whether Greek students attend such *Gymnasien*, we have demonstrated that the Greek educational pattern—in relation to cultural variables, for instance—is quite unlike that of other non-German groups. Given the facts that such a separate system exists and that Greek students are more likely than others to attend *Gymnasien*, the conclusion that Greek *Gymnasien* play a significant role seems unavoidable. If it is correct, then the degree of Greek advantage in German *Gymnasien* is unclear and so, for the moment, does not challenge our central conclusion that the children of the main foreign groups are, in varying degrees, disadvantaged in German schools.

On a more positive note, we have found that cultural factors, such as the language spoken in the home, and the child's school career, particularly whether it is divided between Germany and the home society, are strongly associated with ethnic disadvantage. The question that must now be asked is: what larger interpretation should be placed on these findings? At first sight, they seem to fit best with conventional explanations of disadvantage that focus on characteristics of ethnic minorities, such as their cultural heritage and their intentions to return eventually to their homelands. Thus language is probably the most important medium for communicating ethnically distinctive aspirations, values, and so on—cultural configurations, in sum—that may affect the ways different groups make use of schools. (Of course, speaking a non-German tongue at home may also frequently lead to educational disadvantage because it is linked with an imperfect knowledge of German.) A school career that is divided between two societies may reflect the intentions of parents to return to the homeland.

Nevertheless, we wish to caution against too quick an acceptance of such conclusions. Cultural traits may also stand out as visible signs of foreignness and thus may be pivotal to the often subtle discriminations that engender school disadvantage for minorities (this is suggested by U.S. research summarized by Persell 1976). Moreover, the intention to return and the tenacity with which some families hold on to ethnic identities and aspects of their ethnic cultures could reflect the ultimate uncertainty they feel about their long-term prospects in a society where they are subject to social stigma and a variety of disadvantages because of their foreignness. We therefore believe that the questions about the role of discrimination and broader social (and, for some groups, legal) disadvantage must remain open. They should not be foreclosed by our findings.

Another question that must remain open for the moment is whether ethnic disadvantage for the groups analyzed here is likely to decline in the future. In terms of generational change, our results are quite consistent with assimilation theories: for example, the educational disadvantage of second-generation children is, in general, considerably less than that of children who migrated after the onset of schooling (see also Esser 1990). Generation matters, in short. Moreover, the second generation may not be the best for testing the ultimate socioeconomic integration of an immigrant group; it may be still too marked by cultural and social distinctiveness to fit easily into the receiving society. Further changes can be expected in the third generation, which has not yet emerged in sufficient numbers in Germany to assess its situation. In the United States, the Italian group, for example, also stood out for its disadvantage in school (see Perlmann 1988), until, in the post-World War II period, the third generation came of school age (Alba 1985). In other words, parity in schooling came only after a half century had elapsed from the high point of Italian immigration to the United States. Nevertheless, there is also a counterbalancing force in view: that of continued immigration into Germany. Virtually all sober forecasts indicate that Germany will need immigration for the foreseeable future to maintain its economic and demographic vitality (for an overview of the latest prognoses, see Bade 1994b). Thus the generational distribution of the foreign population may not shift radically in the direction of the third and later generations, because new immigrants will repopulate the first and second. Accordingly, critical questions about the ultimate trajectory of immigrant groups in Germany must remain open for the time being.

Notes

1. For work that addresses the integration of ethnic German groups, see Lüttinger 1986; Handl and Herrmann 1994; and Rainer Münz and Rainer Ohliger, "Long-Distance Citizens: Ethnic Germans and Their Immigration to Germany," ch. 6 in this volume.
2. There is, in truth, a still more disadvantaged track of the German school system, the so-called special schools (*Sonderschulen*), for children who not able to keep pace in the regular schools, because of learning disabilities, for instance. Immigrant children are overrepresented in these schools, but we are not able to address issues of placement in them using the Microcensus data. Nevertheless, only a small fraction—less than 6 percent—of all immigrant children are found in special schools (Zentrum für Türkeistudien 1994), so these schools do not rival the *Hauptschulen* as determinants of the educational attainments of foreign children in Germany.
3. A few simplifications have been imposed to make the distributions in table 5.1 more readily intelligible. The most important is that students currently in comprehensive schools (i.e., *integrierte Gesamtschulen*) were assigned to the category for the middle branch of the system, the *Realschulen*. This affects 5 percent of the thirteen- to fifteen-year-olds, 2 percent of the sixteen- to eighteen-year-olds, and none of the nineteen- to twenty-one-year-olds. Since these percentages are quite similar across ethnic groups (except for an unusual concentration in comprehensive schools of children in the

residual non-German category), the practical effect on ethnic comparisons is minimal.

4. The percentage differences associated with variables in table 5.2 are approximations. The more precise effects are expressed in the coefficients of a logistic regression analysis, which implies the effects of variables, and have been translated into the approximate differences in table 5.2 by assuming that the members of a reference category for each variable have the same probability of *Hauptschule* placement as the average German student (.354 or 35.4 percent in table 5.1). As is well known, the translation of logistic regression coefficients into percentages or probabilities depends on the reference value chosen. Given our choice of an average value, the effects depicted in the table are reasonably representative.

References

Alba, Richard. 1985. *Italian Americans: Into the Twilight of Ethnicity*. Englewood Cliffs: Prentice-Hall.

_____, Johann Handl, and Walter Müller. 1994. "Ethnische Ungleichheit im Deutschen Bildungssystem." *Kölner Zeitschrift für Soziologie und Sozialpsychologie* 46, no. 2: 209–37.

Allmendinger, Jutta. 1989. *Career Mobility Dynamics: A Comparative Analysis of the United States, Norway, and West Germany*. Berlin: Max-Planck-Institut für Bildungsforschung.

Bade, Klaus J., ed. 1994a. *Ausländer—Aussiedler—Asyl: Eine Bestandsaufnahme*. Munich: Beck.

_____. 1994b. *Das Manifest der 60: Deutschland und die Einwanderung*. Munich: Beck.

Baker, David, Yilmaz Esmer, Gero Lenhardt, and John Meyer. 1985. "Effects of Immigrant Workers on Educational Stratification in Germany." *Sociology of Education* 58 (Oct.): 21–27.

Baker, David, and Gero Lenhardt. 1991. "Nationalismus und Arbeitsmarktintegration in der BRD(alt)," *Zeitschrift für Soziologie* 20 (Dec.): 463–78.

_____. 1988. "Ausländerintegration, Schule, und Staat." *Kölner Zeitschrift für Soziologie und Sozialpsychologie* 40, no. 1: 40–61.

Blauner, Robert. 1972. *Racial Oppression in America*. New York: Harper and Row.

Boos-Nünning, Ursula. 1994. "Familie, Jugend, Bildungsarbeit." In *Das Manifest der 60: Deutschland und die Einwanderung*, ed. Klaus J. Bade, 43–48. Munich: Beck.

Boos-Nünning, Ursula, Alice Jaeger, Renate Henscheid, Wolfgang Sieber, and Heike Becker. 1990. *Berufswahlsituation und Berufswahlprozesse griechischer, italienischer und portugiesischer Jugendlicher*. Beiträge zur Arbeitsmarkt und Berufsforschung 140. Nüremberg: IAB.

Brubaker, Rogers. 1992. *Citizenship and Nationhood in France and Germany*. Cambridge: Harvard University Press.

Büchel, Felix, and Gert Wagner. 1996. "Soziale Differenzen der Bildungschancen in Westdeutschland: Unter besonderer Berücksichtigung von Zuwandererkindern." In *Lebenslagen im Wandel: Sozialberichterstattung im Längsschnitt*, ed. Wolfgang Zapf, Jürgen Schupp, and Roland Habich, 80–96. Frankfurt: Campus.

Deutsches Institut für Wirtschaftsforschung. 1994a. "Ausländerintegration und Bildungspolitik." *Wochenbericht*, 20 Jan., 33–38.

———. 1994b. "Nach wie vor Rückstände in der Schul- und Berufsausbildung junger Ausländer." *Wochenbericht*, 14 July, 486–92.

Esser, Harmut. 1990. "Familienmigration und Schulkarriere ausländischer Kinder und Jugendlicher." In *Generation und Identität: Theoretische und Empirische Beiträge zur Migrationssoziologie*, ed. Hartmut Esser and Jürgen Friedrichs, 127–46. Opladen: Westdeutscher.

Esser, Hartmut. 1980. *Aspekte der Wanderungssoziologie: Assimilation und Integration von Wanderern, ethnischen Gruppen und Minderheiten*. Darmstadt-Neuwied: Luchterhand.

Esser, Hartmut, and Jürgen Friedrichs. 1990. *Generation und Identität: Theoretische und Empirische Beiträge zur Migrationssoziologie*. Opladen: Westdeutscher.

Faist, Thomas. 1993a. "Ein- und Ausgliedrung von Immigranten: Türken in Deutschland und mexikanische Amerikaner in den USA in den achtziger Jahren." *Soziale Welt* 44: 275–99.

———. 1993b. "From School to Work: Public Policy and Underclass Formation among Young Turks in Germany during the 1980s." *International Migration Review* 27 (summer): 306–31.

Gans, Herbert. 1982. *The Urban Villagers*. Rev. ed. New York: Free Press.

Geiersbach, Paul. 1989. *Warten bis die Züge Wieder Fahren: Ein Türkenghetto in Deutschland*. Berlin: Mink.

———. 1982. *Bruder, Musszusammen Zwiebel und Wasser Essen: Eine Türkische Familie in Deutschland*. Berlin/Bonn: Dietz.

Gordon, Milton. 1964. *Assimilation in American Life*. New York: Oxford University Press.

Handl, Johann, and Christa Herrmann. 1994. *Soziale und berufliche Umschichtung der Bevölkerung in Bayern nach 1945*. Munich: iudicium.

Heckmann, Friedrich. 1992. *Ethnischer Minderheiten, Volk, und Nation*. Stuttgart: Enke.

Herrmann, Helga. 1995. "Ausländische Jugendliche in Ausbildung und Beruf." *Aus Politik und Zeitgeschichte* B35: 23–29.

Hirschman, Charles. 1983. "America's Melting Pot Reconsidered." *Annual Review of Sociology* 9: 397–423.

Hopf, Diether. 1987. *Herkunft und Schulbesuch ausländischer Kinder: Eine Untersuchung am Beispiel griechischer Schüler.* Berlin: Max-Planck-Institut für Bildungsforschung.

Köhler, Helmut. 1992. *Bildungsbeteiligung und Sozialstruktur in der Bundesrepublik: Zu Stabilität und Wandel der Ungleichheit von Bildungschancen.* Berlin: Max-Planck-Institut für Bildungsforschung.

Korte, Elke. 1990. "Die Rückkehrorientierung im Eingliederungsprozess der Migrantenfamilien." In *Generation und Identität: Theoretische und Empirische Beiträge zur Migrationssoziologie,* ed. Hartmut Esser and Jürgen Friedrichs, 207–60. Opladen: Westdeutscher.

Kugler, Roland. 1993. *Ausländerrecht: Ein Handbuch.* Göttingen: Lamuv.

Lewis, Oscar. 1965. *La Vida.* New York: Vintage.

Lieberson, Stanley. 1980. *A Piece of the Pie.* Berkeley: University of California Press.

Light, Ivan. 1984. "Immigrant and Ethnic Enterprise in North America." *Ethnic and Racial Studies* 7 (Apr.): 195–216.

Lüttinger, Paul. 1986. "Der Mythos der schnellen Eingliederung: Eine empirische Untersuchung zur Integration der Vertriebenen und Flüchtlinge in der BRD bis 1971." *Zeitschrift für Soziologie* 15: 20–36.

Massey, Douglas, and Nancy Denton. 1993. *American Apartheid.* Cambridge: Harvard University Press.

Max Planck Institute for Human Development and Education. 1979. *Between Elite and Mass Education.* Albany: SUNY Press.

Müller, Walter, Susanne Steinmann, and Renate Eli. Forthcoming. "Education and Labour Market Entry in Germany."

Nauck, Bernhard, and Sule Özel. 1986. "Erziehungsvorstellungen und Sozialisationspraktiken in türkischen Migrantenfamilien: Eine individualistische Erklärung interkulturell vergleichender empirischer Befunde." *Zeitschrift für Sozialisationsforschung und Erziehungssoziologie* 6: 285–312.

Neidert, Lisa, and Reynolds Farley. 1985. "Assimilation in the United States: An Analysis of Ethnic and Generation Differences in Status and Achievement." *American Sociological Review* 50 (Dec.): 840–50.

Perlmann, Joel. 1988. *Ethnic Differences: Schooling and Social Structure among the Irish, Italians, Jews and Blacks in an American City, 1880–1935.* New York: Cambridge University Press.

Persell, Caroline. 1976. *Education and Inequality*. New York: Free Press.

Piore, Michael. 1979. *Birds of Passage: Migrant Labor and Industrial Societies*. New York: Cambridge University Press.

Portes, Alejandro, and Robert Bach. 1985. *Latin Journey: Cuban and Mexican Immigrants in the United States*. Berkeley: University of California Press.

Portes, Alejandro, and Rubén Rumbaut. 1990. *Immigrant America*. Berkeley: University of California Press.

Rosen, Bernard. 1959. "Race, Ethnicity, and the Achievement Syndrome." *American Sociological Review* 24 (Feb.): 47–60.

Sanders, Jimy, and Victor Nee. 1987. "Limits of Ethnic Solidarity in the Ethnic Enclave." *American Sociological Review* 52(Dec.): 745–67.

Schiffauer, Werner. 1991. *Die Migranten aus Subay: Türken in Deutschland: Eine Ethnographie*. Stuttgart: Klett-Cotta.

Seifert, Wolfgang. 1996. "Zunehmende Arbeitsmarktintegration bei anhaltender sozialer Segregation." *Informationsdienst Soziale Indikatoren*, no. 15: 7–11.

_____. 1992. "Die zweite Ausländergeneration in der Bundesrepublik: Längeschnittbeobachtungen in der Berufseinsteigsphase." *Kölner Zeitschrift für Soziologie und Sozialpsychologie* 44, no. 4: 677–96.

Spaich, Herbert. 1991. *Fremd in Deutschland: Auf der Suche nach Heimat*. Weinheim/Basel: Beltz Quadriga.

Steinberg, Stephen. 1989. *The Ethnic Myth: Race, Ethnicity, and Class in America*. Boston: Beacon.

Vallet, Louis-André, and Jean-Paul Caille. 1995. "Les carrières scolaires au collège des élèves ,étrangers ou issus de l'immigration." *Education et Formations* 40: 5–14.

Wagner, Gert, Jürgen Schupp, and Ulrich Rendtel. 1993. "The English Language Public Use File of the German Socio-Economic Panel." *Journal of Human Resources* 28, no. 2: 429–33.

Wilson, William J. 1987. *The Truly Disadvantaged: The Inner City, the Underclass, and Public Policy*. Chicago: University of Chicago Press.

_____. 1978. *The Declining Significance of Race*. Chicago: University of Chicago Press.

Zentrum für Türkeistudien. 1994. *Ausländer in der Bundesrepublik Deutschland: Ein Handbuch*. Opladen: Leske and Budrich.

Chapter 6

Long-Distance Citizens
Ethnic Germans and Their Immigration to Germany

Rainer Münz and Rainer Ohliger

State—Nation—Migration

Ethnic Migration as a Consequence of Europe's New Geopolitical Order, 1918–1945/49

State and nation were never identical in modern German history. After the first German nation-state was created in 1871, a considerable number of ethnic Germans continued to live outside its borders, most of them in the Austro-Hungarian Empire and in czarist Russia. Moreover, the 1919 treaties of Versailles, Saint-Germain, and Trianon, which formally ended World War I and reshaped European political geography, left large numbers of ethnic Germans living outside the borders of Germany and Austria. A direct consequence of the establishment of new borders was not only the creation of ethnic German minorities in Poland, Czechoslovakia, Yugoslavia, Romania, France, and Italy but also an increase in emigration to Germany and Austria. Ethnic migration between 1919 and 1923 mainly affected state officials in the administration, the military service, the educational system, and the railway and postal services. These ethnic migrants belonged to the state elite in the German or Austro-Hungarian empires before 1918. The total number of such (re)migrants stood at 1.3 million (Münz and Fassmann 1994, 22). In 1937 approximately 8.5 million people of German descent lived in the countries to the east of Germany and Austria—i.e., Poland, Czechoslovakia, Hungary, and Yugoslavia—as well as Romania, the Soviet Union, the Baltic states, and the Free City of Danzig. Some of these people were resettled to Germany (or territories occupied by Germany) during the Second World War (see table 6.1). This was true for ethnic Germans in the Baltic states, Bessarabia, Bukovina, the Gottschee area, Krain, the southern Tyrol, and Volhynia. However, the main collective resettlement only took place after the end of the Second World War. In 1945 9.3 million Germans were living within the territories annexed by Poland and the USSR. Another 3.2 million were living in the reestablished Czechoslovakia. Between 1945 and 1949 these discrepancies between state and nation[1] were largely but not completely eliminated as a result of World War II and decisions taken by the Allies at Yalta and Potsdam.[2] Germany's eastern borders were moved westward, and most German citizens living on the former eastern German territories ceded to Poland and the USSR (eastern Brandenburg, Pomerania, East Prussia, and Silesia) were expelled.[3] The Allies also allowed Poland, Czechoslovakia and Hungary to expel all ethnic Germans (not holding German citizenship) living on their territories.[4] At the same time, the Tito government expelled all ethnic Germans (and most Italians) living in Yugoslavia (Hersak 1983, 131–39). Taking a somewhat different approach, in 1941 Stalin ordered the internal deportation of ethnic Germans, especially from such traditional settlement areas as the Volga region and the district of Leningrad, to Siberia, Kazakhstan, and Kyrgyzstan.

In total, some 1.8 million ethnic Germans were resettled between 1940 and 1944, and some 12 million German citizens and ethnic Germans were expelled to the American, British, and Soviet zones of occupied Germany and Austria (see Klaus J. Bade, "From Emigration to Immigration: The German Experience in the Nineteenth and Twentieth Centuries," and Rainer

Münz and Ralf Ulrich, "Changing Patterns of Immigration to Germany, 1945–1995," chs. 1 and 3, respectively, in vol. 1 of this series) or had fled the region between 1945 and 1949 (see table 6.1).[5] Almost 2 million were killed or died of other causes during the last months of the war, just afterward, or during deportation (Statistisches Bundesamt 1958, 29–37).

Table 6.1 German Resettlers, Refugees, and Expellees, 1940 to 1949

Areas of Origin	Resettlers (1940–44)	Refugees/Expellees (1945–49)
Poland		
Interwar Poland		672,000
Former German territories and Danzig		6,198,000
USSR		
Baltic states[1]	77,000	25,000
Interwar USSR	1,500,000[2]	65,000[3]
Former German territories		ca 1,000,000
Czechoslovakia		2,921,000
Yugoslovia	36,000[4]	287,000
Hungary		206,000
Romania	200,000[5]	100,000
Total	**1,878,000**	**ca 11,409,000[6]**

1. Including the Memel region.
2. People resettled within the USSR.
3. Ethnic Germans from Volhynia resettled either to Germany or to areas occupied by Germany (Polish territory).
4. Of these, 15,000 from the Gottschee area, 17,000 from Bosnia-Herzegovina and Croatia, and 3,000 from Serbia.
5. Rettlers from Bessarabia, Bukovina, and Dobrudja, territories that were annexed partly or completely by the USSR or Bulgaria in 1940.
6. The discrepancy here with the figure of 12 million German refugees and expellees cited in the text has to do with the difficulties of accounting exactly for ethnic German POWs and forced laborers who were not in their areas of origin in 1945 and thus were not expelled from those areas.
Source: Brandes 1992; Filaretow 1990; Statistisches Bundesamt 1958.

Ethnic Migration since 1950: Ethnic German Immigrants

But flight, evacuation, and expulsion from 1945 on did not affect all Germans on former German territory nor did they affect all German minorities in Central and East European countries. Between 2.5 and 3 million of them remained, predominantly in Poland, Romania, and the USSR, as well as in Hungary and Czechoslovakia. Herein lies the origin of the potential for ethnic German immigration into Germany that started in the 1950s and continues to the present.

With Allied consent, Poland expelled the majority of its German population but also tried to reclassify some of them as so-called Germanized Poles. This reclassification was mainly applied to Catholic Germans in Upper Silesia, to Protestant Mazurs in the southern part of East Prussia, and to people living in mixed marriages and the offspring of mixed marriages. The policy was legitimized by the fact that several million Polish citizens had been naturalized by Nazi authorities because of their supposed German origins between 1940 and 1944 (*Volksliste* I and II) or because they had been classified as "germanizable," being of German origin (*Volksliste* III and IV).[6] Among the latter many were made into German citizens and thus exempted from the repression imposed on the remainder of the Polish population (this policy of germanization was answered by a policy of forced polonization after 1945). In total, about 1 million people of German or mixed descent remained in Poland despite expulsion measures.[7]

The Soviet Union expelled 1 million German citizens from former German territories (i.e., the northern part of East Prussia, now the Kaliningrad district), while approximately 1.5 million ethnic Germans continued to live inside the Soviet Union as internally displaced persons. Romania did not engage in any systematic expulsions of its remaining 400,000 ethnic German citizens. They were accused of having sympathized with Germany during the war, however, and in 1945 the USSR put 70,000 ethnic Germans from Romania to forced labor as some sort of reparation (Oschlies 1988, 74–75; Weber 1996).[8]

Historically and legally, the Federal Republic of Germany (FRG), which was founded in 1949, considered itself to be the only legitimate successor state of Nazi Germany. It thus assumed the responsibility for ethnic Germans in the East. In 1949 Germans still living on former German territories were constitutionally granted citizenship in West Germany.[9] In 1953 ethnic Germans living in Central and Eastern Europe and in Central Asia were also constitutionally included under the definition as Germans and subsequently able to apply for admission to (West) Germany under special laws.[10] A privileged gate of entry for ethnic Germans from Central and Eastern Europe was thus created and has since been maintained to a greater or lesser extent. The traditional German notion of nationhood and citizenship, characterized by inclusion through descent, was thus preserved and reinvigorated.

After 1950 ethnic German migration depended on East-West relations, especially foreign relations between West Germany, on the one hand, and Poland, Romania, and the Soviet Union, on the other. During the cold war, migration flows were regulated by bilateral agreements regarding the numbers of ethnic German immigrants, or *Aussiedler*.[11] In the case of communist Poland, migration also depended on a willingness to admit officially the very existence of a remaining ethnic German diaspora. As a consequence, ethnic German migration from these three principal sending countries has undergone significant variations and fluctuations. But the situation changed fundamentally with the end of the cold war, when the role of foreign and international relations began to lose its importance in this context.

Before 1989 the migration process was explained and interpreted within the framework of competition between two political and ideological systems. Ethnic German immigration, as well as migration from East to West Germany, had distinctive, political connotations and was understood in the West to be the result of individual decisions in favor of liberal democracy and a market economy. At the same time, however, the East German government explained the migration of ethnic Germans to West Germany as involving the importation and exploitation of cheap labor by West German capital (Zentralkomitee der SED 1988).[12] (For more on this, see Münz and Ulrich, "Changing Patterns of German Immigration," ch. 3 in vol. 1 of this series.)

During the cold war the number of ethnic German immigrants to Germany was comparatively small: before 1988 it never exceeded 140,000 per year. In 1990, however, the figure skyrocketed to almost 400,000.[13] During the thirty-seven years between 1950 and 1987, a total of 1,420,000 ethnic Germans migrated to Germany, an average of only 38,000 per year. The nine years between 1988 to 1996, however, saw 2,267,000 ethnic German migrants move to Germany, an average of 252,000 per year. Since 1990 German legislation has responded to the growing flows of ethnic German immigrants by making recognition and admission as *Aussiedler* more difficult. As a result of these legal changes, ethnic Germans living in the successor states of the Soviet Union are almost the only ones still eligible for guaranteed admission into Germany.[14] Moreover, the number of *Aussiedler* admitted yearly has been limited to 220,000 since 1993, and recently the number of ethnic German immigrants as well as new applicants for *Aussiedler* status has decreased. Whereas 218,000 *Aussiedler* immigrated to Germany in 1995, only 178,000 arrived in 1996, among them 97 percent from the successor states of the Soviet Union (CIS). An analysis of areas of origin shows that 1.44 million *Aussiedler* came from Poland between 1950 and 1995. Another 1.38 million came from the USSR or CIS, 321,000 from Romania, and 105,000 from Czechoslovakia. Until 1990 immigration from Poland was dominant; since then immigration from Russia, Kazakhstan, and Kyrgyzstan had led. *Aussiedler* from Romania arrived in Germany predominantly between 1977 and 1991, while those from Czechoslovakia mostly arrived in the fifties and between 1965 and 1969 (see figure 6.1).

Among the stock of Germany's immigrant population, ethnic Germans number about 3 million and compose the second largest group today, the largest being the labor migrants of the sixties and seventies (about 6 million). In fact, in terms of current flows, they have become the largest. Unlike the labor migrants of the 1960s and early 1970s and the asylum seekers of the 1980s and early 1990s, these new immigrants are considered prospective permanent residents and German citizens. Ethnic Germans from Eastern Europe and Central Asia admitted as *Aussiedler* have immediate access to German citizenship. This has made them a privileged group among immigrants.

Figure 6.1 Immigration of Ethnic Germans to the FRG by Country of Origin, 1950–1996 (in thousands)

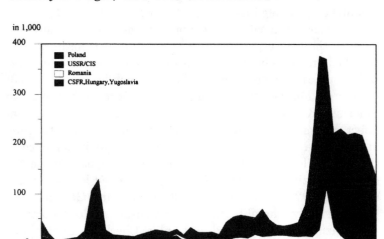

Source: Information from Bundesverwaltungsamt, Bundesministerium des Inneren.

Ethnic Germans in the East: Assimilation, Reethnicization, or Exodus

Questions of ethnic German identity are contested, and the nature of the German element of ethnic German ethnicity remains controversial. Throughout the twentieth century, conflicting processes of assimilation, ethnicization, and reethnicization can be observed among the many different groups within the ethnic German diaspora. A short discussion of ethnic German minorities in Poland, Romania, and the former Soviet Union will help to illustrate the problems involved.[15]

Ethnic Germans in the USSR and the CIS

During the 1920s and 1930s Germans in Soviet Russia enjoyed far-reaching cultural and territorial autonomy until 1941, when they faced severe discrimination on ethnic and political grounds immediately after Germany invaded the Soviet Union. After the USSR entered World War II, being German in the Soviet Union meant being labeled as a fascist. It was in this context that Stalin ordered the collective deportation of all ethnic Germans because they were perceived as (potential) collaborators with the Nazi enemy. The subsequent expulsion of ethnic Germans from the autonomous German Volga Republic, the district of Leningrad, Moscow, the Ukraine, and the Crimean peninsula to Siberia,[16] Kazakhstan, and Kyrgyzstan had the paradoxical effect of simultaneously increasing the importance of ethnic identity as a political category and lessening its importance at the cultural level. The political stigma of having been suspected of sympathizing with Nazi Germany continued long after the end of World War II, and only in 1964 were ethnic Germans as a group formally rehabilitated and the accusation of collaboration with Nazi Germany rejected. But unlike Chechens, Ingushians, Crimean Tatars, and Balts, ethnic Germans never managed to return to their pre-1941 settlement areas.

In cultural terms, deportation to Siberia and Central Asia was the turning point in ethnic Germans' gradual assimilation. Their political as well as their cultural autonomy were entirely abolished between 1941 and 1955; use of the German language was restricted to the home (Pinkus and Fleischauer 1987, 303–39). Assimilation of the younger generation, often supported by the parents, rapidly increased. Only from the mid-1950s on has cultural life among ethnic Germans gradually recovered. German language newspapers and broadcasting were facilitated. Instruction of German in schools was once more made possible, although a lack of German-language teachers and textbooks and continuous resistance by local administrations made the recovery difficult (Brandes 1992, 130–31).

As a result the German-language proficiency of the ethnic German population has gradually declined over the course of two generations. In the last USSR census of 1989, only 48.7 percent of the ethnic Germans in the Soviet Union declared German to be their mother tongue (Brunner 1993, 123). Furthermore, such declarations were often simply meant as claims of German identity that did not necessarily reflect the respondents' actual language competence.

Despite obvious signs of russification, however, complete assimilation was not achieved, for two reasons. First, religion remained a point of divergence. Most ethnic Germans, irrespective of their mother tongue or family language, remained Lutherans, Roman Catholics, Mennonites, or Pentecostals, while Russians were either atheists or Orthodox and Kazakhs were Muslim. Second, the Soviet ID and passport system continued to classify citizens according to ethnic background, with ethnicity being a category noted on the passport and other documents. Thus the Soviet administration itself preserved the notion of a formal ethnic German identity. When German as the community language gradually lost its importance, ethnic identity was transformed from a self-ascribed, predominantly cultural frame of reference to a more politically and administratively defined category, partly ascribed to the group from outside. As a consequence, in Siberia and Central Asia, social barriers between Germans and other ethnic groups have been reshaped and lowered since World War II. Comparatively high intermarriage rates are a result. Among the ethnic German immigrants from the former Soviet Union, approximately 40 percent stem from mixed marriages ("Rationale Zuwanderungssteuerung" 1996, 420).

Emigration from the Soviet Union was possible during times of domestic liberalization and international détente. During the thaw at the beginning of the Khrushchev era in 1958/59 more than 12,000 ethnic Germans were able to leave the country. Similarly, between 1972 and 1980 62,000 people emigrated; however, the yearly number of emigrants never exceeded 10,000. Only with the implementation of perestroika under Gorbachev did emigration become a real alternative, and the number of emigrations increased rapidly. Whereas only 753 ethnic Germans left the Soviet Union for Germany in 1986, this number skyrocketed to 14,000 the following year. Emigrations peaked in 1994, when 213,000 people left the country. In future years, the number of ethnic German emigrants from the CIS is expected to fluctuate between 100,000 and 200,000.

Ethnic Germans in Romania

The case of ethnic Germans in Romania was different. Culture and language retained their importance for individual and group identity. For the majority of this group, assimilation to Romanian language and culture was not an issue. Even after 1944, when Romania switched allegiance from Nazi Germany to the Allies, there was no stigmatization or discrimination against ethnic Germans in Romania comparable to that seen in the Soviet Union. And although ethnic Germans in Romania suffered economic deprivation after 1945, cultural autonomy continued to be granted to a certain extent.[17] Minority schools, traditionally administered by churches and local communities, were taken over by the central government but continued to use German as the main language of instruction. For these reasons, German-language proficiency was and is much higher among ethnic German immigrants from Romania than it is among those from Russia and Kazakhstan. In fact, ethnic Germans from Romania, as well as those still living in Romania, are generally bilingual, speaking both German and Romanian fluently.

The emigration of ethnic Germans from Romania took a different course from that in Poland or the USSR. It started after the beginning of the Second World War, when approximately 200,000 ethnic Germans from Bukovina, Dobrudja, and Bessarabia were resettled by Nazi authorities. Moreover, about 100,000 ethnic Germans were evacuated from Romania in 1944, when the German army withdrew from the country. Ethnic German men who had served in the German army, especially in the Waffen-SS, remained in Germany after the war. Thus an ethnic bridgehead favoring ethnic German migration from Romania was created even before the foundation of the Federal Republic. From the late fifties to the midsixties around 15,000 ethnic Germans from Romania moved to West Germany by way of family unification facilitated through the Red Cross. With the establishment of diplomatic relations between Romania and West Germany emigration became easier from the late sixties on. Beginning in 1970, several thousand *Aussiedler* moved from Romania to Germany yearly, with the number of ethnic German emigrants from Romania exceeding 10,000 for the first time in 1977. In 1978 West Germany and Romania came to an agreement facilitating emigration for 10,000 to 15,000 ethnic Germans per year; in return, West Germany compensated Romania with per capita payments. Only after the fall of the Ceauãescu regime in 1989, however, did a mass emigration of ethnic Germans take place. In 1990 111,000 ethnic German emigrants from Romania came to Germany; this was half the ethnic German population then remaining in Romania.

An exception among the ethnic Germans in Romania[18] are the so-called Swabians living in the district of Satu Mare (*Sathmarer-Schwaben*). Although originally a subgroup within the German minority in Romania, they had been assimilated to Hungarian language and culture in the late nineteenth century and thus had almost completely integrated into what became, after 1918, the Hungarian minority in Romania. This process of assimilation went on until the 1980s. Only since 1989/90,[19] when the German government started to offer economic help to ethnic Germans in Romania, has reethnicization become an important phenomenon among the Swabians of Satu Mare. Despite the massive emigration of ethnic Germans from Romania between 1989 and 1991, the 1992 Romanian census showed an increase of more than 500 percent in the number of people declaring themselves as German in the area of Satu Mare (Comisia Nationala 1994, 708). Being of German ethnicity had become an instrument to gain access to resources. Recognition by German authorities, in combination with the availability of economic privileges, thus has the potential for increasing ethnic German identification among Romanian citizens. Although ethnic Germans in Romania no longer have easy access to *Aussiedler* status and the claim to subsequent legal immigration, a trend back to Germanness could spread among certain groups in response to the possibility of receiving financial and political assistance from Germany.

Ethnic Germans in Poland

The case of ethnic Germans in Poland is different. From 1945 to 1947 Poland, unlike the Soviet Union and Romania, expelled most of its German population. However, more than a million ethnic Germans stayed in Poland, along with several million Polish citizens who had been classified by Nazi authorities as persons of German descent, or "germanizable," and were subsequently offered German citizenship from 1940 to 1944. The official Polish policy after 1945 denied the very existence of a German minority, while endeavoring to make it vanish. German family names were polonized, or, as the official claim went, "repolonized." Following primordial assumptions about ethnicity, the communist Polish governments considered the remaining ethnic Germans in Upper Silesia and East Prussia to be autochthonous Poles who had lost their Polish language and culture as a result of German assimilation policy. After 1945 a verification policy was implemented through which individuals purportedly belonging to this group as well as those classified by Nazi Germany as "germanizable" were identified, exempted from expulsion, and (re)polonized (Urban 1993, 67ff.). German-speaking Catholics and people stemming from or living in mixed (i.e., ethnic Polish-German) marriages were subjects for such (re)polonization. The same was true for people whom the Nazi authorities had classified as members of the Volksliste III and IV.

Only after 1956 did questions regarding a remaining German minority and its emigration become an issue between the governments of Poland and West Germany. In the "more liberal" climate of the mid-1950s, more than 250,000 ethnic Germans and bilingual Protestants (mainly from the Warmia and Mazury regions) applied for emigration to West Germany (Korcelli 1994; Sakson 1986). Despite its continued denials of the existence of an ethnic German diaspora, the Polish government tolerated emigration, hoping in this way to solve its ethnic German minority problem. In many cases Polish authorities accepted emigration not on ethnic grounds but for reasons of family reunification. In the late 1950s, however, the government abandoned this more liberal policy because of fears of a continuing brain drain (Urban 1993, 85). Even with the greater restrictions, several thousand ethnic Germans still managed to emigrate from Poland every year. In 1977 the number stood at 30,000 and fluctuated over the next decade between 30,000 and 50,000 per year, before climbing to 140,000 in 1988, 250,000 in 1989, and 133,000 in 1990. After 1990 emigration of ethnic Germans from Poland declined sharply, since it was made much more difficult for ethnic Germans from Poland to apply for

Aussiedler status; successful applications are now very rare. It is worth noting that a considerable number of ethnic Germans in Poland were granted *Aussiedler* status but did not emigrate, while others remigrated to Poland after short stays in Germany. Moreover, German citizenship is given to people who were classified as German citizens before 1945, during the German occupation, and to their descendants.[20] According to the German Foreign Ministry annually some 20,000 Poles claim German citizenship for this reason. As a consequence Poland now has some 250,000 residents holding dual citizenship. These dual citizens can emigrate to Germany whenever they want and are not treated as *Aussiedler* or foreigners.

Change Versus Preservation of Identity

After the fall of communism and the dissolution of the USSR, the legal and social status of ethnic Germans underwent significant changes in their home countries. The most important change was a new freedom of movement, including the right to emigrate or leave the country for extended periods of time. Prior to 1989 the procedure for leaving the Soviet Union, Romania, or Poland had been difficult, often accompanied by administrative sanctions and discrimination, particularly job related, during the application process. Ethnic German emigrants were forced to renounce their Polish, Romanian, or Soviet citizenship before emigrating. This situation has changed for the better since 1990. The legal procedures are comparatively easy; potential emigrants are no longer threatened with losing their jobs. Citizenship no longer needs to be renounced; indeed, many recent ethnic German immigrants now also have a Polish, Russian, or Kazakh passport. Moreover, it is possible for ethnic Germans to keep their property in the countries of origin, whereas under communist rule they were generally forced to sell it to the state or to members of the ruling nomenklatura. As a consequence, a growing number of *Aussiedler* keep in contact with their regions of origin or even commute back and forth. This is less common for ethnic Germans from Romania, but more so for those from Poland.[21] The prejudices against Germans in Russia, Kazakhstan, and Kyrgyzstan, who, as noted, have been labeled as fascists, have increasingly diminished in the last decades, and for the younger generations such discrimination is no longer a factor (Dietz and Hilkes 1994, 22–23).

No single ethnic identity unites the various groups of the German diaspora in the east. Assimilation, as well as persistence of ethnic identity, dual citizenship, and even dual ethnic identities can be found. Ethnic German identities in Eastern Europe and Central Asia have always been exposed to different processes of change. Not surprisingly, such changes continue after ethnic Germans have entered Germany as *Aussiedler*. The *Aussiedler* do not constitute a homogeneous group, either in terms of identity or socially, despite the similar legal conditions under which their cases are processed (Bade and Troen 1993, 7; Bade 1994; Graudenz and Römhild 1996, 29). Their diverse cultural backgrounds actually separate the various groups more than their common legal status unites them. Rivalries, competition, and social conflict among subgroups of ethnic German immigrants living together in reception camps are well documented (Ministerium für Arbeit 1992, 115).

In addition, the notion of most ethnic Germans that they are returning to their ancestral homeland in order to live as "Germans among Germans" (Ludwig 1978) in many cases is heavily challenged after immigration. The *Aussiedler* quickly recognize that mainstream German society perceives them as being different. In the best case, they are viewed as hyphenated Germans (Romanian-Germans, Russian-Germans, Polish-Germans). In the worst case, they are labeled as Russians, Romanians, or Poles and exposed to the prevailing negative stereotypes many Germans associate with these nations.

This perception of *Aussiedler*, and their subsequent treatment in Germany, could conceivably lead to the formation of a minority group if the integration process were slowed down. This new formation would be based on the fact that the *Aussiedler* are perceived as strangers by native-born German citizens, as well as on the *Aussiedler's* inclination to continue to identify with the culturally defined minority group that had served as the basis for ethnic self-definition in their countries of origin. Victimhood's status as a symbolic resource could become a collective response to integration problems in Germany; overemphasized Germanness could be another.

Legally Privileged Immigration

"The ethnocultural, differentialist understanding of nationhood in Germany is embodied and expressed in a definition of citizenship that is remarkably open to ethnic German immigrants from Eastern Europe and the Soviet Union, but remarkably closed to non-German immigrants" (Brubaker 1992, 3). German citizenship law follows jus sanguinis not jus soli principles. Thus descent, not place of birth, is the primary criterion for the acquisition of German citizenship (see Gerald L. Neuman, "Nationality Law in the United States and Germany: Structure and Current Problems," ch. 8 in this volume). Unlike Anglo-Saxon countries, Germany perceives itself as an ethnocultural nation, i.e., as a state of and for the German people. This construction is the basis for the inclusion of ethnic Germans and for the exclusion of other migrants, i.e., labor migrants and refugees and their descendants.[22] Once ethnic Germans from Eastern Europe and Central Asia are recognized as *Aussiedler,* they have an immediate legal claim to German citizenship (*Anspruchsein-bürgerung*). Other migrants are eligible for discretionary naturalization after ten years of continuous residence and can claim German citizenship after fifteen years.[23]

The double standard inherent in the definition of German citizenship, which includes ethnic Germans but excludes other immigrants, has the following implications for integration policy. First, ethnic German immigrants are immediately part of the German electorate, which tends to make politicians, particularly conservative politicians, more prone to address their problems. Second; Germany provides special absorption programs for these groups, as it is presumed that they will remain in Germany. Other immigrants, e.g., labor migrants and their family members, as well as refugees, are not eligible for these programs.

The high numbers of foreigners residing for more than a decade in the country, a growing share of children born as foreigners in Germany, as well as the continued influx of ethnic German immigrants, stirred a new and continuing debate about citizenship at the beginning of the nineties (Spevack 1996, 72). A first result of this debate was a partial rejection of the prevailing jus sanguinis principle that makes descent the key to citizenship. Now children of foreigners born or predominantly raised in Germany can apply for German citizenship after eight years of residence, while foreign adults can apply after ten years. In a growing number of cases, dual citizenship is tolerated. If German citizenship is defined more politically and territorially than ethnically future ethnic German immigration would likely decrease given that such a legal change would end ethnically privileged migration.

Legal Framework of Immigration and Integration

The immigration and incorporation of ethnic Germans are regulated under special laws. One set of laws regulates the issues of citizenship and residence; another set regulates issues relating to integration, recognition of diplomas, and claims to social security, welfare, and pension funds. The three legal documents that are of central importance for admission and citizenship issues are Article 116 of the German Constitution, the expellee law of 1953 (Bundesvertriebenen- und Flüchtlingsgesetz), and the citizenship law of 1913 (Reichs- und Staatsangehörigkeitsgesetz). In 1949 Article 116, together with the citizenship law, established the criteria according to which people were officially considered to be Germans. Included under this definition (which between 1949 and 1990 represented only the West German point of view) were German citizens living in Germany, as well as the refugees and postwar expellees who had been transferred to Germany (within its boundaries as of 1937). In combination with the citizenship law of 1913, which is still in effect, this meant that citizenship either was conferred by reason of German descent or could be acquired as a result of belonging to the German people. The West German construction of citizenship thus included until 1990 citizens of East Germany because they belonged to the German people.[24] In 1953 the expellee law put ethnic Germans remaining in Central and Eastern Europe or Central Asia on the same level as postwar expellees and refugees by defining them as "Status Germans" (*Statusdeutsche*). Thus ethnic Germans living in regions outside German boundaries as of 1937 were also included in the definition of Article 116 as Status Germans. Out of regard for the sensibilities of the Western Allies, this status only applied to ethnic Germans living under communist rule in Central and Eastern Europe and Central Asia, because they suffered from the consequences of national socialism, the lost war, and collective discrimination.[25] Ethnic Germans could therefore be termed "long-distance citizens," because they were considered to be potential German citizens and could claim German citizenship when and if they decided to emigrate to Germany.

In recent years, however, the law governing the admission of *Aussiedler* (*Aussiedleraufnahmegesetz* 1990) and the law dealing with late consequences of World War II (*Kriegsfolgenbereinigungsgesetz* 1992) have established restrictions for the admission of ethnic Germans as *Aussiedler*. Without formally changing the German Constitution and the law on citizenship, these restrictions have nevertheless led to a redefinition of German citizenship at the margins by excluding most ethnic Germans still living in Poland and Romania and, in general, all descendants of ethnic Germans born after 1992, with the exception of those citing reasons of family unification.

As noted, the integration of ethnic German immigrants into German society is facilitated through a set of laws and regulations that make special provisions for *Aussiedler* only. The law for adapting integration measures (*Eingliederungsanpassungsgesetz*) establishes special financial subsidies and the law on foreign pensions (*Fremdrentengesetz*) makes retired *Aussiedler* eligible for pensions in Germany even if they have not contributed to the public pension system. Furthermore, ethnic German immigrants are eligible for language courses and are given preferential access to public housing. Such integration measures have been scaled back, however, under the law dealing with late consequences of World War II. Language courses, for instance, were gradually cut from twelve to six months, and direct financial assistance was reduced as well. Pensions of newly immigrating ethnic Germans who have acquired a legal claim to pensions in their countries of origin had already been reduced 30 percent in 1991. In spring 1996 the law on foreign pensions (*Fremdrentengesetz*) was again modified, and in October of that year the reduction was increased to 40 percent; thus ethnic German immigrants who only contributed to the pension systems in their countries of origin receive 60 percent of the comparable pension given to native-born recipients. This new regulation applies only to *Aussiedler* who immigrated before May 1996 and retire afterward. For ethnic Germans immigrating since May 1996 different legal regulations apply; they are not covered by the 40 percent regulation but nonetheless receive only a minimum pension. Moreover, since March 1996 some of the financial benefits are only granted if ethnic German immigrants stay within the provinces (*Länder*) and districts to which they were assigned by federal and local authorities upon their arrival. The law on allocation of housing (Wohnraumzuweisungsgesetz) obliges them to stay in the district to which they were originally directed if they do not want to lose their claim to public support. This regulation aims at preventing regional concentrations of *Aussiedler* who have not yet been integrated economically.

Integration or Ghettoization?

Socioeconomic Profile of Ethnic Germans

The social, economic, and demographic profile of ethnic German immigrants differs from that of native-born Germans. Data of the Federal Administration Office (Bundesverwaltungsamt), through which the immigration of ethnic Germans is handled, show that in comparison with native-born Germans the labor force participation of ethnic Germans was much higher in the countries of origin and remains higher after immigration. Ethnic Germans also engage in economic activities that differ from those pursued by native Germans (see table 6.2). The higher employment ratio is predominantly an effect of the younger age structure of the immigrant population and of higher labor force participation among ethnic German women in their countries of origin. Whereas West German women show a significantly lower employment ratio than do men, ethnic German women had roughly the same employment ratio as men did in their countries of origin.

Table 6.2 Sectors in which Ethnic German Immigrants
worked in the Countries of Origin (percentages)

	1988	1989	1990	1991	1992	1993	1994	1995
Agriculture/ Mining	4.0	5.9	6.1	6.3	6.9	7.4	6.9	7.7
Manufacturing/ Construction	47.2	43.7	41.4	40.4	37.2	35.4	33.9	35.1
Services	48.8	49.3	46.7	50.6	55.8	57.2	59.2	51.3
Unknown	0	1.1	5.8	2.7	0.1	0	0	5.9
Total	100	100	100	100	100	100	100	100

Jahresstatistik *Aussiedler* 1989–95.

The share of ethnic Germans having immigrated between 1988
and 1995 and having worked in the primary, secondary, and ter-
tiary sectors in their countries of origin also varies from the pattern in Germany. Ethnic Germans (especially those who came
prior to 1992), like other Polish, Romanian, and Soviet citizens,
tended to be employed more often in agriculture (4–7 percent) or
manufacturing (34–47 percent) than in the service sector (47–58
percent), whereas in the German economy in general more than
60 percent of the workforce is employed in the growing service
sector.[26] As a consequence, their skills often do not match the
requirements of the German labor market and are even devalued
(Dunn, Kreyenfeld, and Lovely 1996, 16). Moreover, different levels of qualification seem to prevail despite the formal recognition
of degrees acquired in the country of origin, so that it is often not
obvious to German employers which qualification should be associated with a given degree. These structural differences lead to
problems for social and economic integration. In Germany ethnic
German immigrants are more likely to be employed in blue-collar
jobs or to be unemployed and even on welfare. This is especially
true for immigrant women, whose comparatively high employment ratio in their countries of origin is transformed into high
unemployment in Germany (Koller 1993, 207–21).

Adaptation to the German labor market also often means
dequalification and periods of unemployment (Seifert 1996, 195),
as well as vocational retraining (Bade 1990, 141). It is not
unlikely, for instance, for a former engineer from Russia or Kazakhstan to end up working as a mere technician or electrician in

Germany, despite the fact that his or her Soviet degree is formally recognized by German authorities.[27] Growing levels of unemployment indicate that integration into the labor market and German society has become more difficult for ethnic Germans in the 1990s. As discussed earlier, whereas before 1993 special vocational (re)training programs were offered for *Aussiedler* in Germany, legal changes legitimated by the current fiscal crisis and subsequent scarcity of public funds have put an end to these privileges. A kind of affirmative action that tries to encourage self-employment and the creation of new businesses among *Aussiedler* is still in effect; for example, state commissions are given to them by preference.

Labor market integration of ethnic German immigrants also depends on country of origin, time of immigration, and region of settlement in Germany. German immigrants from Romania have better chances on the German labor market than do Germans from Russia and Kazakhstan since the former usually speak, read, and write German fluently and are thus more eligible for jobs in the service sector. Of those who came before 1989 59 percent were employed and about 10 percent were loking for work in the midnineties. Of those who came between 1991 and 1995 only 39 percent were employed in 1995, while one-third (31 percent) were looking for work. Based on the labor force potential this meant an unemployment ratio of 15 percent for the immigrant cohort of 1984–88 in 1995 but an unemployment ratio of 44 percent for the 1991–95 cohort (see table 6.3). Moreover, the earlier cohorts had better chances of entering higher labor market positions. Only 37 percent of them worked as unskilled workers, while 22 percent worked as mid- and high-level white-collar employees. By contrast, members of the 1991–95 cohort who had already found work in the midnineties worked more often as unskilled workers than as mid- and high-level white-collar employees (66 percent vs. 5 percent; see table 6.4).

In terms of access to the labor market, housing availability, and social integration, German unification in 1990 was a turning point. In the main, ethnic German immigrants who arrived in the country before that year had better chances of being integrated than did those who came later. The early 1990s were characterized by fierce competition in the housing and labor market, a competition that predominantly took place between ethnic Germans, foreign workers, and native-born Germans belonging to the lower strata of society. The preferential access of *Aussiedler* to the public housing market, for example, gave rise to negative attitudes toward this group. As a result, parts of the German public hold ethnic German immigrants, along with foreign immigrants, responsible for a variety of domestic problems. They serve to a certain extent as scapegoats, which in turn makes the process of social integration even more difficult.

Table 6.3 Labor Force Participation of Ethnic German Immigrants in Germany in 1995 According to Period of Immigration (percentages)

	1984–88	1989–90	1991–95
Employed	59	54	39
Looking for work	11	13	31
Unemployed	30	33	30
Total	100	100	100
Employment ratio	70	67	70
Unemployment ratio	15	20	44

Sample D (Zuwandererstichprobe) of the 1995 German Socioeconomic Panel (GSOEP). *N=437.*

Table 6.4 Labor Market Position of Ethnic German Immigrants in Germany in 1995 According to Period of Immigration (percentages)

	1984–88	1989–90	1991–95
Unskilled workers	37	43	66
Skilled workers	28	26	20
Low-level white-collar workers	11	12	9
Mid- and high-level white-collar workers	22	17	5
Self-employed	2	2	0
Total	100	100	100

1995 GSOEP, sample D. N=240.

The chances for rapid integration have become smaller as a consequence of high German unemployment rates, budget constraints, and a decrease in language skills among recent ethnic German immigrants. Again those who came before 1990 are today much better integrated than those who emigrated to the united Germany (Dietz and Hilkes 1994, 117).[28]

Spatial Distribution and Social Segregation

The *Aussiedler* are not evenly distributed across Germany. There are two distinctive patterns of spatial segregation: an east-west split and a north-south split.[29] *Aussiedler* generally prefer the western parts of Germany over eastern Germany, and, within West Germany, the southern and southwestern regions over those in the north. Ethnic German immigrants generally avoid eastern Germany—i.e., the territory of the former GDR—because of its lower living standards, significantly fewer job opportunities, and lack of ethnic networks on which newly arriving *Aussiedler* can rely. The absence of networks is a late consequence of the cold war era, when two German states existed. Before 1990 emigration to Germany was generally associated for ethnic Germans with moving to the capitalist West. Migration within the communist sphere, e.g., from Poland to the GDR, was not generally perceived as an attractive alternative. The ethnocultural German identity of German diasporas usually went hand in hand with anticommunist sentiments. Thus, the GDR was labeled negatively. These negative feelings have outlasted the dissolution of the East German state. In fact, although the eastern *Länder* now take part in a quota system through which *Aussiedler* are geographically distributed throughout Germany in order to facilitate some burden sharing, this system has not been fully effective, because of the considerable internal migration of *Aussiedler* from East to West Germany. This pattern might change in the future because, as noted earlier, social benefits for *Aussiedler* are now linked to the place to which they were first assigned via regional quota distribution.

The north-south divide is neither as pronounced nor as distinctive as the east-west divide. Nor is it easy to explain. Migration to the southern parts of Germany has taken place among German immigrants from Romania, who have preferred to settle in the states (*Länder*) of Bavaria and Baden-Württemberg. This can be explained in part by the fact that Baden-Württemberg has served as a patron for these immigrants. This is also true for the province of North Rhine-Westphalia, which has set up yet another partnership for this group, leading to agglomerations in certain districts.

The political preferences of *Aussiedler,* who tend to vote for the conservative parties that are in power in the southern provinces, might be an additional reason for the north-south bias. At the same time, mental maps of sectors within the ethnic German diaspora associating the southern areas with the traditional homeland of their ancestors play a role. Once a regional link had been established, the effects of chain migration and the emergence of a social infrastructure of ethnic German immigrants in the various parts of Germany became an additional pull factor. Within the processes of migration and integration, *Aussiedler* draw considerably on ethnic networks (Bauer and Zimmermann 1995, 4–7).

The extent to which internal migration by *Aussiedler* follows economic push and pull dynamics is controversial. Their concentration in the economically more advanced south of Germany seems to be evidence for labor market factors pulling migrants to these regions. However, *Aussiedler* tend to be relatively stable spatially once settled in the south and west of the country. The low interregional migration rates could develop into an obstacle to better integration if this pattern prevents *Aussiedler* from responding to labor market dynamics (Klös 1992, 264).

A relatively new phenomenon is the concentration of *Aussiedler* in cities where French, Canadian, and U.S. troops had been based. After these troops were withdrawn following German reunification and the Multilateral Balanced Force Reduction (MBFR) treaty for Europe, garrisons and housing facilities were and are still being used to accommodate ethnic German immigrants, especially those coming from the CIS. In some cities this has led to considerable ghettoization of the new immigrants. This was a well-known pattern among labor migrants of the 1960s and 1970s, but the pattern is new for *Aussiedler.* The process has had a further negative impact on attitudes among local populations toward ethnic German immigrants and on the willingness to incorporate them. At the same time, it reinforces the social segregation of ethnic German immigrants and their non-German family members.

A study of the geographic mobility of ethnic German immigrants from Poland has shown that there is a tendency among the group to concentrate spatially and socially in minority communities (Hofmann 1995; Hofmann, Bürkner, and Heller 1992). Interaction among ethnic German immigrants originating from the same region is more common than interaction between *Aussiedler* and native-born Germans. However, the informal interaction among *Aussiedler* prevails over formal or institutionalized interaction. Since ethnic Germans, unlike labor migrants, are largely integrated into the legal and social system of the Federal Republic of Germany, there is no necessity for formalized local structures to replicate services already provided by the state or by local authorities. Thus, in comparison to foreign labor migrants and their families, ethnic German communities tend to concentrate themselves in "incomplete ethnic neighborhoods" that lack typical immigrant self-organizations (Hofmann 1995, 208).

A high degree of informal interaction, as well as both social and spatial concentration, can particularly be found among ethnic German immigrants from the CIS, as was shown by Dietz and Hilkes (1994, 117). Dietz and Hilkes prefer to speak of "isolation" rather than "ghettoization" because of what they see as relatively smooth integration despite spatial and social segregation. Her study, however, draws on findings for people who immigrated between 1975 and 1985. Since 1985 almost 1.3 million ethnic German immigrants from the CIS have arrived, and these individuals, because of lower proficiency in German, reduced absorption measures, and a more hostile German environment, tend not only to cluster spatially but also to have to rely more heavily on ethnic networks. For them, then, "ghettoization" might be the more appropriate label at present.

Furthermore, unequal regional distribution has an institutional aspect related to the division of responsibilities among different levels of government in the German federal system. This also increases debate over the costs of integration measures. For example, the federal government regulates the admission and distribution of *Aussiedler,* while the local communities (*Gemeinden*) have to pay welfare and provide housing. Local communities have thus repeatedly complained about what they see as an unequal division of responsibility and financial burdens.

Political and Cultural Integration

German refugees and expellees of the postwar era and ethnic German immigrants have organized themselves into political pressure groups called compatriots' associations (*Landsmannschaften*). Membership in these organizations is based on ethnic origin and descent. Within the spectrum of political pressure groups, these compatriots' associations exercise an important, at times reactionary influence on the conservative parties, to which they have political affinities (see table 6.5). While members of ethnic German pressure groups were running as candidates for Social Democrats and Liberals until the seventies, today they are only being found as MPs for the Conservative Party. This situation reflects political attitudes among *Aussiedler*. As a result of their mostly agrarian backgrounds, more Christian and traditional value orientations, and aversion to left-wing parties, shaped in their countries of origin, most *Aussiedler* sympathize with the CDU or CSU, if they have a political preference at all. Data of the German Socioeconomic Panel (GSOEP) show that three of four *Aussiedler* who had a political preference supported conservative parties (74 percent) but only one in six (17 percent) supported the Social Democrats. Political preference thus constitutes a huge difference between ethnic Germans and the labor migrants of the 1960s and 1970s, who have tended to sympathize more with the Social Democrats and the Green Party than the German electorate does (Münz, Seifert, and Ulrich 1997; see also Dietz and Hilkes 1994, 89).

Table 6.5 Political Preferences of Ethnic German Immigrants and of Labor Migrants from Mediterranean Countries (percentages)

PartyPreference	*Aussiedler*	Labor Migrants	1994 Federal Elections
CDU	74	39	41.4
SPD	17	41	36.4
Greens	5	18	7.3
Others	4	2	14.9

Note: Because of the small case numbers in the sample of *Aussiedler* and labor migrants, the "Others" category comprises preferences for the FDP and PDS (federal elections 1994: FDP: 6.9 percent; PDS: 4.4 percent; Others: 3.6 percent).
Source: 1995 GSOEP, sample D; Statistisches Bundesamt 1995.

In contrast to expellees of the postwar period and their descendants, today's *Aussiedler* maintain rather limited political involvement with the established party system. Currently, there are no *Aussiedler* spokespeople in any of the German political parties, whereas expellees of the postwar era and their descendants and second-generation labor immigrants have some political representatives in the federal and a number of provincial parliaments. A dominant pattern among the new *Aussiedler* population is their withdrawal into the sphere of family and privacy (Ministerium 1992, 117); they do not directly exercise the privilege of full citizenship through political participation.

Culture and language set ethnic Germans apart from mainstream German society. This is a result of social distance and communication barriers. A certain number of them speak, read, and write good standard German. As noted, this is generally true, for instance, of ethnic Germans from Romania (92 percent fluent in spoken German; 80 percent in written), but to a much lesser extent of ethnic Germans from Poland (46 percent fluent in spoken German; 28 percent in written) and from the former Soviet Union (57 percent fluent in spoken German; 34 percent in written; see tables 6.6 and 6.7).[30] Younger members of these last two groups assimilated linguistically to Polish or Russian or stem from mixed marriages, while some members of the older generation only speak archaic German dialects inherited from their ancestors and have never had the opportunity to learn adequate standard German. German language education ceased being offered in the USSR in 1941 and in Poland in 1945, and this continues to have an impact for many of them. Among recent immigrants, the share of *Aussiedler* with a good knowledge of German is declining, and even those who speak fluent German can be identified because of their different word usage, pronunciation, and accents. This has led to a situation in which some 90 percent of recent *Aussiedler* from the CIS need to participate in German language courses, whereas on average only two-thirds of *Aussiedler* arriving during the late eighties and early nineties had to take such courses (Seifert 1996, 190).[31]

Table 6.6 Self-Rated German Speaking Proficiency of Ethnic German Immigrants According to Country of Origin (percentages)

	Country of Origin			
	Romania	**Poland**	**USSR**	**total**
Very good	46	7	6	12
Good	46	39	51	46
Fair	4	45	38	36
Poor	4	9	5	6
Not at all	0	0	0	0
Total	100	100	100	100

Source: Buechel and Wagner 1996. Data based on 1995 GSOEP, sample D.

Table 6.7 Self-Rated German Writing Proficiency of Ethnic German Immigrants According to Country of Origin (percentages)

	Country of Origin			
	Romania	**Poland**	**USSR**	**total**
Very good	38	7	5	10
Good	42	21	29	28
Fair	12	42	50	42
Poor	8	23	16	17
Not at all	0	7	0	3
Total	100	100	100	100

Source: Buechel and Wagner 1996. Data based on 1995 GSOEP, sample D.

Ethnic Germans preserved and prolonged a more traditional German culture that was less affected by modernization. In general, this leads to misperceptions of Germany among potential migrants. Twentieth-century German reality often clashes with older traditions, customs, mentalities, and attitudes among ethnic Germans (Röh 1982), leading to alienation and a rejection of Americanized forms of German mass culture among *Aussiedler*.[32] On average, ethnic Germans are less secularized and more inclined to traditional social and religious values and patterns of family life than are native-born Germans. Among ethnic Germans from Russia and Kazakhstan, about 10 percent belong to small and very conservative Protestant denominations (Baptists, Pentecostals, and Mennonites), which until their arrival were almost nonexistent in Germany (Müller 1992).[33]

Immigration to Germany is thus usually experienced as a transplantation to a modern or even postmodern culture and society. Self-organized institutions among *Aussiedler* along cultural lines are an important response to these challenges. Cultural suborganizations, newspapers, and cultural politics run by the compatriot associations play a central role here, at least for the first generation of ethnic German immigrants. In general, however, these immigrants' cultural traditions are not preserved indefinitely; instead, they gradually assimilate to mainstream German culture (Tolksdorf 1990, 122).

Ethnic German immigration needs to be interpreted as a migration between different cultures. The asserted Germanness of these immigrants does not necessarily make their absorption much easier than that of other recent immigrants.

Sociopsychological Integration

Despite their clear aim to live as Germans among other Germans, their long-cherished images about the land of their ancestors, now partly revealed as misconceptions, can become social and psychological obstacles in the process of absorption. Ethnic German immigrants are confronted with questions and problems of integration similar those facing labor migrants, but their processes of adaptation and integration differ. Since *Aussiedler* have been admitted as ethnically privileged immigrants, for ethnic reasons, their countries of origin generally lose their importance as positive reference points or are even devalued explicitly. Yet German society is experienced as distant, indifferent, or sometimes even hostile. Although they perceive Germany as their true homeland, they are confronted with the fact that they are, in many instances, strangers in Germany (Bade 1992, 19–23) who remain at the margin of society (Masumbuku 1994, 78–79). As a consequence, many *Aussiedler* find themselves struggling to establish new identities. They cannot easily rely on their countries of origin to define their identities, but in many cases they are not offered a positive alternative by their new society.

German officials claim that ethnic Germans are migrating to live and be accepted as Germans among Germans; this may be the case, but the experience of many *Aussiedler* reveal the difficulties of realizing this ambition.[34] Nowadays the majority of the German population does not perceive recent ethnic German immigrants as fellow countrymen. Some *Aussiedler,* like foreign labor migrants and asylum seekers, have even become the objects of hostility and targets of xenophobic attacks. Opinion polls of the mid-1990s showed that a majority of the German population is opposed to continued ethnic German migration. In 1996, when Social Democrats proposed a decrease in ethnic German migration, 68 percent of those polled were in favor of such a measure (Institut für Demoskopie Allensbach 1996). Ethnic German immigrants themselves also have mixed feelings about the integration process. In a 1995 poll, 57 percent of ethnic Germans from the CIS said that they did not feel accepted as fellow citizens by Germans. Only 16 percent stated they were treated like other Germans. Forty-two percent of those polled said they were not satisfied or rather unsatisfied with their new life in Germany; 48 percent, however, stated that they were satisfied, or more or less satisfied (Institut für Deutschland- und Osteuropaforschung 1995, 76).

The reservations and sometimes even hostility of native Germans toward immigrants are thus one barrier to successful integration. At the same time, the antiquated notions of Germanness often prevalent among ethnic German immigrants are a source of conflict not only between *Aussiedler* and native-born Germans but also between *Aussiedler* and other immigrants. Acceptance of legal foreign residents is lower among *Aussiedler* than among native-born Germans (Ministerium 1992, 120). Conflict over the distribution of public funds and other resources, rather than solidarity, has often been the norm among the diverse immigrant groups in Germany. At the same time, tension between young ethnic Germans from the CIS and second-generation Turks in Germany might be interpreted not only as the result of competition for access to resources within the lower strata of German society but also as a struggle for recognition. In this respect, cultural patterns also play a role. Forty-seven percent of the ethnic Germans from the former Soviet Union lived in Kazakhstan in 1989, living alongside Kazakhs, who speak a Turkic language (Dietz and Hilkes 1992, 32). As Europeans in Central Asia, the ethnic Germans considered and still consider the Kazakhs to be inferior. After having migrated to

Germany, however, they found the existing social hierarchy to be at variance with such prejudices, for Turkish labor migrants and their descendants have been in Germany much longer than recent *Aussiedler,* they are for the most part more fluent in German, and are usually better integrated into the German labor market.

Immigration Policy in a Nonimmigration Country: Political Rhetoric, Social Policy, and Lines of Conflict

The statement "Ethnic Germans, a benefit for our country" (Waffenschmidt 1989, 18; Institut für Deutschland- und Osteuropaforschung 1995, 14–15) expresses a longstanding position of the (West) German government with respect to the immigration of ethnic Germans over the last decades. During the 1990s, however, this position has been contested. With the growth of immigration, unprecedented budgetary constraints, and rising social tensions between Germans and immigrants, the discussion now focuses more on cost and benefit. In this context, ethnic German immigration has become a highly controversial issue. Questions concerning integration and integration policy are deeply embedded within the public perception of immigration to Germany, which does not officially consider itself to be an immigration country.

In general terms, two lines of argument can be distinguished. The pro-ethnic German argument emphasizes Germany's responsibility for these coethnics, especially those ethnic Germans who suffered ethnic discrimination and collective persecution in the aftermath of World War II. In this perspective, it is not a question of whether ethnic Germans should have a right to immigrate but rather in what quantities and particularly how integration can be achieved quickly (Waffenschmidt 1989; Institut für Deutschland- und Osteuropaforschung 1995, 15; von Laer 1993, 164). The opposite perspective, however, is also concerned with the ifs: in debates concerning the legal and quantitative regulation of future immigration and the modification of German citizenship law, they question the very right of ethnic

German immigrants to privileged immigrant status and social and economic assistance (Otto 1990, 3–9; Bade and Troen 1994, 16–27, 147–74).

The first position holds that ethnic German immigrants are or will eventually bring benefits to Germany and stresses positive demographic and labor market effects to support its claim (Lebok 1994, 73; Hof 1989). The second position focuses more on the costs of integration, housing problems, and the creation of a new underclass. These socioeconomic and demographic arguments for or against ethnic German immigration reflect corresponding debates about the German concept of nation and citizenship. Thus, whereas the first perspective favors a rather exclusive, more ethnonational definition of the nation, the second is inclined to make changes on the basis of a more inclusive French or Anglo-Saxon political concept that would make it easier for foreign immigrants and their children to become German citizens and exercise political rights.

In addition to the political argument that Germany has historic responsibilities for German minorities in Eastern Europe and Central Asia, demographic, socioeconomic, and cultural arguments are made for privileged ethnic German immigration. One point cited in favor of ethnic German immigration relates to age structure. Since *Aussiedler* are on average younger than Germany's native population, they have a positive demographic effect, slowing down the pace of the aging process by supplementing the smaller birth cohorts of the 1970s and 1980s. Ethnic German immigrant cohorts are balanced in terms of sex ratio, which is an effect of family migration (Velling 1994, 283). Moreover, ethnic Germans had and continue to have a comparatively high fertility rate in their countries of origin, especially those living in Russia and Kazakhstan. Recent studies on fertility transition among *Aussiedler*, however, show that the immigrant cohorts quickly adapt to the German demographic regime, with their fertility rates falling below replacement level (Dinkel and Lebok forthcoming). Indeed, at least temporarily, total fertility rates among *Aussiedler* cohorts have fallen below the West German level, drawing close to levels in eastern Germany, which reached a historical low in the mid-1990s. Still, in the future *Aussiedler* fertility rates may return to higher levels, once they and their descendants have adapted to the West

European fertility pattern of later births; the same may be true for East Germans.

In any case, the entire argument favoring ethnic German immigration as a means to counterbalance demographic change depends on two assumptions. First, it posits that there will continue to be a high share of younger age cohorts among ethnic German immigrants; however, the age composition of prospective immigrants can be expected to grow older. The case of Germans from Romania serves to corroborate this: Until 1991/92 emigration among retired Germans from Romania was comparatively high, though still falling below levels among the younger generation, whereas groups between age forty-five and sixty were more inclined to stay in Romania. This latter age group, which was and is the most disadvantaged in the German labor market, probably anticipated problems in labor market integration, and some of them will likely try to realize the possibility of emigration after retirement. If they do not qualify for *Aussiedler* status, most of the remaining ethnic Germans in Romania will have the opportunity to apply on the basis of family reunification. The average age of ethnic German immigrants from the CIS will also increase as a consequence of the fact that ethnic Germans born after 1993 will not have an independent claim for *Aussiedler* status. The recent modification of the *Fremdrentengesetz* reduced pensions for ethnic German immigrants, but they can still claim pensions in Germany even if they have not contributed to any pension fund. Thus there remains an economic incentive for retired ethnic Germans to immigrate to Germany.

The second argument in favor of privileged ethnic German immigration is their contribution to the German economy. *Aussiedler* are, of course, only beneficial to the German economy and welfare state if they are integrated into the labor market, i.e., if they pay taxes and contribute to social security instead of receiving welfare benefits. From today's perspective, it is obvious that this was much more the case for ethnic Germans coming from Poland and Romania in the eighties than for those coming from Russia and Kazakhstan in the nineties.

A cultural aspect within the broader argument in favor of ethnic German immigration is that ethnic Germans are close to German culture and thus might be integrated more easily. In the first half of the 1990s, however, this claim has come into question, because the overwhelming majority of ethnic German immigrants are from Russia or Kazakhstan, where cultural Germanness has substantially faded. Furthermore, the argument of cultural proximity leading to smoother social integration is easily conflated with normative arguments concerning immigration. Politicians and even some analysts draw the conclusion that ethnic German immigrants, being culturally close to native Germans, should be seen offering a welcomed contribution to the German society, while asylum seekers and others should be excluded. This inherently ethnocentrist view can only be understood as a normative statement, even if it appears in a scientific context (see, e.g., von Laer 1993).

Current and Future Migration Potentials

The official construction of *Aussiedler* policy as different from regular immigration policy has legal ramifications, which in turn raise problems for the integration of immigrants. The law dealing with late consequences of World War II, discussed above, established an admission quota of up to 220,000 ethnic German immigrants per year. This quota is an administrative regulation used as a political steering device; it can influence only the yearly number of *Aussiedler* admitted to Germany and not the overall number of future applications.[35] Nor does the quota take German labor market dynamics into account. But the current legal situation reflects the recent political changes in Europe. Ethnic Germans from Poland, Romania, and other East Central European countries are no longer eligible for *Aussiedler* status if they cannot prove that they personally suffer from ethnic discrimination or the consequences of earlier discrimination.[36] This change is in line with Germany's more restrictive asylum procedures, which declare Poland, the Czech Republic, Slovakia, Hungary, and Romania to be safe countries of origin where no political persecution is to be expected (see Kay Hailbronner, "New Techniques for Rendering Asylum Manageable," ch. 4 in vol. 4 of this series).

The law dealing with the late consequences of World War II basically restricts ethnic German immigration to members of German diasporas living within the territory of the former Soviet Union, who now account for some 97 percent of ethnic German immigration. The law also establishes an end to future ethnic immigration: after the year 2010 all ethnic Germans born after 1992 will no longer have an independent claim to *Aussiedler* status, although the door will remain open for reasons of family unification and for those born before January 1993.

The quota system itself is controversial among political parties. On the one hand, the governing conservative parties see it as an exception that should only be applied to ethnic German immigrants. On the other hand, the Social Democrats and the Green Party argue that the quota for *Aussiedler* should be lowered and that admission on a quota basis should also apply to other immigrant groups within the framework of immigration law.

The migration of ethnic Germans to Germany is often interpreted as a consequence of World War II and the discrimination against these diaspora groups since 1945. There is no doubt that this interpretation, which has been upheld by the (West) German government since 1949, has explanatory value.[37] However, World War II and its impact are not the only explanation for trends in ethnic German migration. At least two other factors seem to be of importance.

First, ethnic discrimination, socialist economies, and the hardships of postsocialist transformation deprived and indeed continue to deprive people in Eastern Europe and Central Asia of their hope for a better future. A few ethnic minorities—e.g., Germans, Jews, Armenians, Finns, Hungarians, and Greeks— are granted legal opportunities to escape these hardships by migrating to the West. Ethnic German migration is thus only one facet of larger migration patterns in Europe and must also be viewed as an offshoot of economically spurred east-west migration (Vishnevsky and Zayonchovskaya 1994, 244–46; Fassmann and Münz 1994, 524–25).

Table 6.8 Ethnic German Minorities in Poland, Romania, and the USSR/CIS, 1938/39–1995[1]

	Romania	Poland	USSR/CIS
1938/39	800,000[2] (1939)	1,371,000 (1938)	1,427,200 (1939)
1950	400,000[2]	1,100,000 (est.)[3]	1,500,000 (est.)[4]
1989	200,000	500,000[5]	2,038,603
1995	60,000	350,000 (est.)	more than 1,000,000

1. As defined by contemporary borders.
2. 1930 census: 745,421; 1948 census: 343,913.
3. Plus several million people whom Nazi authorities classified as ethnic Germans or as being of mixed ancestry (according to the Volksliste) and offered German citizenship.
4. 1949 census: 1,035,701; 1959 census: 1,619,655.
5. Plus around 300,000 people who could apply or have applied for German citizenship.

Source: Own calculations based on Statistisches Bundesamt 1958 and *Jahresstatistik Aussiedler* 1995.

Second, and more important, ethnic migration is itself producing further migration flows. Massive emigration has deeply affected the social structures and cultural networks of ethnic Germans as in the case of the Germans in Romania, for example, where cultural and religious institutions were so severely weakened by emigration that even those who had strongly opposed leaving Romania ultimately decided to emigrate after their everyday life changed dramatically and ethnic German communities in Transylvania and the Banat entirely collapsed (Sterbling 1994).

Between 1950 and 1996 some 3.7 million ethnic Germans left their home countries. Today's migration potential is estimated to amount to 1 to 2 million ethnic Germans (and an as yet unknown number of their non-German family members) in Russia, Kazakhstan, Kyrgyzstan, and small numbers living in Tajikistan and Ukraine (*Jahresstatistik Aussiedler* 1995, 1).

The opportunity to emigrate may revive ethnic identity among assimilated German minorities, children living in ethnically mixed families, and people with more remote German ancestry.[38] For a certain part of the population in Russia and Kazakhstan, ethnic identification is and will remain a matter of choice as long as they can opt for either their mother's or their father's ethnicity. In the context of postsocialist transformation, economic hardship, and rising nationalism, however, and given the possibility of improving one's circumstances through migration, the German option might become more attractive from a purely rational perspective. But since ethnic Germans born after 1992 are legally barred from applying for *Aussiedler* status after the year 2010, the number of potential ethnic German immigrants is limited.

The other question is whether families of mixed ethnic background coming to Germany might build an ethnic bridgehead for future chain migration from the CIS. The high intermarriage rate among ethnic Germans in Russia and Kazakhstan could represent a starting point for new networks, so that future family reunification and new family formation would ultimately lead to new immigration flows.

How many ethnic Germans will eventually decide on and succeed in immigrating is a matter of controversy. German government officials are inclined to stress that financial support for ethnic Germans and their relocation in compact, self-administered settlement areas in Siberia (Omsk, the Altai district, etc.) are creating the possibility of staying in the country of origin and thus reducing migration pressure (Gassner 1992, 256), although one could also argue that Germany is merely subsidizing them while they wait in line (and acquire German language competence).[39] Nevertheless, the current flow of ethnic German immigrants into Germany will continue for quite a while. So far, certainly, the number of applications has not decreased significantly: the present backlog of undecided cases stands at approximately 520,000, while more than 100,000 people have been granted *Aussiedler* status but continue to stay in their home countries.

Conclusion

The cold war and iron curtain reduced east-west migration in Europe but never stopped it. Several waves of east-west migration were characteristic after 1950, some directly linked to political crises in communist countries and some resulting from political negotiations between countries of origin and countries of destination. Between 1950 and 1992 the documented number of east-west migrants was more than 14 million, and the total number must have been higher (between 15 and 16 million), given that cumulative data are only available for legal or regular migrants. About 75 percent of European east-west migrants between 1950 and 1995 can be labeled as ethnic migrants. This classification is not always exact, however. Many people came as ethnic migrants but were also motivated to leave their home countries for economic reasons. Still, this migration was less an effect of economic disparities than of political relations, bilateral negotiations, and trade-offs between countries of origin and countries of destination. As a result, the majority of east-west migrants were ethnic migrants who had support from a Western country or a well-organized lobby; only this privileged status opened up the possibility of legally leaving the restrictive communist states.

With the political changes between 1989 and 1992 ethnic migration developed a new dynamic. After the fall of the iron curtain, migration between the eastern and western portions of the European sphere was no longer restricted or prevented by countries of origin but by countries of destination. Again, exempted from these restrictions were members of ethnic or religious minorities with caring nation-states or powerful lobbies behind them. Most prominent among ethnically privileged migrants before and after 1989 are Jewish, Armenian, Greek, and German minorities. In some cases, this kind of migration results from a legal claim; in others, it is simply due to domestic or international political considerations in the country of destination. Israel, for example, guarantees the right of immigration to everyone of Jewish origin, and Jewish organizations succeeded, with the help of the USA, in extracting concessions from the USSR even before the era of perestroika. And Germany had an unrestricted right of immigration for ethnic Germans from Eastern Europe and Central Asia until 1992. Since 1993 this right has been limited primarily to ethnic Germans from the CIS (especially Russia, Kazakhstan, and Kyrgyzstan). Members of these German minorities were and are considered as potential German citizens by German authorities, even if they hold another citizenship. German citizenship, however, is only given after individuals are recognized as *Aussiedler* and have immigrated to Germany.

Despite their privileged immigration status, *Aussiedler* have to overcome significant social and cultural barriers if they wish to integrate fully into German society. This integration has become more difficult since the late eighties as a consequence of increased immigration since 1989 and a weak German labor market. Moreover, the situation has become worse since the reduction of integration measures, especially language courses. All of this leads to increased competition among ethnic German immigrants, foreign migrants, and unemployed Germans for jobs and public resources. This adds to the danger that a growing number of *Aussiedler* will be marginalized socially or even made into a minority within Germany: the very status from which they are seeking to escape by immigrating.

Notes

1. A more appropriate term would be German *Volk*, which means "people of a certain origin," not "nation" in the political sense of the term.
2. The historical difference between state and nation is characteristic of most central and east-central European nation-states. It generated conflict when nation-states have been established that have tried to homogenize nation-alize their populations culturally, thus assimilating ethnic minorities or expelling them. Political mobilization and the migration of minorities throughout the twentieth century is closely related to this process. A thoughtful theoretical and historical analysis of these questions is provided in Brubaker 1996. For ethnically motivated resettlements and expulsions in Eastern and Central Europe, see Fassmann and Münz 1994.
3. In 1945 around 9 million Germans were living within territories subsequently annexed by the Soviet Union (ca. 1 million) and Poland (ca. 8 million) as well as in the rest of Poland and the former free city of Danzig. For official figures, see Statistisches Bundesamt 1958.
4. In 1945 some 3.4 million ethnic Germans were living in reestablished Czechoslovakia, some 400,000 in Romania, 590,000 in Hungary, and more than 300,000 in Yugoslavia. Most of them were expelled. See Dövényi and Vukovich 1994, 187–205; Stanek 1985; Hersak 1983; Statistisches Bundesamt 1958. The numbers given by different authors vary. The German Statistical Office calculated the postwar population on the basis of prewar

censuses, but the actual numbers were supposedly lower than the Statistical Office calculated, because it included ethnic German soldiers in the German army and war victims in its tally even though the soldiers were usually not at home and the victims were dead. In the case of Yugoslavia the actual ethnic German population was 300,000 rather than 500,000, as assumed by the Statistical Office for 1945.

5. The French authorities ony allowed the resettlement of a few German expellees (around 350,000) in their occupation zone (Rhineland-Palatinate, Baden, South Württemberg) or in the Saar region that was temporarily annexed to France (1945–1957).

6. The *Volksliste*, established by Nazi authorities, comprised five categories:
   Volksliste I and II: People ethnically belonging clearly to the German nation.
   Volksliste III and IV: People who were classified as "germanizable" because of Germany ancestry, ethnopolitically German attitudes, and/or "racial" characteristics.
   Volksliste V: People with German ancestors who were classified as "lost to Germandom" or as "Slavs."

7. German officials estimated the number of ethnic Germans in Poland (including the interwar German territories annexed to Poland) in 1950 to be 1.1 million. Some Polish officials set the number at only 2,500. See Urban 1993, 12, 57, 80–81.

8. Nazi Germany already had reduced the number of ethnic Germans in Romania through systematic population transfers in 1940, when approximately 200,000 were moved from Bukovina, Dobrudja, and Bessarabia to Germany and occupied territories in Poland. See Jachomowski 1984.

9. These individuals were defined as (former) citizens living within territories that had belonged to Germany in 1937 and distinguished from people living in Austria, Bohemia, Moravia, South Tyrol, France, Luxembourg, and Slovenia who had become German citizens after (parts of) their countries were formally annexed to Germany (Austria, the Sudeten area, West Prussia, northern Slovenia, Alsace-Lorraine, Luxembourg) or administered by Germany (the so-called *Generalgouvernement* in Poland and Czech parts of Bohemia and Moravia).

10. Some of them also had acquired German citizenship during the annexation or occupation of their countries by Nazi Germany. Among them were people of Slavic origin who had been classified by German authorities as "germanizable" (in Poland and Slovenia, the so-called *Volksliste* III and IV).

11. Ethnic German immigrants from the East who came to West Germany after 1950 were legally classified as *Aussiedler,* or resettlers. Since 1993 the legal term has been *Spätaussiedler*, or late resettler. In this text, we use *"Aussiedler"* to refer to ethnic German immigrants, whereas the term "ethnic Germans" denotes the diaspora that has not yet emigrated.

12. East Germany did not see ethnic Germans as potential citizens to whom privileged access was guaranteed. The main possibility to acquire East German citizenship was by the same naturalization process applied to foreign immigrants in general. Only West Germans immigrating to the GDR had immediate access to GDR citizenship. See Ruhrmann 1994, 139–41.

13. In 1988 the number stood at 202,645, in 1989 at 377,055, and in 1990 at 397,073. For ethnic German immigration figures, see *Info-Dienst Deutsche Aussiedler* 1994 and Münz, Seifert, and Ulrich 1997.

14. Applicants from other Central and East European countries have to give evidence that they personally suffer from discrimination for ethnic reasons or from consequences of earlier discrimination.

15. Identity formation along ethnocultural lines among ethnic Germans is an underlying pattern that can partly explain the direction of the migration flow. However, (West) Germany's privileged legal inclusion of ethnic Germans after 1949 is the more important cause explaining the migration process. For the postwar German legislation concerning ethnic Germans, see Bade, "From Emigration to Immigration," ch. 1 in vol. 1 of this series.

16. In some areas of Siberia ethnic German settlers have been present since 1890/91, when they colonized land given to them.

17. Ethnic Germans in Romania were completely expropriated in 1945 as retribution for their alleged collaboration with Germany. Only in 1956 was some property given back. See Ohliger 1996, 293.

18. Religious, spatial, social, and linguistic differences segregated the ethnic Germans in Romania more than ethnicity united them.

19. In 1990 the (West) German government started programs offering economic aid to ethnic Germans in Eastern Europe and Central Asia; DM 200 million were spent on these programs in 1994. See *Info-Dienst* 1994a, 8. In 1996 DM 84 million were budgeted for ethnic Germans in Siberia and Central Asia. In contrast, the money the federal government spends on the integration of *Aussiedler* alone amounts to DM 3 billion per year, plus expenses for unemployment, social security, and welfare. However, the expenses for the integration of (younger) ethnic German immigrants could be counted as an investment that will pay off in the future.

20. This is particularly true for people whom Nazi authorities considered to be "germanizable" and subsequently gave German citizenship (*Volksliste* III and IV).

21. In 1992 ethnic German remigrants founded the association Noah's Ark, which takes care of remigrants, new immigrants, and their problems.

22. In 1991 a reform was proposed in the German parliament that would have changed the definition of citizenship (Art. 116 of the German Constitution) into "A German is someone who has German citizenship." The proposed new version did not get a majority in the German parliament (see Heinelt and Lohmann 1992, 247). It would have ended direct access to German citizenship for ethnic Germans as Status Germans.

23. Second-generation immigrants who are not ethnic Germans can claim German citizenship after eight years of residence before age twenty-three. First-generation migrants are subject to discretionary naturalization after ten years of residence. They have a claim for citizenship after fifteen years of residence in Germany. In both cases, as a rule, they have to renounce their original citizenship.

24. West Germany never recognized the notion of separate East German citizenship.

25. This implicitly excluded the German-speaking populations of Austria, Belgium (Eupen-Malmédy, Arlon), Denmark (North Sleswig), Luxembourg, France (Alsace-Lorraine), and Italy (the southern Tyrol), who collectively became German citizens between 1938 and 1943 and remained Germans until 1945.

26. The sharp decrease in the number of ethnic Germans in the secondary sector is an immediate consequence of the collapse of manufacturing in the CIS.

27. Recognition of degrees is legally granted, although the process can be quite lengthy. In some cases, however, the legal claim to citizenship can be a decisive advantage. For example, in the case of law graduates, ethnic Germans who received their degrees in Romania, Poland, or Russia are eligible for immediate entrance into practical legal training (*Referendariat*), whereas immigrants of Romanian, Polish, or Russian ethnicity with the same degrees are not.

28. The most recent bibliography on integration of *Aussiedler* is Kiefl 1996.

29. The official German statistical records do not provide data on spatial distribution of *Aussiedler*. However, a pattern can be located indirectly by analyzing the distribution of newspapers published by compatriots' associations (*Landsmannschaften*). According to this analysis, 4 percent of ethnic Germans from the CIS and 1 percent of ethnic Germans from Romania live in East Germany, and 49 percent of the former and 78 percent of the latter are residents of Bavaria or Baden-Württemberg. In comparison, 22 percent of Germany's population lives in East Germany, including Berlin, and 27 percent lives in Bavaria or Baden-Württemberg. The analysis is based on the distribution of the newspapers *Siebenbürgische Zeitung*, *Banater Post*, and *Volk auf dem Weg* for 1996.

30. The results could be methodologically biased: the survey was taken in German, which means that people without knowledge of German are underrepresented.

31. The data is based on sample D of the 1995 GSOEP. Other surveys for the same period conclude that up to 80 percent of *Aussiedler* need to participate in language courses (see Koller 1993).

32. See the 31 July 1983 letter to the editor of the *Siebenbürgische Zeitung*, in which the author complains about the cold, materialistic West German host society consisting of selfish, soulless individuals.

33. In the sixteenth and seventeenth centuries, dissenting Protestant denominations were first oppressed and later outlawed and persecuted in Germany, the Netherlands, and Switzerland, which ultimately led members of these groups to relocate to czarist Russia, North America, and occasionally Transylvania in the eighteenth century. See Brandes 1992. 101–7.

34. See the interviews in Ferstl and Hetzel 1990, e.g., "Another problem is that we are considered Russians in Germany. In Russia we were considered to be Germans" (68) and "It was almost a crisis of identity for myself. I came from Romania, thus I was considered to be Romanian here. In Romania, however, I was always considered to be German. . . . For the Romanians in Romania, I am German. In Germany, I am Romanian" (181).

35. According to the German Ministry of the Interior, the number of undecided applications for *Aussiedler* status stood at 520,000 in mid-1995 (Münz, Seifert, and Ulrich 1997).

36. However, social isolation after other ethnic Germans have left is also recognized by German authorities as being, in effect, another form of discrimination.

37. It has made its way into science as well. See, e.g., Dietz and Hilkes 1994, 13, in a modest form, or von Laer 1993, 140–49, in an extreme form.

38. As was the case for Jews from the former Soviet Union, who began to reassert their Jewishness after migration to Israel (and other countries) became an option, the option to emigrate to Germany or draw on economic support from Germany has led to an increasing return to German identity. In the Romanian case, the *Sathmarer-Schwaben*, mentioned above, are the most striking example. In Poland not only autochthonous Germans but more and more people who were classified by Nazi authorities as "germanizable" (*Volksliste* III and IV), and their offspring lay claim to the rights stemming from their German roots. In Siberia and Kazakhstan, the large number of children being raised in ethnically mixed families is an interesting and critical case. In the Jewish case, it is worth noting that the number of Jews in the city of Brest (Belarus) doubled between 1989 and 1996, despite emigration (Institut für Deutschland- und Osteuropaforschung 1995, 9–11).
39. Since 1996 language tests are mandatory in order to obtain *Aussiedler* status.

References

Bade, Klaus J. 1994. *Ausländer-Aussiedler-Asyl: Eine bestandsaufnahme.* Munich: Beck.

_____. 1992. "'Einheimische Ausländer' und 'fremde Deutsche' im vereinigten Deutschland." *Jahrbuch für Wirtschaftsgeschichte*, no. 2: 9–27.

_____. 1990. "Aussiedler: Rückwanderer über Generationen hinweg." In *Neue Heimat im Westen*, ed. Klaus J. Bade, 128–49. Münster: Westfälischer Heimatbund.

Bade, Klaus J., and Ilan Troen, eds. 1994. *Returning Home: Immigration and Absorption into their Homelands of Germans and Jews from the Former Soviet Union.* Beer Sheva: Hubert A. Humphrey Institute for Social Ecology, Ben Gurion University of the Negev.

Bauer, Thomas, and Klaus F. Zimmermann. 1995. "Network Migration of Ethnic Germans." Discussion Paper. Munich: SELAPO, Universität München.

Beer, Mathias. 1991. "'Das unsichtbare Gepäck': Drei Thesen zur kulturellen und sozialen Integration der *Aussiedler* aus Rumänien in der Bundesrepublik." *aktuelle ostinformationen*, no. 23: 49–60.

Brandes, Detlev. 1992. "Die Deutschen in Russland und der Sowjetunion." In *Deutsche im Ausland-Fremde in Deutschland:*

Migration in Geschichte und Gegenwart, ed. Klaus J. Bade, 85–134. Munich: Beck.

Brubaker, Rogers. 1996. *Nationalism Reframed: Nationhood and the National Question in the New Europe.* Cambridge: Cambridge University Press.

———. 1992. *Citizenship and Nationhood in France and Germany.* Cambridge: Harvard University Press.

Brunner, Georg. 1993. *Nationalitätenprobleme und Minderheitenkonflikte in Osteuropa.* Gütersloh: Bertelsmann Stiftung.

Buechel, Felix, and Gert Wagner. 1996. "Educational Prospects of Children of Immigrants in West Germany." Deutsches Institut für Wirtschaftsforschung, Berlin. Photocopy.

Bundesministerium für Raumordnung, Bauwesen und Städtebau. 1993. *Integration von Aussiedlern und anderen Zuwanderern in den deutschen Wohnungsmarkt.* Weimar: Weimardruck.

Comisia Nationala Pentru Statistica, ed. 1994. *Recensamantul Populatiei din 7 ianuarie 1992.* Vol. 1. Bucharest: Comisia Nationala Pentru Statistica.

Dietz, Barbara, and Peter Hilkes. 1994. *Integriert oder isoliert? Zur Situation russlanddeutscher Aussiedler in der Bundesrepublik Deutschland.* Munich: Olzog.

———. 1992. *Russlanddeutsche: Unbekannte im Osten. Geschichte, Situation, Zukunftsperspektiven.* Munich: Olzog.

Dinkel, Reiner H., and Uwe Lebok. Forthcoming. "The Fertility of Migrants Before and After Crossing Border: The Ethnic German Population from the Former Soviet Union as an Example." *International Migration Review.*

Dövényi, Zoltan, and Gabriella Vukovich. 1994. "Hungary and International Migration." In *European Migration in the Late Twentieth Century: Historical Patterns, Actual Trends, and Social Implications*, ed. Heinz Fassmann and Rainer Münz, 187–205. Aldershot: Edward Elgar Publishing.

Dunn, Thomas A., Michaela Kreyenfeld, and Mary E. Lovely. 1996. "Communist Human Capital in a Capitalist Labor Market: The Experience of East German and Ethnic German Immigrants to West Germany." Working Paper, Center for Policy Research and Department of Economics, Syracuse University.

Fassmann, Heinz, and Rainer Münz. 1994. "European East-West Migration, 1945–1992." *International Migration Review* 28 (Fall): 520–38.

Ferstl, Lothar, and Harald Hetzel. 1990. *Wir sind immer die Fremden: Aussiedler in Deutschland.* Bonn: Dietz.

Filaretow, Bastian. 1990. *Kontinuität und Wandel: Zur Integration der Deutsch-Balten in die Gesellschaft der BRD*. Baden-Baden: Nomos.

Gassner, Hartmut. 1992. "Die Aussiedlerpolitik der Bundesregierung." *Sozialer Fortschritt: Unabhängige Zeitschrift für Sozialpolitik* 41: 256–58.

Graudenz, Ines, and Regina Römhild. 1996. "Grenzerfahrungen: Deutschstämmige Migranten aus Polen und der ehemaligen Sowjetunion im Vergleich." In *Forschungsfeld Aussiedler: Ansichten aus Deutschland*, ed. Ines Graudenz and Regina Römhild, 29–67. Frankfurt am Main: Peter Lang.

Heinelt, Hubert, and Anne Lohmann. 1992. *Immigranten im Wohlfahrtsstaat: Rechtspositionen und Lebensverhältnisse*. Opladen: Leske and Budrich.

Hersak, Emil. 1983. "Migracijska razmjena izmedu Italije i Jugoslavije." *Migracije* (Zagreb) 1: 131–39.

Hof, Bernd. 1989. "Die Auswirkungen einer verstärkten Aussiedlerzuwanderung auf Bevölkerung, Wachstumspotential und Arbeitsmarkt." In *Die Integration deutscher Aussiedler: Perspektiven für die Bundesrepublik Deutschland*, ed. Institut der deutschen Wirtschaft, 152–99. Cologne: Institut der deutschen Wirtschaft.

Hofmann, Hans-Jürgen. 1995. "Soziale Binnenstrukturen von Aussiedlern aus Polen in niedersächsischen Städten: Ansätze zu Einwandererkolonien?" *Erfurter Geographische Studien* 3: 197–211.

Hofmann, Hans-Jürgen, Hans-Joachim Bürkner, and Wilfried Heller. 1992. *Aussiedler —eine neue Minorität: Forschungsergebnisse zum räumlichen Verhalten sowie zur Ökonomischen und sozialen Integration*. Praxis Kultur und Sozialgeographie, vol. 9. Göttingen: Geographisches Institut der Universität Göttingen.

Info-Dienst Deutsche Aussiedler (Bonn). 1994a. No. 46.

_____. 1994b. No. 57.

Institut für Deutschland- und Osteuropaforschung, ed. 1995. *Informationsdienst Deutsche in der ehemaligen Sowjetunion: Dokumente, Berichte, Meldungen, Kommentare, Meinungen, Zahlen*. no. 28/29 (December).

Institut für Demoskopie Allensbach. 1996. *IfD-Umfrage 6027*. Allensbach: Institut für Demoskopie Allensbach.

Jachomowski, Dirk. 1984. *Die Umsiedlung der Bessarabien-, Bukowina-, und Dobrudscha-Deutschen: Von der Volksgruppe in Rumänien zur Siedlungsbrücke an der Reichsgrenze*. Munich: Oldenbourg.

Jahresstatistik Aussiedler. 1989–1995. Bonn: Bundesministerium des Innern.

Kiefl, Walter. 1996. *Bibliographie zur Integration von Aussiedlern in Deutschland*. Wiesbaden: Bundesinstitut für Bevölkerungsforschung.

Klös, Hans-Peter. 1992. "Integration der Einwanderer aus Ost/Südosteuropa in den deutschen Arbeitsmarkt." *Sozialer Fortschritt: Unabhängige Zeitschrift für Sozialpolitik* 41: 261–70.

Koller, Barbara. 1993. "*Aussiedler* nach dem Deutschkurs. Welche Gruppen kommen rasch in Arbeit?" *Mitteilungen aus der Arbeitsmarkt- und Berufsforschung* 2, no. 26: 207–21.

Korcelli, Piotr. 1994. "Emigration from Poland after 1945." In *European Migration in the Late Twentieth Century: Historical Patterns, Actual Trends, and Social Implications*, ed. Heinz Fassmann and Rainer Münz, 171–85. Aldershot: Edward Elgar Publishing.

Lebok, Uwe. 1994. "Die Auswirkungen von Aussenwanderungen für die deutsche Bevölkerungsdynamik unter besonderer Berücksichtigung der Aussiedler." *Acta Demographica* 1993: 61–78.

Ludwig, Egon. 1978. *Als Deutsche unter Deutschen leben: Eingliederung der Aussiedler*. Bonn: Bundeszentrale für politische Bildung.

Masumbuku, Jean Rahind. 1994. "Psychosoziale Probleme von Aussiedlern in der Bundesrepublik Deutschland." In *Probleme der Zuwanderung*, ed. Arthur Cropley, Hartmut Ruddat, Detlev Dehn, and Sabine Lucassen, 72–95. Göttingen/Stuttgart: Verlag für angewandte Psychologie.

Ministerium für Arbeit, Gesundheit und Soziales des Landes Nordrhein-Westfalen, ed. 1992. *Ausländer, Aussiedler und Einheimische als Nachbarn: Ermittlung von Konfliktpotentialen und exemplarischen Konfliktlösungen*. Wuppertal: Ministerium für Arbeit, Gesundheit und Soziales des Landes Nordrhein-Westfalen.

Müller, Johannes Stefan. 1992. "Mennoniten in Lippe: 'Gottes Volk unterwegs zwischen Verfolgung und Verführung': Milieustudie in einer ethno-konfessionellen Gemeinschaft russlanddeutscher Aussiedler." Ph.D. diss., Universität Bielefeld.

Münz, Rainer, and Heinz Fassmann. 1994. "Geschichte und Gegenwart europäischer Ost-West-Wanderung." In *Internationale Wanderungen*, ed. Rainer Münz, Hermann Korte, and Gert Wagner, pp. 20–40. Demographie aktuell 5. Berlin: Humboldt University.

Münz, Rainer, Wolfgang Seifert, and Ralf Ulrich. 1997. *Zuwanderung nach Deutschland: Strukturen, Wirkungen, Perspektiven*. Frankfurt am Main and New York: Campus.

Ohliger, Rainer. 1996. "Vom Vielvölkerstaat zum Nationalstaat: Migration aus und nach Rumänien im 20. Jahrhundert." In *Migration in Europa, 1945–2000: Aktuelle Trends, soziale Folgen, politische Reaktionen*, ed. Heinz Fassmann and Rainer Münz, 285–302. Frankfurt am Main and New York: Campus.

Oschlies, Wolf. 1988. *Rumäniendeutsches Schicksal, 1918–1988*. Cologne and Vienna: Böhlau.

Otto, Karl A. 1990. *Westwärts-Heimwärts? Aussiedlerpolitik zwischen "Deutschtümelei" und "Verfassungsauftrag."* Bielefeld: AJZ.

Pinkus, Benjamin, and Ingeborg Fleischhauer. 1987. *Die Deutschen in der Sowjetunion: Geschichte einer nationalen Minderheit im 20. Jahrhundert*. Baden Baden: Nomos.

"Rationale Zuwanderungssteuerung: In Deutschland tabu? Streitgespräch zwischen Kerstin Müller und Cornelie Sonntag-Wolgast." 1996. *Blätter für deutsche und internationale Politik* (Apr.): 416–26.

Röh, Susanne. 1982. "Heimatvorstellungen von Spätaussiedlern: Ein Spiegel der Integrationsproblematik." *Jahrbuch für ostdeutsche Volkskunde* 25: 139–201.

Ruhrmann, Ulrike. 1994. *Reformen zum Recht des Aussiedlerzuzugs*. Berlin: Duncker und Humblot.

Sakson, A. 1986. *Migration of the Population of Warmia and Mazury to the FRG*. Monografie i Opracowania 212. Warsaw: Academy of Planning and Statistics.

Seifert, Wolfgang. 1996. "Neue Zuwanderergrupen auf dem westdeutschen Arbeitsmarkt: Eine Analyse der Arbeitsmarktchancen von Aussiedlern, ausländischen Zuwanderern und ostdeutschen Übersiedlern." *Soziale Welt* 2: 180–201.

Spevack, Edmund. 1996. "Ethnic Germans from the East: *Aussiedler* in Germany, 1970–1994." *German Politics and Society* 14, no. 1 (Spring): 71–91.

Stanek, Eduard. 1985. *Verfolgt-verjagt-vergessen: Flüchtlinge in Österreich*. Vienna: Europa.

Statistisches Bundesamt, ed. 1995. *Statistisches Jahrbuch für die Bundesrepublik Deutschland 1995*. Wiesbaden: Metzler und Poeschel.

_____. 1958. *Die deutschen Vetreibungsverluste*. Stuttgart: W. Kohlhammer.

Sterbling, Anton. 1994. "Die Aussiedlung der Deutschen aus Rumänien: Motive, Randbedingungen und Eigendynamik eines Migrationsprozesses." In *Internationale Wanderungen*, ed. Rainer Münz, Hermann Korte, and Gert Wagner, 66–74. Demographie aktuell 5. Berlin: Humboldt University.

Tolksdorf, Ulrich. 1990. "Phasen der kulturellen Integration bei Flüchtlingen und Aussiedlern." In *Neue Heimat im Westen*, ed. Klaus J. Bade, 106–27. Münster: Westfälischer Heimatbund.

Urban, Thomas. 1993. *Deutsche in Polen: Geschichte und Gegenwart einer Minderheit*. Munich: Beck.

Velling, Johannes. "Zuwanderer auf dem Arbeitsmarkt: Sind die neuen Migranten die 'Gastarbeiter' der neunziger Jahre?" *ZEW-Wirtschaftsanalysen* 3: 261–95.

Vishnevsky, Anatoli, and Zhanna Zayonchovskaya. 1994. "Emigration from the Former Soviet Union: The Fourth Wave." In *European Migration in the Late Twentieth Century: Historical Patterns, Actual Trends, and Social Implications*, ed. Heinz Fassmann and Rainer Münz, 239–59. Aldershot: Edward Elgar Publishing.

von Laer, Hermann. 1993. "*Aussiedler* und Übersiedler, Gastarbeiter und Asylanten: Die wirtschaftliche Bedeutung der Zuwanderung für die Bundesrepublik Deutschland." In *Zwischen Heimat und Fremde: Aussiedler, Ausländer, Asylanten*, ed. Wilfried Kürschner and Hermann von Laer. Vechtaer Universitätsschriften. Cloppenburg: Runge.

Waffenschmidt, Horst. 1989. "*Aussiedler* ein Gewinn für unser Land." *Eichholz Brief. Beiträge zur politischen Bildung und Information für die Mitarbeiter, Teilnehmer und Förderer der politischen Akademie und des Bildungswerkes der Konrad-Adenauer-Stiftung*, no. 2.

Weber, Georg. 1996. *Die Deportation von Siebenbürger Sachsen in die Sowjetunion, 1945–1949*. 3 vols. Cologne, Vienna, and Weimar: Böhlau.

Zentralkomitee der SED, ed. 1988. *Was und Wie: Informationen, Argumente, Übersichten für den Agitator*. East Berlin: Zentralkomitee der SED.

Chapter 7

The Treatment of Aliens in the United States

Peter H. Schuck

Throughout our history, most Americans have viewed the poly-
glot character of our population as a source of strength and
vitality. The iconography of welcome, succor, and assimilation—
Miss Liberty guiding the huddled masses to safe American
shores; the melting pot constantly transforming a vigorous
hybrid people; the "new race" of (hyphenated) Americans that
the eighteenth-century French immigrant Crevecoeur envisioned—is perhaps our most enduring cultural motif. Americans
love to recount stories about the rags-to-riches journeys of immigrants. We recall with pride our own immigrant ancestors'
courage and their success, achieved against great odds. Immigration, most Americans believe, has been very good for American society; it has fueled our economy, enriched our cultural life,
and nourished our tolerance for diversity. In 1990 Congress
demonstrated the continuing power of this ethos by enacting, at
a time of economic recession, what was probably the most pur-
posefully expansive immigration law in U.S. history (Schuck
1992). In 1996 the most energetic restrictionist campaign in
decades failed to reduce legal immigration levels significantly,
although it did succeed in denying to many legal resident aliens
equal access to governmental benefits and some of the procedural protections that they have long enjoyed. The immigrant

---

Notes for this chapter begin on page 239.

mythos, then, remains vibrant; even its ardent opponents must treat it with political respect. (Schuck 1998a).

But this celebration of our immigrant past is only part of the story. Immigrants have always inspired fear in some Americans, and these fears have often taken ugly, even violent forms. Profound ambivalence about immigrants can be traced back to the English Puritans, who idealized their own experience as the first refugees in America while practicing intolerance toward newcomers whose religious values differed from their own. Later in the colonial period, expansion-minded politicians, land speculators, and merchants welcomed settlers from the British Isles, France, Germany, and other European countries, but many colonists denounced Germans, whose language was thought to make them socially unassimilable, and non-English groups were often deemed incapable of sustaining liberal political institutions. During the nineteenth and twentieth centuries, governments and growth-minded entrepreneurs welcomed each new group of immigrants, while many Americans who had arrived in earlier waves reviled them. (Smith 1997).

This ancient ambivalence continues today. Many of the values, beliefs, and emotions that underlie Americans' attitudes toward immigration are familiar; they probably differ little from those harbored by earlier generations. We continue to ascribe industry, frugality, and other virtues to immigrants in general, while remaining anxious about their assimilability, loyalty, fertility, exotic ways, and willingness to work at wages with which native labor will not, and perhaps should not, compete.

For all this continuity, however, certain attitudes are relatively new, reflecting the dramatically changed social and policy contexts in which immigration issues now arise. Some of the most significant contextual shifts occurred (or at least culminated) only after the most recent wave of immigration to the United States began in the late 1960s. These include the rapid rise of the welfare state, which crested only in 1996; the unprecedented racial, ethnic, and linguistic diversity of the migrant streams; massive worldwide refugee flows with strong humanitarian claims that even realpolitik cannot easily ignore; and a technological revolution in communications and transportation that affects the motives and opportunities to migrate and the incentives of immigrants after they arrive.

This paper explores what is sometimes called "immigrant"—as distinct from "immigration"—policy: it discusses how Americans view legal and illegal migrants and how U.S. law treats them once they enter the country. The paper has three main sections. The first discusses Americans' attitudes toward immigration and immigrants, distinguishing among different ideological stances and then summarizing the public opinion data. The next section explores what a sociologist might call (following Robert Merton) the "manifest functions" of immigrant policy: the self-conscious allocation of status and rights to the different categories of aliens in the United States, an allocation that is now under severe political challenge.[1] The final section addresses four highly controversial issues with which policymakers are now grappling: (1) the treatment of aliens who commit crimes in the United States; (2) aliens' access to public benefits; (3) the allocation of immigrant-related costs among different levels of government; and (4) the significance of citizenship.

Public Attitudes

Almost all Americans favor some restrictions on immigration. The principal public debates center on the questions of how much immigration should be permitted, the appropriate criteria and mix for whatever immigration is permitted, and the moral and policy justifications for these criteria. Virtually all Americans want stronger enforcement of existing restrictions, and most also favor reducing legal immigration below current levels, which in 1996 totaled 915,900 aliens admitted as legal permanent residents.[2] Congress recently considered a number of proposals for restrictions on legal immigration, ranging from modest adjustments to major reductions, but these proposals were defeated. (Schuck 1998a).

Although those who favor restrictions are commonly seen as monolithic in their views, they are actually a diverse group motivated by different emotions, principles, and interests, some of which are misrepresented in public debate. In order to understand restrictionists' views, it is useful to distinguish broadly among four ideological positions, which I call xenophobia, nativism, principled restrictionism, and pragmatic restrictionism. Although these positions can be distinguished analytically, they are often conflated in the political debate over immigration policy. This conflation occurs both because advocates of different positions may advance similar policy proposals and justifications and because conflating them may confer rhetorical and political advantage on particular groups in the intense policy debate.

Although I focus here on restrictionist views, the diversity of expansionist positions should also be noted. Some (like the author) favor moderate increases in legal immigration but tighter controls on illegal aliens. Principled expansionists—libertarians, some economists, and the editorial page of the *Wall Street Journal*—assert that essentially open borders will maximize individuals' rights to engage in voluntary transactions with other individuals and otherwise to do as they like; government, they believe, should not limit these rights by impeding such transactions. Pragmatic expansionists, including many agricultural and other business interests seeking cheap labor or skills in short supply, ethnic groups desiring more members in the United States, and human rights organizations advocating larger refugee quotas, also favor increased immigration.

Xenophobia is an undifferentiated fear of foreigners or strangers as such. Who counts as a foreigner or stranger, of course, depends on the domain of one's primary reference group, which is usually much smaller than the nation-state. It may be that the sources of xenophobia are congenital, reflecting some deeply embedded, universal feature of human psychology and identity by which individuals seeks to distance themselves from those whom they define as "others" or "strangers." Fortunately, most Americans seem capable of overcoming or "unlearning" this fear as they are exposed to those outside their primary group. In this sense, the scope of xenophobia—the domain of perceived "otherness"—seems to be contracting over time.

One might predict, then, that the development of the so-called global village through advanced communications and transportation technologies and the integration of the world economy would tend to homogenize cultures and reduce the fear of otherness on which xenophobia feeds. No doubt this has occurred to some extent. Public attitudes toward Asians, for example, have grown markedly more favorable and less fearful than they were several decades ago, even as heightened economic competition between the United States and Japan has strained the newer tolerance.

On the other hand, the advance of transcendent, cosmopolitan values can engender a sharp backlash in the more parochial enclaves where xenophobia tends to flourish. Sudden migration flows can inflame these attitudes, as has occurred recently in the United States and especially in Europe, including Germany. Some people in these enclaves engage in violence against those whom they view as foreign because of their race, language, appearance, or behavior. This may explain some of the crimes committed in recent years by blacks against Korean-Americans and other immigrant minorities in Los Angeles and Washington, D.C. In general, however, the level of xenophobia in the United States has steadily declined and is probably not a significant force today.

Nativism is a more discriminating, specific position than xenophobia. Nativists believe in the moral or racial superiority of the indigenous stock. (In the U.S. context, this refers not to the indigenous stock, which was of course Native American, but to the Anglo-Saxons who became demographically, politically, and culturally dominant). Nativism holds that members of this stock alone exemplify the distinctive values that the nativist associates with the nation-state. The nativist insists that immigrant cultures are inimical to these values and, at least in that sense, inferior. Nativism, then, is a species of racism; it maintains that cultural values inhere in particular racial, ethnic, or national groups and cannot be learned. It demands not only exclusion of the inferior groups but leads ineluctably to doctrines that justify nativist domination of the members of the other groups who are already inside the country.

Nativism, unlike xenophobia, has been a perennial theme in U.S. history; it is as constant as the motifs of welcome, succor, and assimilation mentioned earlier. It has erupted with special force during periods of social upheaval and economic crisis. But even in more stable times, groups of Americans have organized politically for the explicit purposes of ostracizing, excluding, and repatriating immigrants. In his classic study of American nativism during the late nineteenth and early twentieth centuries, John Higham (1970) showed that nativism has appealed to all strata of society at different times. But it has especially attracted those whose economic and social positions are the least secure and who search most desperately for simple explanations, scapegoats, and conspiracies to assuage their painful sense of status vulnerability.

American nativism has assumed many repellent forms. Before (and even after) the Civil War, prominent Americans, including President Abraham Lincoln, proposed sending U.S. blacks back to Africa. Nativist premises have led the federal and state governments to enact harshly discriminatory laws, among them the Chinese Exclusion acts, the national origins quotas, and anti-Japanese policies such as the Gentleman's Agreement and World War II internment. Nativist groups have fomented violence against Catholics, Jews, and other immigrant groups. (Smith 1997).

As with xenophobia, however, nativism—as distinct from other restrictionist theories—is probably not a significant force in U.S. politics today. Although the question is controversial among immigration scholars and the answer is far from clear (Schuck 1996a, 1966 n. 18), I believe that the support for Proposition 187 in California in 1994 is best understood as an expression of widespread public frustrations with the failures of federal immigration enforcement and the perceived erosion of U.S. sovereignty and control over its borders and demographic destiny, not as a spasm of nativist hatred (Schuck 1995). The openly nativist candidacy of Patrick Buchanan during the 1992 and 1996 Republican primary campaigns indicates that it does survive and is capable of being mobilized to some extent; the public's decisive rejection of that candidacy, however, suggests that nativism is no longer widespread, even in the conservative wing of the Republican Party. Indeed, some of the most prominent members of that wing, such as the House Majority Leader Richard Armey of Texas, vice presidential candidate Jack Kemp, and commentator William Bennett, are openly pro-immigration, while others such as Speaker Newt Gingrich claim to favor immigration.

In contrast to xenophobia and nativism, *principled restrictionism* is a commonly held position in the United States today. Principled restrictionism is driven neither by a generalized fear of strangers nor by a belief that only certain categories of Americans are capable of civic virtue. Instead, it is the view that current levels of immigration threaten particular policy goals or values advocated by the restrictionist.

Today, the leading principled restrictionists in the United States include some advocates of environmental and demographic controls who maintain that zero (or even negative) population growth is essential to preserve ecological stability and that both the number of immigrants and their high fertility rates threaten that stability. The leading example here is the Federation for American Immigration Reform. Some of FAIR's board members are environmental and population control activists, labor union professionals, demographers, and politicians—for example, presidential candidate and former Colorado governor Richard Lamm—who in other areas subscribe to liberal public policy positions.[3]

Many principled restrictionists also express a concern for the effects of contemporary immigration on the interests of low-income Americans. They believe, with some labor economists, that today's levels of immigration—especially illegal (and some legal) migration by low-skill Mexican and Central American workers—displace native workers from jobs, drain scarce public benefits intended primarily for American indigent citizens, and consume already overburdened public services (primarily education and health care). Some also point to the adverse effects that large numbers of nonvoting aliens (legal and illegal) have on the political effectiveness of Mexican Americans and other new immigrant groups.

Some principled restrictionists place special emphasis on values such as national solidarity, linguistic unity, religious tolerance, or cultural coherence. These themes are commonly sounded in congressional speeches, organization newsletters, and private conversations. An example of such a group is U.S. English, founded by the late senator (and linguist) S. I. Hayakawa. These principled restrictionists are sometimes more conservative in their social policy views than those of the FAIR stripe, but, again, they are well within the mainstream of U.S. politics.

Unlike nativism, which most Americans regard as a disreputable position, principled restrictionism contributes significantly to the overt debate about U.S. immigration policy. Because the etiquette of acceptable public discourse forces nativists' views underground, nativists may seek political legitimacy and influence by publicly couching their racist views in the less objectionable rhetoric of principled restrictionism. Thus it is difficult to determine the extent to which principled restrictionist positions are in fact motivated by nativist and racist views (Schuck 1996a, 1965 n. 14; Smith 1997).

Ideally, only the merits of a speaker's position would be relevant in the public debate over immigration, not the speaker's motives. This debate, however, usually proceeds as if motives matter a great deal. Many immigration advocates seek to stigmatize their restrictionist opponents, whether principled or pragmatic, by tarring them with the nativist brush. The reverse is also true: restrictionists deride those favoring more liberal immigration policies as unpatriotic "one-worlders" and "open-borders" advocates. Principled restrictionists are especially vulnerable to this tactic; they cannot easily refute such charges even when they are false.

Pragmatic restrictionism is a common perspective on immigration levels. It resembles principled restrictionism in the policy positions that it supports, but it differs in one important respect. Where principled restrictionists see the threat that immigration poses to their preferred goals or values as inherent in the nature and fact of immigration, pragmatic restrictionists view such conflicts as contingent, not inevitable.

Pragmatists believe, for example, that immigration's actual effects on population, the environment, national unity, cultural consensus, and so forth are empirical questions whose answers depend on a variety of factors. They do not oppose immigration in principle or in general. They may even be prepared to support it if they can be persuaded, for example, that immigrants actually create jobs rather than taking them away from native workers, that they are mastering the English language without undue delay, and that they do not exploit the welfare system or otherwise threaten social cohesion. Although certain labor unions, taxpayer groups, and other interest groups may have closed their minds on these factual questions, the pragmatic restrictionist remains open to persuasion by contrary evidence.

Most Americans, I suspect, are pragmatic restrictionists, although one cannot be certain. That is, they favor lower levels of immigration but are open to argument and evidence about what those levels should be and about what immigration's actual effects are. Thus their views about the wisdom and level of restriction are capable of being changed.

In a recent study, political scientists Paul Sniderman and Thomas Piazza examined public attitudes toward race-oriented policy issues and found them notably tractable to counterargument.[4] The evidence just cited did not specifically concern attitudes toward immigration policy. But if Americans are open to argument and evidence with respect to the explosive issues surrounding race and welfare, issues on which they presumably have already developed firm attitudes, it must be even truer of immigration about which (as I discuss immediately below) they are already profoundly ambivalent. Attitudes toward aliens, of course, are not the same as attitudes toward either racial minorities or welfare recipients. Nevertheless, two central facts about American society—that white Americans' hostility toward blacks and other racial minorities has declined sharply and that public benefits for the poor sharply increased between the 1960s and the enactment of the 1996 welfare reform law (Schuck 1996a, 2010–11)—suggest that negative attitudes toward aliens (as distinguished from attitudes concerning the optimal number who should be admitted to the U.S.) have probably softened as well. I have already noted the markedly more favorable views of Asians since 1965, when they began immigrating to the United States in large numbers.

Surveys of public opinion that specifically inquire about immigration tend to support my claim that most Americans are pragmatic restrictionists (Espenshade and Hempstead 1996). Survey data about many public policy issues often seem puzzling or even incoherent, of course, and those concerning attitudes toward immigration are no exception. These data are sensitive to the respondent's own perceptions about economic and social conditions, the specific wording of the question being asked, and the respondents' willingness to share strong, sometimes stigmatized feelings with interviewers who are strangers (Lewontin 1995). In part, however, the data are hard to interpret because of Americans' ambivalent views about immigration.[5]

Some of the evidence of ambivalent or conflicting American attitudes toward immigration may reflect this propensity to draw subtle but important distinctions. According to the survey data, for example, Americans like immigrants more than they like immigration, favor past immigration more than recent immigration, prefer legal immigrants to illegal ones, prefer refugees to other immigrants, support immigrants' access to educational and health benefits but not to welfare or Social Security, and believe that immigrants' distinctive cultures have enriched American life and that diversity continues to strengthen American society today. At the same time, they overwhelmingly resist any conception of multiculturalism that discourages immigrants from learning and using the English language.[6]

One tension invariably pervades current immigration policy debates: Americans treasure their immigrant roots yet believe that current immigration levels are too high. Anxiety about immigration, it seems, is aroused by the newer immigrant groups, a bias that a 1982 Gallup poll places in a revealing historical light. When asked about its views on the contributions of particular immigrant groups, the public gave the highest scores to precisely the groups that had been widely reviled in the nineteenth and early twentieth centuries; the lowest scoring groups were the newer arrivals (in 1982 Cubans and Haitians). Professor Rita Simon has captured this ambivalence in an arresting metaphor: "We view immigrants with rose colored glasses turned backwards" (1995). The optimist might infer from this that seventy-five years hence the public will view today's newcomers—who by then may be seen as old, established groups—with the same solicitude and admiration now generally reserved for Italians, Jews, Slovaks, and other well-assimilated groups. The pessimist, of course, will reject this attitudinal prediction, insisting that things really have changed for the worse.

When viewed over time, however, the polling evidence suggests that in attitudes toward immigration as in so many other areas, the more things seem to change, the more they stay the same. The public, it appears, has *always* thought that the immigration levels of their day were too high. Over the course of the past fifty years, Americans asked (in slightly different formulations) whether immigration levels should be increased, reduced, or kept the same have responded in fairly similar ways. During that period, only 4 to 13 percent have favored an increase, while 33 to 66 percent have favored a decrease. In 1993 only 7 percent favored an increase, 61 percent favored a decrease, and 27 percent preferred no change.[7] The trend in attitudes has been toward greater negativity. In 1965 the percentage favoring reduced immigration began rising steadily; this continued until the late 1970s, when it rose more sharply until the mid-1980s, at which point it declined somewhat for several years, fluctuating until the early 1990s, when it again rose sharply. Since about 1980, this attitudinal trend has tracked the movements in the unemployment rate very closely. Hence attitudes about immigration levels can and do change abruptly. (Espenshade and Hempstead 1996, 539, 557).

In sum, the survey data indicate that Americans are quite favorably disposed in principle to legal immigration and to cultural diversity but want less of them. They harbor concerns about the impact of immigration and diversity on specific aspects of American life and also worry about how quickly and completely the newer immigrant groups can be assimilated. As I have noted, these concerns troubled earlier generations of Americans as well.

These data raise another intriguing question: if Americans are indeed ambivalent about immigration and desire even less *legal* immigration, how can we explain the adoption of the Immigration Act of 1990? This was a law, after all, that expanded immigration levels by about 40 percent and will continue those higher levels for the foreseeable future, a law that will thus maintain and perhaps even increase the ethnic and racial diversity of the immigration streams to the United States.[8] This puzzle only deepens when we note that Congress passed the 1990 act during a national and international economic recession, a time when virtually all other immigrant-receiving countries were moving to restrict normal immigration and limit asylum claiming. Why did these enormous anti-immigration pressures fail to convince Congress to follow suit, as so many restrictionists (principled and pragmatic alike) strongly urged it to do? And why did a strenuous restrictionist effort in

1996 fail to cut back these higher legal immigration levels even as it succeeded in restricting legal immigrants' procedural and substantive rights?

One answer is that restrictionist pressures, which often build up in particular regions and localities as a result of the high residential concentration of immigrants in a handful of states and localities, tend to dissipate somewhat when legislation is considered at the national level, where the U.S. Constitution lodges exclusive jurisdiction over immigration policy. In 1995 two-thirds of the legal immigrants intended to settle in only six states: California, New York, Texas, Florida, New Jersey, and Illinois. Almost one in four hoped to live in either of two metropolitan areas, New York or Los Angeles (U.S. Dept. of Justice 1996, 8). The pronounced regionalization of immigration means that the majority of Americans (and their political leaders) who reside elsewhere feel its effects on jobs, public service budgets, and cultural unity only in an indirect, muted form. Public attitudes about desired immigration levels vary by region (Espenshade and Hempstead 1996, 546, 548). In addition (and not surprisingly), immigrant enclaves are in precisely those areas where the political groups with a powerful stake in increased immigration, such as growers, church groups, and ethnic organizations, are located.[9] These groups, which enjoy excellent access to the mass media, are often strong enough to counteract the restrictionist pressures that concentrated immigrant populations generate.[10] For whatever reasons, national political leaders, media, prominent commentators, business executives, and other elite groups generally support immigration more than the general public does, and immigration policy tends to reflect their pro-immigration positions.[11]

The Law's Treatment of Aliens

Since 1980 the institutional, legal, and political contexts in which the rights of citizens and various categories of aliens are defined and enforced (and all too often violated) have changed in a number of important ways. Together, these changes have given great prominence to the public debate over the character and extent of these rights.

During the 1980s a more cosmopolitan legal culture began to permeate the parochial bureaucratic culture of the INS. For a variety of reasons, immigration law began to shed its shadowy reputation as a backwater legal specialty of interest largely to marginal, low-status practitioners and the INS. More lawyers of demonstrated professional competence and high repute were attracted to the private, public-interest, and government sectors of immigration practice. Some of the elite law schools began to offer academic and clinical courses in immigration law. Legal scholars began to scrutinize the INS and immigration law more carefully. Publications devoted to monitoring and reporting on the INS and the courts' immigration decisions were established (Schuck 1989a).

An analogous change occurred during the 1980s in the federal courts, which have exclusive jurisdiction over immigration law (Schuck 1984; Schuck and Wang 1992). Abandoning much of their traditional deference to the INS, they were drawn into a more detailed supervision of the agency's administration of the law. They entertained a flood of immigration cases, which mirrored the rising immigration levels. Although the government won the vast majority of these cases, the courts did invalidate statutory provisions and INS procedures and policies with an alacrity that would have astonished an earlier generation of immigration lawyers.

Still, old habits are hard to change, especially in law, and the long tradition of judicial deference to Congress (as distinguished from deference to the INS) continues in matters of immigration policy. The Supreme Court has strongly reaffirmed this tradition in a number of its recent decisions.[12] Even so, the new judicial assertiveness in immigration cases is unmistakable. Indeed, the courts are likely to engage in even closer constitutional review as Congress, driven by deep public anxieties about drug trafficking, smuggling, and terrorism, increasingly emphasizes the use of criminal sanctions against aliens. Many of the far-reaching enforcement provisions of the 1996 immigration reforms, including unprecedented restrictions on judicial review of deportation decisions, are being challenged in the courts.

A third factor that has conditioned immigrants' rights, of course, is politics (Schuck 1992). The forces favoring immigration restriction and those favoring immigration expansion are always in tension in the United States, and the balance of power changes over time. During much of the 1980s the interests that traditionally favor liberal immigration policies—primarily western growers and many business organizations—were joined by newer, less conventional allies: ethnic groups, religious organizations, libertarians, the influential *Wall Street Journal*, human rights activists, and many politicians in both parties. These interests gained greater power at the expense of traditional restrictionists such as organized labor. Black civil rights organizations, which historically looked askance at immigration (Fuchs 1990), joined the expansionist coalition. In many states and localities, opposition to U.S. policies in Central America led many citizens with little interest in immigration policy to favor sanctuary for asylum claimants and to advocate other forms of noncooperation with the federal immigration authorities, all in furtherance of immigrant rights and ultimately of expanded immigration through the legalization under the 1986 law of millions of unsuccessful asylum claimants and other illegals. As noted earlier, the 1990 act further increased immigration levels well into the future.

By the 1994 congressional campaign, the expansionist tide had receded as many erstwhile proponents of liberal immigration policies began to join restrictionists in demanding curtailment of the rights of illegal, and in some cases even legal, aliens.[13] This reversal was first evident in California, which was suffering from a protracted economic recession, but it became manifest on a national scale in 1996 with the enactment of three statutes—the Anti-Terroriam and Effective Death Penalty Act, the welfare reform legislation, and the Illegal Immigration Reform and Immigrant Responsibility Act—that sharply limited the procedural and substantive rights of both legal and illegal aliens under the federal immigration laws as well as their eligibility for many governmental benefits. These developments underscore the larger point that within the leeways permitted by the Constitution—and indeed beyond those leeways, as the legally doubtful Proposition 187 suggests (Terry,

1997)—immigrant rights are inevitably shaped by the forces of public opinion.

In the discussion that follows, I focus on the legal rights of legal resident aliens and illegal aliens. Other papers in this volume deal with the rights of U.S. citizens and those who seek asylum and refugee status.

Resident Aliens

Until very recently, the differences in legal rights between legal permanent resident aliens (LPRs) and citizens in the United States were quite modest, more political than legal or economic. These differences, however, increased dramatically in 1996 when Congress, in a series of bipartisan votes, sharply reduced LPRs' legal rights. This issue is discussed at greater length in Current Immigrant Policy Issues, below.

Earlier, U.S. courts had established that the constitutionality of government-imposed discriminations between citizens and aliens turned on whether the discrimination being challenged was imposed by the federal government or by a state, and in certain circumstances also on the strength of the justifications for the discrimination advanced by the enacting government.

In several Supreme Court decisions during the 1970s, the Court held that Congress could exclude some LPRs from public benefits under Medicare (and presumably under other federal programs as well) but that the states could not do so (*Mathews v. Diaz*, 426 U.S. 67 [1976]; *Graham v. Richardson*, 403 U.S. 365 [1971]). Since then, the constitutional rationale for decisions restricting the states' power to discriminate may have changed. The Court in *Graham* originally seemed to view state law discriminations on the basis of alienage as a "suspect classification" like race, which would impose a very heavy, probably impossible, burden on the state to demonstrate that its interest in discriminating against aliens was "compelling" and narrowly tailored to achieve its purpose. But in subsequent cases, the Court seemed to favor a different constitutional theory, one based on the Supremacy Clause rather than the Equal Protection Clause. Stressing the dominant federal interest in regulating immigration, this "federal preemption" theory holds that a state cannot legislate about aliens if doing so could interfere with this federal interest. On the other hand, states may enact legislation that merely mirrors or reinforces federal immigration policy (Tribe 1988). It seems to follow that federal law may constitutionally *require* the states to discriminate against legal aliens or *authorize* them to discriminate. In the 1996 Welfare Reform Law, which differentiates among benefit programs and between federal and state laws, the federal government did both.

Even before the 1996 law was enacted, some noteworthy differences in legal rights existed, and each of them remains. Three are political in nature: the right to vote, the right to serve on federal and many state juries, and the right to run for certain high elective offices and to be appointed to some high (and not-so-high) appointive ones. Each of these restrictions seems to be premised on one or more of the following assumptions: that aliens' political socialization is too fragmentary and embryonic to be trusted in matters of public choice; that confining political participation of this kind to citizens carries an important symbolic message about the value and significance of full membership; and that exclusion of aliens from such participation encourages them to naturalize as soon as possible (Schuck 1989b).

Although aliens enjoyed the franchise in some states until 1926, when Arkansas repealed its law, only U.S. citizens may exercise it today, a limitation adopted in virtually all countries, at least in national elections.[14] Tacoma Park, Maryland, and some other communities have granted aliens the right to vote in their local elections, and similar proposals have been advanced in some larger cities including Washington, D.C. and Los Angeles. Some academic commentary supports such a reform as well (Rosberg 1977; Raskin 1993). In the current political climate, however, extending the vote to aliens is highly unlikely.

The individual LPR (as distinct from immigrants' rights advocates) probably does not view this inability to vote or serve on juries as a significant, unfair deprivation. Aliens' inability to vote certainly limits their collective political influence qua aliens, but their collective political identities have focused more on their ethnicity than on their alienage. Even so, the welfare reform law and other measures pending that would disadvantage legal aliens broadly as a class have clearly increased the political salience of alienage per se and hence the value that aliens will place on the vote in the future (Verhovek 1995).

Citizenship requirements for jury service are not much of an issue in the United States. In the framing of the Bill of Rights, which protected the right to trial by jury in both criminal and civil cases, jury service was seen as an important political, as well as legal, institution protecting the people from the oppression of governmental and private elites (Amar 1991). Today, Americans continue to esteem juries and serve on them conscientiously. Still, many view such service as less a privilege than a burden; Americans, after all, generally refer to it as jury *duty*. Unlike the right to vote, the notion of extending jury service to aliens has not surfaced in the public debate about improving the jury system.

Aliens' ineligibility for federal employment, which is similar to the practice in virtually all nations (Schuck 1994a), is likely to be of greater concern to many of them than is their inability to serve on juries. As a practical political matter, few LPRs would seek high elective or appointive offices during the period prior to naturalization even if the law permitted them to do so, but many might want to pursue immediate employment in the federal, state, and local civil service systems. In the mid-1970s two Supreme Court decisions elaborated the constitutional principles relating to discrimination against aliens in the civil service setting. The Court held that the Constitution permitted Congress and the president to limit federal civil service jobs to citizens (which has been done since the 1880s) but that the states could not impose citizenship requirements for their civil service systems (*Hampton v. Mow Sun Wong*, 426 U.S. 88 [1976]; *Sugarman v. Dougall*, 413 U.S. 634 [1973]). Although it emphasized the exclusive federal interest in regulating immigration, a principle that is discussed more fully below, the Court did recognize the states' power to exclude LPRs from particular job categories that represented their "political function," such as schoolteaching and police work. This distinction has proved difficult to apply but continues to enjoy the Court's support (Tribe 1988, 1544–53).

Two other inequalities are worth mentioning. First, LPRs have a lesser right to sponsor their family members for immigration than do U.S. citizens. "Immediate relatives" of citizens receive preferred immigration status without regard to numerical quotas, and citizens' siblings and adult children have preferred status under the numerical quota system. In contrast, the spouses and unmarried children of resident aliens qualify for only a numerically limited preference, and their siblings receive no preference at all (Aleinikoff, Martin, and Motomura 1995).

Second, citizens and LPRs differ with respect to their right to remain in the United States. Citizens, whether through birthright or naturalization, are not subject to deportation but LPRs are. Deportation of a long-term resident can wreak enormous deprivation on aliens and their families and friends. Although the Supreme Court has repeatedly held that deportation is not punishment and therefore does not implicate the due process and other constitutional guarantees that surround the imposition of criminal sanctions, the fact is that, as Justice Douglas put it, deportation "may deprive a man and his family of all that makes life worthwhile" (*Harisiades v. Shaughnessy*, 342 U.S. 580 [1952], Justice Douglas, dissenting)

Still, this risk should be viewed in a realistic context. Deportation may indeed be devastating to individual aliens and their families and friends. Before Congress amended the immigration laws in 1996, however, the probability of an LPR actually being deported was in fact exceedingly low, unless he or she had been convicted of a serious crime. Moreover, the courts require government to observe high standards of procedural fairness in adjudicating individual rights, including the qualified right of deportable LPRs to remain in the United States. Deportable LPRs can also invoke extensive procedural safeguards established by statute and regulation, as well as by judicial decision.[15]

In truth, long-term resident aliens faced a vanishingly small risk of deportation unless they were convicted of certain crimes. In 1996, for example, only 54,000 aliens were formally deported or removed "under docket control," and virtually all of these were illegal entrants, out-of-status nonimmigrants, violators of narcotics laws, or convicted criminals. A far larger number (1.5 million) were expelled without formal proceedings, but almost all of these were undocumented aliens.[16] In addition, relatively few of those who were deported or expelled had been in the United States for a long period of time. Finally, severe administrative failures and resource constraints limit the INS's ability to implement even the relatively few formal deportation orders, and the far more numerous informal departure agreements that it does manage to obtain. The INS's current efforts to improve its dismal removal record are focused almost entirely on deportable aliens who commit crimes in the United States. As a practical and legal matter, then, the ability of noncriminal long-term resident aliens to remain in the United States if they wish is remarkably secure, although they do not quite equal those of U.S. citizens.

The 1996 changes to the immigration statute sharply limited the procedural rights and ability to avoid deportation of even long-term LPRs if they are convicted of an "aggravated felony." As noted below, this category has been steadily expanded to encompass a large number of offenses punishable by more than one year of imprisonment, including a broad range of weapons and drug offenses. It is not yet clear how many LPRs will be affected by these changes.

Today, the most controversial issue concerning the rights of LPRs (and other alien categories) involves their eligibility for social benefits, an issue discussed in more detail in Current Immigrant Policy Issues, below. Until federal law was amended in 1996, LPRs were entitled to many cash assistance, medical care, food, education,[17] housing, and other social programs. These benefits were often also available to certain other categories of aliens who were present in the United States legally and would probably gain LPR status in the future, though they did not enjoy it yet: family members of amnestied aliens, refugees and asylees, parolees, Cuban/Haitian entrants, and so-called PRUCOLs (individuals "permanently residing under color of law" whom the INS knows to be illegal but declines to deport). In addition, LPRs were often eligible for state benefit programs such as low tuition in state university systems.

Even before the 1996 changes, these rights were limited in certain respects. First, so-called deeming provisions applied to many federal and state benefit programs. Even aliens with visas to enter as LPRs could be excluded from the United States if they were "likely at any time to become . . . public charge[s]," and LPRs or other aliens already in the country could be deported if they had become public charges within five years after entry, unless they could show that their poverty was caused by conditions that arose *after* entry. Very few deportations were enforced under this provision. All entering aliens (except for refugees) had to show that they would maintain a steady source of support through employment, family resources, or otherwise. If they could not do so, a portion of the income of their U.S. resident sponsors was deemed to be available to the alien for a number of years after arrival, which would ordinarily render him or her ineligible for public benefits. Until the 1996 welfare reforms, the deeming period was five years in the case of SSI, a means-tested cash assistance program for the aged, blind, and disabled that was used by a rapidly growing number of elderly aliens, much to the consternation of Congress. An alien who received welfare would probably be unable to sponsor other family members as immigrants. Finally, aliens who received legal status under the 1986 amnesty program were not permitted to receive most federal benefits, except emergency health care, for five years after they were legalized, a period that has now ended for almost all of them.

These older limitations, as well as the new ones adopted in 1996, are palliated somewhat by the fact that they need only be temporary. The vast majority of LPRs can easily remove them by naturalizing in five years (three if they have a citizen spouse), although fewer than 10 percent of LPRs have naturalized that quickly prior to 1995. Indeed, the median period of U.S. residence was nine years for those individuals who naturalized in 1996, and only 45.9 percent of the cohort that was admitted as LPRs in 1977 had naturalized by the end of 1995, more than eighteen years later (U.S. Dept. of Justice 1997, 139, 141). Although naturalization rates vary a great deal among different nationality groups, even those groups that traditionally naturalized at relatively low rates have recently begun to petition for naturalization at much higher levels.[18]

The marginal incentive of LPRs to naturalize is presumably affected by the importance of the rights they can obtain only by becoming citizens. Many Americans, noting the low naturalization rate among LPRs as a group, believe that U.S. citizenship, as a distinctive status carrying special rights, counts for less than it once did or perhaps than it should. This belief, among others, has fueled a debate over the significance of citizenship and the appropriateness of imposing disadvantages on LPR status, a debate that culminated in the 1996 statutory changes that sharply curtailed certain rights of LPRs, especially those receiving public assistance. I discuss these changes further in Current Immigrant Policy Issues, below.

Another legal regime bearing on the rights of resident aliens in the United States is the corpus of antidiscrimination law. In 1986, as part of IRCA, Congress adopted an antidiscrimination remedy for aliens in order to balance the employer sanctions program and fill a remedial gap in employment discrimination law. Many immigrant advocates feared that the new employer sanctions provisions would encourage employers to discriminate against job applicants, especially Hispanics, whose national origin or citizenship status made them statistically more likely to be undocumented. These groups also argued that existing remedies for such discrimination were inadequate since Title VII of the Civil Rights Act of 1964, which bars discrimination on the basis of race and national origin (among other factors), has been held to be inapplicable to alienage-based discrimination.

When these concerns threatened to fracture the coalition supporting the legislation, a compromise was forged. In the end, IRCA created a Special Counsel for Immigration-Related Unfair Employment Practices in the U.S. Department of Justice. The special counsel is authorized to investigate and prosecute alienage-based discrimination claims against employers, referral agencies, or recruiters. Enforcement activity by the special counsel appears to have been very limited so far.[19] It is hard to know, however, whether that is because alienage discrimination is rare or because the new antidiscrimination program has simply been ineffective. In 1996, moreover, Congress amended this law to make it easier for employers to defend against discrimination complaints. A decade after IRCA, then, the issues of how much alienage-based job discrimination exists, how much of that is caused by employer sanctions, and how the law should be enforced remain hotly contested.

The employer sanctions program itself has been only indifferently enforced, as a steady stream of congressional reports and private studies has established. Employer noncompliance is due to several factors, including ignorance about the program's complex provisions, the inadequate penalties assessed against violators, and the notorious document fraud that the program has engendered. In any event, employer sanctions have squandered whatever small credibility they began with: employers and illegal aliens know that they have little to fear from them. Perhaps the level of illegal border crossings is lower than it would have been without the program. Illegal entry, however, has returned to pre-IRCA levels.[20] The best estimate is that 3.2 million illegal aliens were living in the United States (more or less permanently) in October 1992. This total grows by about 250,000 each year, for an estimated total of over 4 million in 1998. More than half of these are believed to be illegal entrants, with the remainder being people who entered legally but then overstayed their visas (Espenshade 1995).

Finally, Congress has adopted increasingly stringent provisions governing the deportability of resident aliens who commit crimes in the United States and severely limiting the procedural and other immigration-related rights of those who have committed "aggravated felonies." This category, created in the late 1980s, is peculiar to immigration law. Already defined quite broadly, it was constantly expanded by Congress, most recently in 1996 legislation. The issue of criminal aliens is discussed in Current Immigrant Policy Issues, below.

Illegal Aliens

Many individual rights protected by the Constitution apply to "persons," not just "citizens." For this reason, aliens who are in the United States illegally—whether because they entered illegally or because they remain in violation of their visa restrictions—enjoy some of the basic legal rights of citizens. The question of whether and to what extent government may treat them differently once they are in the country, as distinct from expelling them for their illegal status, has no clear answer.[21] In principle, they are entitled to sue in the courts, claim the protections of the Due Process Clause, and enforce civil rights like anyone else, although as a practical matter they may risk detection if they attempt to do so (unless, for example, they can assert their rights more or less anonymously through class action, an organization, or a "John Doe" claim).

The Supreme Court has directly addressed the question of the rights of illegal aliens in only one case, *Plyler v. Doe*.[22] In

Plyler, illegal alien children challenged the constitutionality of a Texas statute that barred them from attending public schools. A closely divided Court struck down the statute as a violation of the Equal Protection Clause, holding that because the statute failed to further a substantial state interest, it was irrational under equal protection jurisprudence. Texas had cited its interests in deterring illegal migration, its fiscal obligations to its own citizens and resident aliens, and its desire to use its resources to benefit those who were likely to remain in Texas. The Court, however, rejected these reasons, emphasizing that whatever laws their parents might have violated, the children were innocent. To deny them basic education would force them into a permanent caste or underclass, which Texas could not rationally pursue as a public goal.

In order for the Court to strike down the Texas statute, it had to fashion what Professor Laurence Tribe has called a "curious new species of equal protection review" (1988, 1552); this is a kind of "intermediate scrutiny" between the strict scrutiny reserved for racial and other "discrete and insular minorities" (*United States v. Carolene Products*, 304 U.S. 144, 152 n. 4 [1938]) and the minimal scrutiny accorded to most other classifications. The logic of the Court's opinion in *Plyler* is not altogether convincing, but its special solicitude for the "innocent" children of illegal alien parents nevertheless remains attractive. Despite this solicitude, however, the INS can legally deport illegal alien parents even when doing so means that, as a practical matter, their citizen children must also leave the United States.[23]

It is not clear how far the reasoning of *Plyler* extends beyond the category of illegal alien children and the domain of public education. Its logic, however, might conceivably protect illegal alien children's access to other social services on the theory that these services are needed to prevent them from forming a permanent underclass. Public education may indeed be a special case. In 1996 Congress narrowly rejected an effort to deny such children the right to attend public schools, a right that became a central element of the presidential campaign.

Indirect access by illegal alien children to public benefits also occurs in the situation of mixed-status families in which some children may be U.S. citizens, others may be LPRs or in other valid statuses, and still others are illegal aliens. The citizen and LPR children may be entitled to welfare and other public benefits, while the illegal alien children are not—although the parents (who themselves are probably illegal in such cases) will inevitably allocate some of the benefits the citizen and LPR children receive (e.g., cash and food stamps) to their illegal alien children as well. The mixed-status family claiming welfare benefits is increasingly common; citizen children of illegal aliens accounted for an estimated 3 percent of total AFDC benefit costs and 2 percent of food stamp costs in 1993. The 1996 welfare reform legislation, by excluding LPRs from some but not all public benefit programs, will confuse the situation even more.

In recent years, restrictionists and others opposed to the growth of welfare budgets have intensified their efforts to deny access to public programs not only to illegal aliens but also to an ill-defined category of aliens who are not LPRs but whom the government allows to remain in PRUCOL status. Illegal aliens (but not PRUCOLs) are expressly barred from almost all major federal assistance programs with the important exception of emergency services under Medicaid (including labor and delivery services). Before the 1996 welfare reform law was enacted, they still remained eligible for certain other federal programs as well, such as school lunches, Head Start, social services, and earthquake disaster relief.[24] Under the new law, however, both illegal and PRUCOL aliens will be barred from participating in most or all of these programs unless the states enact laws specifically making them eligible.

California has led other states seeking to go beyond these federal restrictions (Rosen 1995). In November 1994 the state's voters, by a margin of 59 to 41 percent, approved Proposition 187, which would deny illegal alien children the right to attend public schools, in apparent violation of their rights under *Plyler*, and allow access only to emergency medical care, while requiring teachers and other social service providers to report suspected illegal aliens to the INS (Schuck 1995). A federal court enjoined enforcement of this law and then held its core provisions unconstitutional (Terry 1997). I discuss the implications of these events below.

Current Immigrant Policy Issues

Some of the developments that contributed to Proposition 187's political success are also shaping the major immigrant policy issues today. Perhaps the most important of these are the large number of illegal aliens in the United States, particularly in California, and voters' opposition to welfare benefits for aliens. Illegal migration to the United States is a striking example of the law of unanticipated and unintended consequences. Few would have predicted that a series of immigration control measures would in fact increase the level of illegal migration. Yet that is precisely what occurred when the federal government terminated the bracero program in 1964, established an asylum program in 1980, and made it easy for agricultural workers (but not their families) to gain legal status and for employers to comply with employment authorization verification requirements in 1986.

All observers now agree that two decades of enforcement reforms, of which employer sanctions formed the centerpiece, have failed to reverse the tide of undocumented workers and visa abusers. Recent data suggest, moreover, that the composition of this flow is changing, as women, children, and the elderly—the very groups most likely both to remain permanently and to demand costly public services—migrate or remain illegally. (Espenshade 1995). This volume and kind of illegal migration, however, is at least as much a political problem as a fiscal one. It inflames Americans' fears and antagonisms by stoking a widespread sense that the United States can no longer control its borders (if it ever did), that U.S. sovereignty is in grave jeopardy, that our national destiny is increasingly in the hands of strangers, and that taxpayers' generosity is being abused by those same strangers.

Several analyses of voters' attitudes toward Proposition 187 shed some additional light on these fears. A still-unpublished analysis of registered voters' reasons for supporting Proposition 187 indicate that 90 percent of them thought (and hoped) that it would send a message to the federal government to do more to protect the border; this was also the consequence cited most frequently (Jack Citrin, unpublished data sent to author on 6 Apr.

1995). Exit polls indicated that the measure attracted the support of a majority of Asian Americans, African Americans, and non-Hispanic whites as well as 22 percent of Latinos. Another survey, conducted by Ron Unz, an immigration advocate who unsuccessfully challenged Governor Wilson in the Republican primary, indicated that Republican primary voters did not feel a generalized anxiety about immigrants or even much concern about their impact on unemployment or crime so much as they resented that illegal aliens were receiving welfare benefits and that both legal and illegal aliens were not learning English in the schools and would benefit unfairly from affirmative action. If this survey is correct, voters' anger may have more to do with concerns about illegal migration, welfare abuse, multiculturalism, and affirmative action than with opposition to legal immigrants per se (Schuck 1995).

In this final section, I briefly discuss four issues that are being shaped by these and other similar anxieties: criminal aliens; aliens' rights to public benefits; the distribution of immigrant-related costs among the various levels of government; and the nature and significance of U.S. citizenship.

Criminal Aliens

No aspect of current immigration policy evokes more public indignation and dismay than the problem of aliens who commit serious crimes but nevertheless remain in the United States. As the Urban Institute demonstrated in the study that I discuss below, the direct cost to states of incarcerating aliens convicted of crimes is quite high; the indirect costs imposed by the crimes themselves, of course, are far higher. Although the vast majority of legal and illegal aliens are law abiding (excepting, of course, for immigration offenses committed by the latter), foreign-born individuals constitute a significant and growing fraction of the inmates in U.S. prisons, federal and state. The overwhelming majority of these inmate aliens, moreover, are legally deportable and have few if any avenues of relief available to them.

Congress has enacted many laws and held many hearings on this issue in the last decade. It has imposed expedited procedures for deporting criminal aliens, required that they be detained and kept in custody until they can actually be removed (which may sometimes mean indefinite or even lifetime incarceration), denied them immigration benefits, made them ineligible for discretionary relief from deportation, imposed severe criminal sanctions on their reentry, and instructed the INS to deport them as swiftly and unceremoniously as possible.

As with so many other immigration policies, however, the INS has failed to implement these congressional directives effectively, although its performance in this respect is improving. Remarkably, no one knows how many convicted criminal aliens are in U.S. prisons and jails. The INS succeeded in deporting 50,165 criminal aliens in 1997, almost seven times as many as it deported in 1989, but this still amounted to fewer than 15 percent of the deportable aliens under criminal justice supervision. According to one newspaper account, 87 percent of the criminal aliens in New York City who received three-day deportation notices (which even the INS calls "run letters") disappeared from the system (Sontag 1994). The INS is now placing a high priority on this problem, expanding a program that commences (and hopefully completes) their deportation hearings while they are still serving their criminal sentences in federal or state prisons[25] (Williams and Schuck 1998).

Some states, tired of waiting for the INS to remove criminal aliens, have taken direct action. In 1992 New York State sued the federal government to force it to take custody of illegal aliens in the state's prisons and deport them (Lyall 1992). In 1994 Florida won the INS's permission to pull convicted aliens out of prison and deport them, and the state announced in October that it would begin to deport aliens accused of minor and nonviolent offenses even before they were tried if they agreed not to return to the United States. Florida claimed to have saved a great deal in incarceration costs through these programs ("Florida" 1994). Other states are probably doing the same.

Aliens' Right to Public Benefits

As noted earlier, federal law bars illegal aliens from participating in the major federal assistance programs (except for emergency medical and disaster relief benefits and public schools), while legal aliens were entitled to participate in all of them (although "deeming" and "public charge" limitations applied) until Congress amended the law in 1996. But while these differences in welfare rights between legal and illegal aliens were clear to lawyers, the public was understandably confused on this point. This confusion contributed to the closer, more hostile scrutiny to which legal aliens' access to public benefits has recently been subjected.

As noted earlier, the public views legal immigrants much more favorably than illegal ones. Even so, politicians who wish to attack illegal aliens must tread carefully in order to avoid antagonizing legal aliens (many of whom will vote soon enough) and citizens (many of whom support legal immigration and may also sympathize with the plight of illegal aliens even while favoring enforcement activity against them). For this reason, politicians across the political spectrum tend to couple any attack on illegal immigrants with expressions of support for the rights of legal immigrants.[26] In the debate over Proposition 187, for example, California governor Pete Wilson and other prominent advocates of the measure took pains to defend and even praise legal immigrants (although the new law's reporting requirements might in fact adversely affect them), pointing out that one of every four Californians is a legal immigrant and that the state had benefited from their presence. Still, the passionate intensity of immigration politics can easily obscure the distinction between legals and illegals, as some of the hostility to the latter spills over and taints the former as well (Schuck 1995).

Another reason why the public conflates legal and illegal aliens is that illegal aliens, who are specifically barred from almost all public programs, nevertheless do receive significant public resources. The precise amount, of course, is impossible to determine because of methodological obstacles and variations among the studies (Vernez and McCarthy 1995). A 1994 study by the Urban Institute provided the first systematic assessment of some (not all) of the fiscal impacts occasioned by illegal aliens.

The study, which has been criticized by restrictionist groups, which think that it underestimates the net costs imposed by illegal aliens, focused on seven states in which an estimated 86.4 percent of the nation's illegal aliens live; the largest, of course, is California, whose 1.4 million illegals constitute 4.6 percent of the state's population. The study found the following costs in the seven states: criminal incarceration, $471 million; education, $3.1 billion; and Medicaid, $200–300 million. (Partly offsetting these costs are $1.9 billion in revenues generated from sales, property, and state income taxes on illegal aliens in the seven states surveyed.) The Urban Institute's estimates focused on illegal aliens' use of those services to which they are entitled (e.g., emergency care under Medicaid); thus they do not include benefits that illegal aliens obtain fraudulently. On this point, congressional testimony in May 1994 indicated that little fraud could be detected by the federal eligibility verification system for aliens (SAVE); the fraudulent claims that SAVE could *not* detect may be much greater (Clark et al. 1994).

Legal aliens, as noted, until recently enjoyed a right to public benefits that was essentially equal to that of U.S. citizens, and a large and growing number of them in fact claimed and received these benefits. With Americans fervently denouncing welfare dependency and desperately searching for spending reductions to lower budgetary deficits, aliens' use of welfare benefits— which is already substantial and seems to be increasing for refugees and certain other subgroups (Schuck 1996a, 1984)— generated considerable public controversy and resentment.

This public opposition has taken an enormous toll on aliens' benefit entitlements in recent years. Congress in 1994 extended the deeming period for SSI benefits for legal aliens from three to five years and limited illegal aliens' access to earthquake disaster funds to emergency relief and temporary housing of up to ninety days. The 1996 welfare reform law adopted far more sweeping restrictions, barring most *current* LPRs (except for refugees/asylees in their first five years in the United States, veterans and soldiers, and those who have worked for ten years in the United States and not taken public assistance during that period) from cash assistance and food stamps, and most *new* LPRs from most federal means-tested programs for five years. It also imposes restrictions on LPR eligibility for most *state* benefit programs. In addition, the new law extends and enforces more rigorously the deeming provisions against the family and employer sponsors of legal aliens who might apply for public benefits, tightens income requirements for sponsors, and requires stricter application of the "public charge" provisions to facilitate deportation of legal aliens who receive benefits, especially during their first few years in the United States. These changes are expected to produce very large budgetary savings (more than twenty billion dollars over five years [Fix and Passel 1994, 65–67]), a factor that makes them politically irresistible to so-called deficit hawks as well as to welfare opponents and immigration restrictionists. In late 1997, however, Congress restored some of these benefits and the President has proposed restoring most of the rest (Schuck 1998a).

Many provisions in the 1996 law raise difficult constitutional questions, which will have to be tested in the courts. As a policy matter, denying public support to LPRs, especially children, will have unpredictable consequences. Enforcing the complex new eligibility restrictions may involve high administrative and political costs. Moreover, federal limits on aliens' benefits will displace many of these costs onto those state and local governments that seek to fill the gap (where the new law permits these governments to do so). This raises the intergovernmental cost allocation issue, to which I now turn.

Intergovernmental Allocation of Immigration-Related Costs

In a federal system, the allocation of costs among different levels of government raises difficult problems. This issue, which the states and localities tendentiously but correctly call the question of "unfunded federal mandates," has several different aspects. First, federal law until 1996 required the states to provide to legal aliens the same welfare, health care, food programs, and other social services that the states provided to their own citizens, while paying only a portion of their cost. Indeed, federal constitutional principles require the states to provide the same benefits and services to legal aliens that they provide to citizens, even if the federal government contributes *nothing* to those benefits and services. The 1996 law permits, and in some cases requires, the states to avoid these fiscal burdens, but as just noted those states and localities that decide to pick up the slack will end up with *greater* burdens. Finally, these principles (as interpreted in *Plyler v. Doe*) still require the state to provide public education, by far the most costly public service of all, even to illegal aliens.

In addition to these features of the system, a large fiscal mismatch exists among the different levels of government. Most of the costs of public benefits and services that legal and illegal aliens use (two-thirds, according to state government estimates) are borne by state and local governments, while most of the taxes (again an estimated two-thirds) paid by those aliens go to the federal government. (The states and localities, however, tend to ignore the likelihood that most of the other economic benefits that aliens generate are received by the local communities in which they live and work.) In the case of illegal aliens, the federal government enjoys a further fiscal advantage; the workers pay Social Security taxes but do not ordinarily claim Social Security benefits.

This mismatch between cost bearers and tax receivers is a subject of bitter intergovernmental dispute, and the 1996 welfare reform law has in some ways exacerbated the conflict (Espenshade 1996). By restricting aliens' access to federal benefits, the law will aggravate the mismatch as states and localities move to defray the costs of indigent aliens through their general assistance and other programs, which are politically unpopular. Although the new law bars the states from assisting some non-LPR aliens with some benefits, it leaves them free to extend many benefits to legal aliens (a number of states have done so) and actually requires them to provide certain benefits, including the very costly Medicaid program, to favored categories of aliens. It is unclear how the new law, which transforms federal entitlements into block grants to the states, will affect those costs. State and local governments' uneasiness over their inability to shift their immigration-related costs to the federal government, which possesses exclusive policy control in this area, mirrors their long-standing frustrations with unfunded federal mandates in numerous other areas of public policy, frustrations that led Congress in 1995 to impose limits on unfunded mandates. This legislation is prospective only, however, and it is not yet clear to what extent it will affect immigration-related costs.

Long before the 1995 unfunded mandate law, some desperate states mounted a number of attention-getting challenges. Florida and California sued the federal government, demanding reimbursement for certain costs generated by both illegal and legal aliens residing in the state. Although these suits will probably fail, they helped to secure the unfunded mandates legislation. In addition, some states are adopting new restrictions on illegal aliens' access to public services. In addition to Proposition 187 in California, Virginia required its schools to verify the legal status of students over eighteen years of age who are enrolled in English as a second language (ESL) programs and of all students over twenty who entered the United States after the age of twelve. Failure to do so might lead to the loss of some state funding. These laws probably foreshadow similar efforts elsewhere.

The Significance of Citizenship

Alexander Bickel, a leading constitutional lawyer, wrote that U.S. citizenship "is at best a simple idea for a simple government" (1975, 54). By this he meant that full membership in the American polity has been widely and easily available (at least to males) since the Fourteenth Amendment was ratified in 1868 and that the nature of this inclusive citizenship—in particular, the legal rights and obligations attached to that status—has long ceased to be an important or divisive issue. In a 1989 essay on U.S. citizenship, I wrote that Bickel's observation "is probably truer today than in 1973 when he made it" (Schuck 1989b, 1).

Now I am not so sure. In the last few years, public discourse about citizenship has returned to first principles: its nature, sources, and significance. This discourse has been prompted by a number of developments since the late 1960s, most of them related to high levels of illegal immigration and of legal immigration by individuals with linguistic and cultural backgrounds vastly different from those of earlier waves of immigrants. These developments have raised concerns about the unity and coherence of the American civic culture, concerns that have in turn raised fundamental questions about how U.S. citizenship affects that culture. I shall briefly note five of these concerns: multicultural pressures; the loss of a unifying ideology; technological change; the expansion and consolidation of the welfare state; and the devaluation of citizenship.

With the enactment of the 1965 immigration reforms law, the composition of the immigration stream to the United States changed radically. Of the top ten source countries, only Jamaica sends predominantly English-speaking immigrants. Bilingual education thus became a major curricular issue in public education, and teaching in dozens of languages became necessary in many urban school systems. With the growing politicization of ethnicity and widespread attacks on the traditional assimilative ideal, anxieties about linguistic and cultural fragmentation increased. These anxieties have led to public measures establishing English as the official language in about half the states. They also prompted House passage of a national official-language requirement in August 1996 and the 1996 restrictions on the rights of legal and illegal aliens. The civil rights movement, moreover, took a turn toward separatism after 1965. African Americans, already severely disadvantaged, were obliged increasingly to cede political and economic influence to more recently arrived Hispanic and Asian voters. Certain economic sectors came to depend almost entirely on immigrant workers, legal and illegal. Relatively parochial immigrant enclaves grew larger. These multicultural pressures caused many Americans to feel more and more like strangers in their own country.

The end of the cold war rendered largely irrelevant the anti-communist ideology that had served for many decades as a unifying, coherent force in American political culture and as an obsessive preoccupation and goal in U.S. foreign policy. No alternative ideology has yet emerged to replace it. Only constitutionalism, the American civic religion, seems potentially capable of performing this function of binding together a nation of diverse peoples.

Rapid changes in transportation and communication technologies have transformed a world of sovereign nations into a global web of interdependent societies and multinational enterprises. Migration is now inexpensive and reversible. Immigrants no longer need to make an irrevocable commitment to their new society; they can more easily retain emotional ties to their countries and cultures of origin. Studies by sociologists of immigration such as Alejandro Portes and others indicate that TV and other cultural forces help to assimilate second-generation immigrant youths into an underclass culture rather than into mainstream American life and that divorce rates and other indicia of social dysfunction tend to increase with the length of immigrants' residence in the United States. With the welfare state's expansion, the behavior, values, and economic progress of immigrants have become matters of fiscal significance and public policy concern. In contrast to the historical pattern, immigration no longer ebbs and flows with the business cycle, presumably because of a stronger social safety net. The welfare state, by pitting citizens and aliens against one another in competition for scarce public resources, has raised the stakes in the perennial debate over how the polity should conceive of community, affinity, and civic obligation.

Until the 1996 legislation reversed the tide, the welfare state's egalitarian thrust, its nourishing of entitlement as an ideal, and the growth of a dependent population had diluted citizenship as a distinctive status bearing special privileges and demanding special commitments and obligations. The rights of legal aliens had converged with those of citizens until there was little to separate them; as noted above, only the franchise, immigration sponsorship privileges, and eligibility for the federal civil service remained the special prerogative of citizens. Americans began to feel that U.S. citizenship had lost much of its value, that it should somehow count for more.[27] As the practice of dual nationality became more widespread and the U.S. government grudgingly acquiesced to it, many U.S. citizens participated actively in the politics of their countries of origin (Schuck 1998b).

These changes led to calls for a revitalization of citizenship. One type of proposal, which prompted the enactment in 1993 of the National Community Service Corps, looks to the creation of a spirit of public service to the nation among young people. Another approach, embodied in the federal welfare reform laws adopted in 1988 and 1996 and in many state programs, sought to undermine the entitlement mentality by insisting that able-bodied applicants for cash assistance perform some kind of socially useful work as a condition of receiving it. The 1996 reform, of course, limited welfare programs for U.S. citizens as well. A further, related strategy, exemplified by the 1996 restrictions on LPRs' rights to public benefits, was motivated by more than the desire to save scarce public resources. Congress also wanted to favor citizens in allocating those resources, to dismantle portions of the welfare state, and to increase citizenship's value by widening the gap between the rights of citizens and aliens, thus strengthening aliens' incentives to naturalize. As noted earlier, the recent spurt in naturalization petitions at least partly reflects the changing incentives generated by policy changes reducing LPRs' eligibility for governmental benefits.

Other types of reforms are aimed directly at citizenship per se. The INS has attempted to make the naturalization process easier, faster, and more attractive. Indeed, the INS has succeeded so well at this that it was accused of tolerating widespread fraud in the naturalization process as a way to attract new voters to the Democratic Party during the 1996 elections. The Commission on Immigration Reform has proposed a 1990s version of the "Americanization" movement that sought to foster rapid assimilation and naturalization around the World War I era. Another approach, which would encourage naturalization but also risk dividing the loyalties of U.S. citizens, would adopt policies more tolerant of dual nationality. It is striking that while Germany and other European states are seriously considering such changes (along with some limited adoption of jus soli principles), the United States continues its official opposition to dual nationality, requiring all who naturalize in the United States explicitly to renounce all other allegiances (Gerald L. Neuman, "Nationality Law in the United States and Germany: Structure and Current Problems," ch. 8 in this volume; Schuck 1994b; Schuck 1998b).

A far more radical proposal, which is not at all inconsistent with the policies designed to encourage naturalization, would deny citizenship to some who, under existing law, are entitled to it. In the traditional understanding of the jus soli rule embodied in the Citizenship Clause of the Fourteenth Amendment, one automatically becomes a citizen merely by being born on U.S. soil, even if one's parents are in the country illegally or only as temporary residents. Those who challenge this understanding emphasize the importance of mutual consent—the polity's as well as the alien's—in legitimating U.S. citizenship. They also point to the perversity of permitting a Mexican woman with no claims on the United States to confer citizenship on her new child simply by crossing the border and giving birth, perhaps at public expense, in a U.S. hospital. While not favoring this common practice, defenders of birthright citizenship wish to avoid creating and perpetuating an underclass of long-term residents who do not qualify as citizens. Many guest workers and their descendants who live in European countries that reject the jus soli principle suffer this disadvantage (Schuck and Smith 1986; Schuck 1996b; Neuman 1996).

This change would require either a constitutional amendment or a Supreme Court reinterpretation of the Citizenship Clause. Congress considered and rejected proposals in 1996 to eliminate birthright citizenship for the children of illegal aliens, although the Republican Party platform supported such proposals in the 1996 presidential campaign (Schuck and Smith 1996). The U.S. is not alone in maintaining a birthright citizenship rule (Adams 1993), and some, notably Germany, have been moving toward—although remaining well short of—the traditional U.S. position (Neuman, "Nationality Law in the United States and the Federal Republic of Germany," ch. 8 in this volume). Nevertheless, some modification of the rule—for example, extending citizenship to those who are born in the United States in illegal status and remain as long-term residents—could possibly attract wider support. A similar change was adopted in France (Schuck 1996b).

Conclusion

The 1980s were years of extraordinary change and expansion in U.S. *immigration* policy, propelled by all three branches of the federal government. Since the enactment of the 1990 law, however, Congress has resisted strong restrictionist pressures to return legal immigration to its pre-1990 and even pre-1980 levels. In the mid-1990s, it has been *immigrant* policy—the treatment of aliens once they are inside the country—that has been the main focus of policy innovation. The INS is intensifying its interior enforcement as well as Border Patrol efforts against undocumented workers. Congress has adopted many harsh, new enforcement rules, subjecting even long-term LPRs to detention and deportation if they commit crimes, regardless of their close familial ties to U.S. citizens. And in the most striking and controversial departure from recent practice, LPRs are now ineligible for a broad range of governmental benefits that they have long been able to claim on an equal basis.

In an important sense, these developments have aligned immigration policy and immigrant policy, perhaps more closely than ever before. Immigration policy—the initial decision about whom to admit and under what conditions—has always placed those admitted on a straight path to full membership if they wished to claim it, while immigrant policy—the treatment of immigrants once they are inside the country—has always shaped their incentives for doing so. In the past, the government did little to influence immigrants' choices about whether to naturalize, and many of them either delayed or declined. In the mid-1990s, the United States suddenly and significantly increased immigrants' material incentives to claim citizenship, and an unprecedented number of them are responding by naturalizing—and more quickly. Americans may come to have second thoughts about the desirability of naturalizations motivated by a concern for governmental benefits and security against deportation, forgetting that immigrants have always had a variety of reasons to naturalize. But for now, immigration and immigrant policies are pushing in the same direction: toward the rapid transformation of aliens into citizens.

Notes

1. Schuck 1996a. The "latent functions" of immigrant policy (to recur to Merton) are more elusive but no less real. They include the economic, demographic, cultural, ideological, and social implications of the way in which the law distributes status and rights among immigrants.
2. U.S. Dept. of Justice 1997, 25.
3. FAIR's former executive director, Roger Conner, now heads a group (the American Alliance for Rights and Responsibilities) that advocates so-called

communitarian norms, especially the promotion of public safety and public values in local public spaces. Here, too, the board members are decidedly mainstream in status and largely liberal in their politics.

4. Employing an unusual methodology, they elicited the respondents' answers to standard survey questions and then followed up with additional questions in a process designed to resemble, albeit crudely, the give-and-take of ordinary conversation about public issues. Sniderman and Piazza found that the respondents' views on race-oriented issues differed considerably from issue to issue. That is, attitudes about affirmative action were not the same as attitudes about fair housing policies or about government spending on behalf of minorities. For my purposes, the more interesting finding is that respondents' initial views on issues (except for affirmative action) changed when those views were even weakly challenged or met with additional information. The authors summarized this finding as follows: "Finally, and perhaps most importantly, the positions that whites take on issues of race are pliable to a degree never suspected. Substantial numbers—on some issues as many as four in every ten—can be talked out of the positions they have taken by relatively weak counter-arguments, affirmative action not surprisingly being a major exception" (1993, 13–14). A somewhat analogous positional shift appears in a recent *New York Times*/CBS opinion poll on welfare reform. When the respondents were asked about their attitudes toward "government spending on welfare," 48 percent favored cuts, and only 13 percent favored increases. But when they were asked about "spending on programs for poor children," 47 percent favored increases, and only 9 percent favored cuts (DeParle 1994).

5. Indeed, the word *ambivalent* appears in the title of a comprehensive survey of public attitudes toward immigration (Simon and Alexander 1993) and in the subtitle of a recent study of Mexican immigrants' political identities in the United States (Skerry 1993).

6. Some of these attitudinal distinctions are arguably inconsistent. Although respondents believe that immigrants take jobs away from Americans, for example, they also believe that immigrants take jobs that Americans do not want and that immigrants threaten neither their own jobs nor the jobs of people whom they know (Simon and Alexander 1993).

7. Even more interesting, roughly similar patterns have been found from polling over time in Canada, Australia, Britain, and France. The survey data discussed in this and the preceding paragraph appear in Simon 1995.

8. Similar questions can be raised about the enactment of the Immigration Reform and Control Act of 1986, which was expansionist on balance although it contained important control measures, notably employer sanctions. For a discussion of both the 1986 and 1990 acts and the role of ideas in immigration politics, see Schuck 1992.

9. Espenshade and Hempstead (1996, 547,548–49, 555), drawing on 1993 polling data, find that Asian and blacks express significantly more pro-immigration views than do whites. They note that, as to blacks, this finding runs counter to earlier data indicating greater opposition to immigration. Hispanics, however, are not significantly different from Anglos in their attitudes toward immigration.

10. This point is not necessarily contradicted by California's adoption of Proposition 187, for the measure was directed not at legal immigrants but at ille-

gal ones, about whom political attitudes are considerably different (Schuck 1995). The political significance of Proposition 187 is discussed below.

11. See Graham 1986. The publications of FAIR, the restrictionist group described above and one of which Graham is a leading member, frequently emphasize this attitudinal gap.

12. Recent examples are *Stone v. I.N.S.*, 115 S.Ct. 1537 (1995) (filing of motion to reopen or reconsider the Board of Immigration Appeals' final deportation order does not toll statute period for seeking judicial review). Lower courts occasionally strike down some legislative provisions, even on constitutional grounds. See, e.g., *American-Arab Anti-Discrimination Committee v. Meese*, 714 F.Supp. 1060 (C.D. Cal. 1989), vacated as moot, 940 F.2d 445 (9th Cir. 1991).

13. Perhaps the most dramatic example of this shift is Pete Wilson, who, as a U.S. senator, obtained expansionist provisions in IRCA at the behest of California growers but less than a decade later made immigration restriction the keystone of his reelection strategy (Schuck 1995).

14. Even U.S. citizens vote at low levels: only 50 percent voted in the 1996 Presidential election. Because of several factors, including the relatively large number of elections in the United States, crossnational comparisons of voting rates should be interpreted with care.

15. For a recent judicial reaffirmation of these rights, see *Arab-American Anti-Discrimination Committee v. Reno*, 883 F.Supp. 1365 (C.D. Cal. 1995).

16. In 1996 two-thirds of the aliens who were deported were charged with crimes or narcotics activity (U.S. Dept. of Justice 1996, 183).

17. According to a summary of a report by the National Center for Educational Statistics, a large number of alien students (including LPRs, nonimmigrants, and perhaps other categories) received sizable educational grants as well as loans on the same basis as students who are U.S. citizens (FAIR 1995). Some of these benefits are being criticized (Johnson 1996).

18. Verhovek 1995. Several reasons may account for this sudden spike in naturalizations: for example, Congress threatened (and in the 1996 welfare reform law fulfilled the threat) to withhold public benefits from LPRs; millions of aliens legalized under IRCA are now becoming eligible to naturalize; and the INS's fees for renewing green cards have made naturalization more of a financial bargain.

19. According to summary data obtained from the special counsel in November 1994, seven years of enforcement have yielded a grand total of $1.5 million in back pay and $550,000 in penalties (U.S. Dept. of Justice, Office of Special Counsel 1994). Many states and localities have established human rights commissions authorized to investigate and prosecute allegations of discrimination based on a number of characteristics, including national origin. It is unclear whether any of these provisions apply to alienage discrimination and, if so, how effectively they have been enforced. New York City has established a Mayor's Office of Immigrant Affairs, which seeks to protect and advance the interests of aliens.

20. The INS reported 1.6 million apprehensions in 1996, slightly less than the figure for 1986, when IRCA was enacted and when an unusual amount of illegal entry probably occurred in anticipation of the new law). The 1995 total was 1.4 million (U.S. Dept. of Justice 1997, 173).

21. The 1996 antiterrorism law permits the government to exclude even long resident illegal entrants rather than deport them with a consequent limitation of their procedural, and perhaps also substantive, rights.
22. 457 U.S. 202 (1982). For discussions of this case, see Tribe 1988, 1551–53; Schuck 1984, 54–58; and Schuck 1995.
23. Under existing law, citizen children cannot petition for an "immediate relative" visa (which is essentially outside the numerical quotas) for their parents until they reach the age of eighteen.
24. It took fifteen years to implement a 1980 statute prohibiting federal housing aid to illegal aliens (*Federal Register* 60 [20 Mar. 1995]: 14816). An amendment to the 1994 crime bill would have barred illegal and PRUCOL aliens from these and other federal programs from which they were not expressly excluded now, but it was ultimately defeated in conference. The 1996 law now bars them.
25. Not all of the incarcerated criminal aliens are subject to immediate deportation in any given year, as their sentences expire at different times.
26. Indeed, former governors Mario Cuomo of New York and Michael Dukakis of Massachusetts, as well as several New York City mayors, including the incumbent Rudolph Giuliani, have voiced vigorous support for *illegal* aliens. See Schmitt 1996. See also Nathan Glazer, "Governmental and Nongovernmental Roles in the Absorption of Immigrants in the United States," ch. 3 in this volume. Leaders in many other communities did the same during the 1980s, when granting sanctuary to asylum-seeking Salvadorans and Guatemalans symbolized opposition to President Reagan's policies in Central America, although many of these same leaders are now in the vanguard of anti-immigration sentiment. In 1997 Congress granted an amnesty to about 400,000 illegal aliens from Central America (Schuck 1998a).
27. Very recently, nationalistic anger, populist resentment, and the politics of tax reform have fused in a bitter condemnation of very wealthy Americans who renounce their U.S. citizenship, apparently in order to reduce their tax liabilities. Many Americans fear that this practice confirms a disturbing trend toward a purely instrumental, self-interested conception of citizenship (De Witt 1995). Another widely publicized example was Rupert Murdoch's decision to naturalize in order to become eligible to purchase additional media properties (Safire 1985). Congress in 1996 amended the tax law to combat this practice (Schuck 1998b).

References

Adams, Sarah A. 1993. "The Basic Right of Citizenship: A Comparative Study." Center for Immigration Studies Backgrounder No. 7-93. Washington, D.C.: Center for Immigration Studies, Sept.

Aleinikoff, T. A., David A. Martin, and Hiroshi Motomura. 1995. *Immigration Process and Policy.* 3d ed. St. Paul, Minn.: West.

Amar, Akhil. 1991. "The Bill of Rights as a Constitution." *Yale Law Journal* 100 (Mar.): 1131–1210.

Bickel, Alexander M. 1975. *The Morality of Consent.* New Haven, Conn.: Yale University Press.

Borjas, George. 1994. "Immigration and Welfare, 1970–1990." National Bureau of Economic Research, Working Paper No. 4872. National Bureau of Economic Research, Cambridge, Mass.

Clark, Rebecca L., Jeffrey Passel, Wendy Zimmermann, and Michael Fix. 1994. *Fiscal Impacts of Undocumented Aliens: Selected Estimates for Seven States.* Report to the Office of OMB and the Department of Justice. Washington, D.C.: Urban Institute.

DeParle, Jason. 1994. "Despising Welfare, Pitying Its Young." *New York Times,* 18 Dec., E5.

De Witt, Karen. 1995. "One Way to Save a Bundle: Become a Former American." *New York Times,* 12 Apr., A1.

Espenshade, Thomas J. 1996. "Fiscal Impacts of Immigrants and the Shrinking Welfare State." Working Paper No. 96-1. Princeton University, Office of Population Research, Princeton, N.J.

_____. 1995 "Unauthorized Immigration to the United States." *Annual Review of Sociology* 21: 195–216.

Espenshade, Thomas J., and Hempstead, Katherine. 1996. "Contemporary American Attitudes Toward U.S. Immigration." *International Migration Review* 30 (summer): 535–70.

FAIR (Federation for American Immigration Reform). 1995. "While Congress Cuts Student Aid, Taxpayers Still Pay Over a Billion Dollars a Year To Educate Foreign Students." FAIR Immigration Report, 2 June.

Fix, Michael, and Jeffrey S. Passel. 1994. *Immigration and Immigrants: Setting the Record Straight.* Washington, D.C.: Urban Institute, May.

"Florida to Try Early Deportation." 1994. *New York Times,* 28 Oct., A25.

Fuchs, Lawrence H. 1990. "The Reactions of Black Americans to Immigration," in *Immigration Reconsidered: History, Sociology, and Politics,* ed. V. Yans-McLaughlin, 293–314. New York: Oxford University Press.

Graham, Otis L. 1986. "Uses and Misuses of History in the Debate Over Immigration Reform." *Public Historian* 8 (spring): 41–64.

Higham, John. 1970. *Strangers in the Land: Patterns of American Nativism, 1860–1925.* 2d ed. New York: Atheneum.

Johnson, Dirk. 1996. "Scholarship Restrictions Make Refugee Feel Scorned." *New York Times,* 12 May, 12.

Lewontin, Richard C. 1995. "Sex, Lies, and Social Science." *New York Review of Books,* 20 Apr., 24

Lyall, Sarah. 1992. "Albany Sues U.S. on Aliens Held in Prison." *New York Times,* 28 Apr., B1.

Neuman, Gerald L. 1996. *Strangers to the Constitution: Immigration, Borders, and Fundamental Law.* Princeton: Princeton University Press.

_____. 1994. "Justifying U.S. Naturalization Policies." *Virginia Journal of International Law* 35 (fall): 237–78.

_____. 1992. "'We Are the People': Alien Suffrage in German and American Perspective." *Michigan Journal of International Law* 13 (winter): 259–335.

Raskin, Jamin B. 1993. "Legal Aliens, Local Citizens: The Historical, Constitutional, and Theoretical Meanings of Alien Suffrage." *University of Pennsylvania Law Review* 141 (Apr.): 1391–1470.

Rosberg, Gerald A. 1977. "Aliens and Equal Protection: Why Not the Right to Vote?" *Michigan Law Review* 75 (Apr.–May): 1092–1136.

Rosen, Jeffrey. 1995. "The War on Immigrants." *The New Republic,* 30 Jan., 22–26

Safire, William. 1985. "Citizen of the World." *New York Times,* 16 May, A31.

Schmitt, Eric. 1996. "Giuliani Criticizes G.O.P. and Dole on Immigration." *New York Times,* 7 June, B3.

Schuck, Peter H. 1998a. "The Open Society," *The New Republic,* April 13, 1998, p. 16.

_____. 1998b. Citizens, Strangers, and In-Between: Essays.

_____. 1996a. "Alien Rumination." *Yale Law Journal* 105, no. 7: 1963–2012.

_____. 1996b. Testimony before House Judiciary Subcommittees on Immigration and Claims and on the Constitution, 13 Dec. 1995, and supplemental letter dated 14 Feb. 1996.

_____. 1995. "The Message of 187." *American Prospect,* no. 21, 85–92

_____. 1994a. Expert testimony delivered Oct. 1994 in *Lavoie v. The Queen,* Federal Court of Canada, Trial Division.

_____. 1994b. "Whose Membership Is It, Anyway? Comments on Gerald Neuman." *Virginia Journal of International Law* 35 (fall): 321–31.

_____. 1992. "The Politics of Rapid Legal Change: Immigration Policy in the 1980s." *Studies in American Political Development* 6: 37–92.

_____. 1989a. "Introduction: Immigration Law and Policy in the 1990s." *Yale Law and Policy Review* 7, no. 1: 1–19.

_____. 1989b. "Membership in the Liberal Polity: The Devaluation of American Citizenship." *Georgetown Immigration Law Journal* 3 (spring): 1–18.

_____. 1984. "The Transformation of Immigration Law." *Columbia Law Review* 84 (Jan.): 1–90.

Schuck, Peter H., and Rogers M. Smith. 1996. Letter to the editor, *New York Times*, 12 Aug., A14.

_____. 1986. *Citizenship Without Consent: Illegal Aliens in the American Polity*. New Haven, Conn.: Yale University Press.

Schuck, Peter H., and Theodore Hsien Wang. 1992. "Continuity and Change: Patterns of Immigration Litigation in the Courts, 1979–1990." *Stanford Law Review* 45 (Nov.): 115–83.

Simon, Rita J. 1995. "Immigration and Public Opinion." Paper presented at National Legal Conference on Immigration and Refugee Policy, Washington, D.C., 30 Mar.

Simon, Rita J., and Susan H. Alexander. 1993. *The Ambivalent Welcome: Print Media, Public Opinion, and Immigration*. Westport, Conn.: Praeger.

Skerry, Peter. 1993. *Mexican Americans: The Ambivalent Minority*. New York: Free Press.

Smith, Roger M. 1997. *Civic Ideals: Conflicting Visions of Citizenship in U.S. History*. New Haven, Conn: Yale University Press.

Sniderman, Paul, and Thomas Piazza. 1993. *The Scar of Race*. Cambridge: Harvard University Press.

Sontag, Deborah. 1994. "Porous Deportation System Gives Criminals Little to Fear." *New York Times*, 13 Sept., A1.

Terry, Don. 1997. "Strong Blow is Delivered to State Law on Aliens," *New York Times*, 15 Nov., A6.

Tribe, Laurence H. 1988. *American Constitutional Law*. 2d ed. Mineola: Foundation.

U.S. Department of Justice. 1996. "Immigration to the United States in Fiscal Year 1995." Washington, D.C.: U.S. Department of Justice, Mar.

_____. 1994. *U.S. Immigration and Naturalization Service, 1994 Statistical Yearbook*. Washington, D.C.: U.S. Government Printing Office.

United States Department of Justice, Office of Special Counsel for Immigration-Related Unfair Employment Practices. 1994. Weekly Report, 28 Nov.

Verhovek, Sam Howe. 1995. "Legal Immigrants in Record Numbers Want Citizenship." *New York Times*, 2 Apr., 1.

Vernez, Georges, and Kevin McCarthy. 1995. "The Fiscal Costs of Immigration: Analytical and Policy Issues." Paper No. DRU-958-1-

IF. RAND Center for Research on Immigration Policy, Santa Monica, Calif., Feb.

Williams, John and Peter H. Schuck. 1998. "Deporting Criminal Aliens: The Perils and Promises of Federalism." *Harvard Journal of Law and Public Policy* 21 (spring).

....

Chapter 8

Nationality Law in the United States and the Federal Republic of Germany: Structure and Current Problems

Gerald L. Neuman[1]

Citizenship, Nationality, Ethnicity

This paper discusses the subject of nationality law in the United States and the Federal Republic of Germany. *Nationality* (*Staatsangehörigkeit*) denotes membership in a particular state in the sense of international law. Before exploring this topic, it is important to discuss the relationship between nationality and the concepts of citizenship (*Staatsbürgerschaft*) and ethnicity.

Nationality and Citizenship

Nationality bears a complex relationship to the multiple meanings of *citizenship* in sociology, political theory, and law. In political theory, *citizen* sometimes serves as an evocative label for elements of a model: the theorist imagines a state in isolation from all other states and refers to all individuals in the model as its citizens. In this scenario citizenship and nationality coalesce, because non-nationals are absent from the model. For other

political theorists, citizenship is an activity—good citizenship—
implying responsibilities as well as rights (Kymlicka and Norman 1995, 286). Not all nationals rise to the level of civic virtue
required for good citizenship.

For many sociologists, and some political theorists, *citizenship* denotes a preferred status in society, ideally but not necessarily available to all nationals (Kymlicka and Norman 1995,
284–85; Marshall 1965). Citizenship entails rights and prestige
and access to resources. There are full, or first-class, citizens,
and then there are lesser members of society whose approxima-
tion to full citizenship is a matter of degree. This hierarchical
conception has deep historical roots reaching back to political
practice in ancient Greece.

In the modern sociological form of this perspective, nationality may not be a prerequisite for citizenship (Barbalet 1988, 99;
Bauböck 1994, 239). Foreign residents may be categorized as
possessing lesser degrees of citizenship, and privileged foreigners may even be hierarchically superior to some nationals. The
operation of immigration law in the United States and aliens
law in the Federal Republic generates multiple ranks of alien
statuses with corresponding bundles of rights. For example, in
the United States today one could focus on permanent resident
aliens, conditionally resident spouses and entrepreneurs, admitted refugees, employees of international organizations and their
families, treaty traders, foreign students, tourists, de facto
refugees in "temporary protected status," asylum applicants,
and undocumented workers, among others. In Germany one
could point to resident European Union nationals, residents
with European Association agreement rights, non-European
residents with residence entitlement (*Aufenthaltsberechtigung*),
non-European residents with limited or unlimited residence permit (*Aufenthaltserlaubnis*), temporary contract workers, asylum
applicants, tolerated de facto refugees, and illegal workers,
among others. In both countries, the different statuses entail
varying consequences with regard to security of residence, labor
market access, and entitlement to government benefits and services. In both countries, the list of statuses and their consequences are constantly changing.

These examples may reinforce the observation that "the
scope of a 'theory of citizenship' is potentially limitless—almost

every problem in political philosophy involves relations among citizens or between citizens and the state" (Kymlicka and Norman 1995, 284). Accordingly this paper will focus on one particular status barrier: the distinction between aliens and nationals.[2] In both the United States and the Federal Republic, even the most privileged categories of aliens differ from nationals in two crucial respects: they lack absolute security of residence, and they lack full rights of political participation.[3] In the Federal Republic, other differences include the fact that aliens do not enjoy the constitutional rights to freedom of assembly, freedom of association, internal mobility, occupational liberty, freedom from extradition, and access to civil service employment (Constitution [GG] arts. 8, 9, 11, 12, 16, 33). Under the United States system of federalism, as Peter Schuck explains in his contribution to this volume ("The Treatment of Aliens in the United States," ch. 7) aliens are more vulnerable to discrimination by the federal government than by the states. They face greater obstacles to arranging for the immigration of their family members than citizens do. They are barred from most positions in state and federal public employment. Resident aliens' eligibility for government benefits is not wholly congruent with citizens', and there is currently a political movement to decrease severely their access to benefits. These differences illustrate what is at stake in access to nationality in the United States and the Federal Republic.

Nationality and Ethnicity

In common U.S. usage, the term *nationality* often carries a different meaning from its legal significance. Most Americans think of themselves as U.S. citizens, not as U.S. nationals, and often employ *nationality* in the sense of *Nationalität*, to describe ethnic origin (or so-called national origin).

The different processes of state formation in the Anglo-American sphere and Germany have led to contrasting assumptions about nationhood (Brubaker 1992; Grawert 1987). English speakers more often equate *nations* with *states* in the international sense and regard a *people* as the population of a given nation or state; in other words, the state defines its people (*Staatsvolk*). By contrast, Germans, like many other Europeans, more easily conceive of a nation (*Nation*) or people (*Volk*) as an aggregate existing independent of state organization, unified by certain commonalities such as language, religion, culture, history, and descent. The romantic nationalism of the nineteenth century insisted that such objectively defined peoples require national states as vehicles for their collective self-determination. This thesis provided the ideological basis for the unification of both Italy and Germany.

The notion of a nation distinct from the population of an existing state remains culturally and politically important in the Federal Republic. The emphasis on collective self-determination is also consistent with the greater strength of the communitarian tradition in German political and legal thought, in contrast to the strength of the liberal individualist tradition in the United States (Grawert 1987, 665–66). At the same time, the postwar repudiation of National Socialist ideology has involved a rejection of excessive *Nationalismus*. Both the United States and Germany have gone through historical periods in which racism played a central role in nationality law, and both countries place great importance on distancing themselves from that approach.

Current German nationality law is characterized by its consistent reliance on jus sanguinis, under which a child's nationality depends on the nationality of its parents, not on its place of birth. Scholars disagree on the extent to which this reliance should be explained historically as a result of nineteenth-century-style nationalism. William Rogers Brubaker's comparative study of French and German nationality law attributes "decisiv[e] influence" to "ethnonational considerations" in Germany's rejection of jus soli proposals in 1913 (Brubaker 1992, 124–37). Not only critics of jus sanguinis (Preuß 1993, 233–34; Rittstieg 1991, 1387–88; Wollenschläger and Schraml 1994, 225) but also some of its defenders (Quaritsch 1988, 496–97; Uhlitz 1986, 146–47; see also Hailbronner 1989, 74, 77) have accepted this explanation. Other scholars have rejected it (Frowein 1994, 100; Löwer 1993, 156–57; see also von Mangoldt 1993, 970–71; but see von Mangoldt 1994, 37). For some critics, the link between jus sanguinis and nineteenth-century nationalism burdens current nationality law with a historical taint (Bryde 1994, 313; Habermas 1994, 144–46). For some defenders, the link associates current nationality law with the positive value of the self-determination of peoples, which commands continued respect in modern human rights law (Bleckmann 1988, 441).

Nonetheless, although the German citizenry is not as ethnically diverse as that of the United States, neither is it ethnically homogeneous. Germans marry foreigners and have children who inherit German nationality (Federal Government's Commissioner 1994, 54, 86). The Federal Republic does naturalize some of its foreign residents (109). It even has ethnic groups with official national minority status in their traditional areas of settlement: the Danes and Frisians in the north, and, since 1990, the Slavic group known as Sorbs (or Wends) in the east (Franke and Hofmann 1992, 402).

United States Nationality Law

A Sketch

Acquisition of Nationality at Birth

United States nationality is acquired at birth by two methods. The dominant rule is a form of jus soli principle, inherited from Great Britain, by which children born within the national territory (with exceptions shortly to be noted) acquire U.S. nationality. U.S. nationality law also has elements of jus sanguinis, by which children born outside the national territory to U.S. parents acquire U.S. nationality. The jus soli principle, unlike the jus sanguinis principle, has constitutional status, being expressed in the first sentence of the Fourteenth Amendment in the following language: "All persons born or naturalized in the United States, and subject to the jurisdiction thereof, are citizens of the United States and of the State wherein they reside" (U.S. Constitution, amend. 14 [adopted 1868]).

In discussing jus soli and jus sanguinis, it should be remembered that neither term designates a single, fully specified rule of nationality law. Rather, these terms refer to categories of rules placing primary emphasis on place of birth or descent, respectively. For example, a jus sanguinis system may require descent from a citizen father or from a citizen mother, or it may allow for both alternatives; a jus soli system may include or exclude births in the territorial sea or in the state's airspace.

The interpretation of the Fourteenth Amendment's jus soli rule involves two subtleties that result in two kinds of exceptions. First, the qualifying phrase "subject to the jurisdiction thereof" excludes certain categories of persons from the constitutional guarantee of birthright citizenship, based on the identity of their parents. Second, the territorial scope attributed to the term *the United States* creates further limitations.

Under the traditional interpretation of the constitution, four categories of persons are not "subject to the jurisdiction" of the United States at birth despite being born there. The first three categories were inherited from England: children born to foreign diplomats, children born on foreign public vessels in territorial waters, and children born to women accompanying an invading army (*United States v. Wong Kim Ark*, 169 U.S. 649 [1898]). These exceptions remain part of current U.S. nationality law. The fourth category was historically important, although it has long been superseded by statute: members of Native American tribes born within the jurisdiction of the tribe were not guaranteed citizenship by the Fourteenth Amendment, because the tribes were then regarded as distinct political societies under the umbrella of U.S. sovereignty.[4] Nonetheless, tribal members were not aliens, either. Rather, they had U.S. nationality in the international sense without having U.S. citizenship in the sense of full membership and political rights in the larger society. In current terminology, they were "noncitizen nationals."

Although Congress extended full citizenship status to all Native American tribes early in this century, the category of "noncitizen national" persists as a relic of U.S. colonialism. When the United States acquired overseas territories at the turn of the last century, a doctrine developed by which many of these territories were regarded as not incorporated into the United States proper and therefore as not counting as the United States for purposes of the Citizenship Clause of the Fourteenth Amendment. The status of persons born within these territories was therefore subject to legislative discretion. In some cases, the inhabitants of these territories were admitted to full U.S. citizenship (e.g., Puerto Rico since 1917); in other cases, they remained noncitizen nationals (e.g., the Philippines during the entire period of U.S. sovereignty there). Under current law, the only U.S. territory where birth leads to the status of noncitizen national is American Samoa (including Swain's Island).[5]

Jus soli nationality is often described in German juristic literature as a device by which countries of immigration seek to increase their population (Löwer 1993, 157; Quaritsch 1988, 489; von Mangoldt 1993, 969–70; Ziemske 1993, 334). This characterization is perplexing from a U.S. perspective, given that the constitutional entrenchment of the jus soli rule was designed as a guarantee of the equality of Americans of African descent, overturning the infamous Dred Scott decision (*Scott v. Sandford*, 60 U.S. [19 How.] 393 [1857]). Moreover, the pivotal interpretation of the Citizenship Clause of the Fourteenth Amendment occurred in a case involving children of Chinese aliens, at a time when the federal government was attempting rigorously to prevent immigration from China (*United States v. Wong Kim Ark*, 169 U.S. 649 [1898] [affirming citizenship of children born to Chinese alien parents]). The constitutional status of the jus soli rule in the United States resulted from its role in protecting residents against hostile government action, not from a desire to acquire new nationals. Jus soli, if consistently followed, prevents the division of the resident population into a superior hereditary class of citizens and an inferior hereditary class of subjects. Current criticisms of jus soli nationality for illegal aliens (see Current Problems in U.S. Nationality Law, below) reflect only the most recent respect in which the protective functions of jus soli conflict with, rather than implement, U.S. immigration policy.

Jus soli nationality also benefits the larger society by facilitating the identification of immigrants' descendants with the United States, even if the immigrants do not naturalize. Although formal nationality cannot guarantee social harmony, it gives ethnic groups access to political rights and an ideological basis for pursuing their interests by emphasizing commonality with the rest of the citizenry. Thus jus soli weakens tendencies to ethnic separatism in the heterogeneous U.S. population (Martin 1985, 283).

The Constitution leaves descent of citizenship by jus sanguinis to the discretion of Congress, and the rules have varied over the years. Prior to this century, jus sanguinis citizenship was acquired only through the father, but since 1934 the rules have been gender neutral, at least prospectively.[6] The U.S. rules have always transmitted jus sanguinis citizenship one generation at a time, requiring the parents to demonstrate sufficient connection to the United States (by periods of residence or certain surrogates) before their citizenship could be inherited by their children. The current prerequisites are fairly minimal. For example, a child born abroad to two U.S. citizens acquires U.S. citizenship at birth if either parent has resided in the United States for any period at any time before the birth of the child (8 U.S.C. §1401[c]); a child born abroad to one U.S. citizen parent and one alien parent acquires U.S. citizenship at birth if the citizen parent has been physically present in the United States for periods totaling five years, at least two of which were after the age of fourteen (8 U.S.C. §1401[g]). Earlier rules sometimes required jus sanguinis citizens to take up residence in the United States for several years in order to preserve their citizenship, but this requirement was repealed in 1978.[7]

Naturalization

The Constitution confers on the Congress the authority to adopt a "uniform rule of naturalization," replacing the independent naturalization authority of the several states. Naturalization is usually defined in U.S. law as the conferral of U.S. citizenship (and therefore nationality) on persons who were not citizens at birth.[8] Naturalization may be individual or collective, as when citizenship is conferred on the inhabitants of a newly acquired territory.

Since 1790 federal statutes have defined criteria that entitle individual resident aliens to acquire naturalization as of right if they meet certain criteria. This regime of naturalization as of right has roots that began in the colonial period but departed from naturalization procedure in Britain itself, which was (and remains) discretionary (Brubaker 1989, 109; Kettner 1978, 69–75, 83–86). U.S. naturalization law also permits exceptional categories of aliens to achieve naturalization more quickly or easily through special statutory provisions or by direct grant from Congress.[9] I will concentrate here on the main legal procedure for individual naturalization.

Under current law, the principal requirements for naturalization include lawful admittance to permanent residence in
the United States; five years' continuous residence (suitably
defined); good moral character throughout the five-year period;
attachment to constitutional principles; being "well-disposed to
the good order and happiness of the United States"; the ability
to speak, read, and write English; knowledge of the "funda-
mentals" of U.S. history and government; and an oath expressing allegiance to the United States and renouncing all prior
allegiances (8 U.S.C. §§1423, 1427, 1448), even if this does not
extinguish the prior nationality.[10] (It may deserve emphasis that
an oath of renunciation of prior allegiance suffices, even if it has
no effect in extinguishing the prior nationality.) Aliens are
barred from naturalization if they have deserted from the U.S.
armed forces (8 U.S.C. §1425) or have successfully asserted
exemption from military service because of nationality, unless
they had previously performed military service in their country
of nationality.[11] The statute also includes a long list of ideological disqualifications, including inter alia aliens who advocate
opposition to all organized government, affiliate with the Communist Party or other totalitarian parties, advocate "the economic, international, and governmental doctrines of world
communism," advocate the forceful overthrow of the U.S. government, advocate the unlawful assault of government officers,
or advocate "the unlawful damage, injury, or destruction of
property" or sabotage. (8 U.S.C. §1424). During wartime, alien
enemies (i.e., nationals of an enemy nation) cannot be naturalized without discretionary authorization from the attorney general (8 U.S.C. §1442).

In one sense, these requirements have been relatively stable
since their recodification in the Immigration and Nationality
Act of 1952. Prior to 1952, racial discrimination played a major
role in U.S. naturalization policy. Between 1790 and 1870, only
"free white persons" were eligible for statutory naturalization;
in 1870 eligibility was extended to persons of African descent,
but most Asians remained ineligible. The last racial exclusions
were gradually repealed between 1943 and 1952. A few statutory
changes have been made since 1952, such as the exemptions
from the English-language requirement for elderly aliens and

the exception from disqualification for aliens who have previously performed military service.

In another sense, the criteria have changed since 1952 because of changes in their meaning. For example, the vague term "good moral character" applies differently in a period of more liberal sexual morality. On the other hand, Congress has recently been expanding the list of criminal offenses that permanently bar an individual from demonstrating good moral character (8 U.S.C. §1101[f]). The requirement of lawful admittance to permanent residence has also had different practical implications over time, depending on the list of statutory grounds for exclusion from the United States. The practical content of the English-language requirement should be changing as a result of efforts to limit the discretion of individual examiners by introducing standardized tests.

Loss of Nationality

Although the U.S. Constitution does not explicitly address loss of nationality, the Supreme Court has interpreted the Citizenship Clause of the Fourteenth Amendment as placing severe limits on the government's ability to deprive U.S. citizens of their nationality (*Afroyim v. Rusk*, 387 U.S. 243 [1967]). Nationality acquired by jus soli under the Fourteenth Amendment cannot be withdrawn by the government at all: it can only be voluntarily relinquished by the citizen. Nationality acquired by valid naturalization also cannot be withdrawn, but the government may later challenge whether the initial grant of naturalization was legally invalid or tainted by fraud. The limits of congressional power to withdraw nationality not covered by the Citizenship Clause of the Fourteenth Amendment are less clear. In the case of nationality by jus sanguinis, the Supreme Court has held that Congress could attach as a reasonable "condition subsequent" the requirement that the child reside for a period of years in the United States on reaching adulthood in order to preserve his or her citizenship.[12] In the past, the United States has extinguished the U.S. nationality of noncitizen nationals on the granting of independence to the territory where they resided (e.g., *Rabang v. Boyd*, 353 U.S. 427 [1957] [Philippines]).

At least for Fourteenth Amendment citizens, the constitutional limits on denationalization in the United States are even stricter than the limits on denationalization in the German *Grundgesetz*. In particular, Congress lacks the power to denationalize a U.S. citizen who voluntarily acquires a new nationality by naturalization in a foreign country, unless the citizen voluntarily relinquishes U.S. nationality in the course of naturalization (*Parness v. Shultz*, 669 F. Supp. 7 [D.D.C. 1987]; Nash 1993). Unlike German constitutional law, modern U.S. constitutional law does not regard voluntary naturalization as necessarily entailing consent to the withdrawal of prior nationality.

U.S. law on loss of nationality has been misunderstood by some German writers. One even finds inaccurate descriptions of U.S. law used to support the argument that countries with jus soli nationality cannot trust in the loyalty of their nationals and therefore provide for denationalization on grounds of disloyalty (Löwer 1993, 159; Ziemske 1993, 230). These accounts are presumably based on statutory provisions that were enacted in 1940 and then invalidated by the Supreme Court in a series of decisions between 1958 and 1967 (*Afroyim v. Rusk*, 387 U.S. 253 [1967]; *Kennedy v. Mendoza-Martinez*, 372 U.S. 144 [1963]; *Trop v. Dulles*, 356 U.S. 86 [1958]). The current U.S. Code takes account of these Supreme Court decisions somewhat obliquely, by adding the element of "intention of relinquishing United States nationality" to each of the former grounds of denationalization (8 U.S.C. §1481).[13] However expressed, the fact remains that jus soli citizens cannot be denationalized for disloyalty, desertion, or treason, unless it can be shown that they actually intended to divest themselves of their U.S. nationality. The possibility of inaccurate determinations of fact creates some risk, but in principle involuntary denationalization is prohibited.

Current Problems in U.S. Nationality Law

There are currently few major sources of dissatisfaction with U.S. nationality law. Some criticisms are primarily of theoretical importance; others focus less on the legal rules than on the context of nationality law, including its administrative implementation. The principal point of controversy is probably the application of the jus soli rule to the children of illegal aliens.

From the theoretical perspective, one recurrent sore point in nationality law concerns constitutional limits on legislative power. The Fourteenth Amendment entrenches the jus soli rule and has been interpreted as barring involuntary denationalization of jus soli citizens and naturalized citizens. Other rules of nationality law, however, are within the power of Congress. The courts have sometimes declined to apply normal standards of judicial review to naturalization criteria, invoking the same notions of extraordinary deference or nonjusticiability that they invoke when immigration criteria are challenged.[14] The suspension of normal constitutional limitations in the field of naturalization, as in the field of immigration, has not been popular with scholars. To give a concrete example, the disqualification from naturalization of persons who advocate communist doctrine (let alone the disqualification of persons who advocate "the unlawful damage, injury, or destruction of property") chafes badly against modern free speech doctrines in the United States, which ordinarily do not allow the government to impose sanctions on political advocacy that does not threaten imminent harm (Neuman 1994, 256–60). The core of this disqualification is far more congenial to German constitutional doctrines of militant democracy than to U.S. constitutional attitudes of free speech absolutism.

The English-language requirement for naturalization has also been criticized, particularly in its application to speakers of Spanish (Gonzalez Cedillo 1983; Perea 1992, 337–40; Select Commission 1981, 403–4 [separate statement of Commissioner Cruz Reynoso]). Spanish speakers are by far the largest linguistic minority in the United States,[15] and large portions of the United States were acquired by purchase or conquest from Spain or Mexico. In 1981 the majority of the Select Commission on Immigration and Refugee Policy defended the requirement on the ground that the English language operates as "a unifying thread of U.S. life ... important for full participation as a citizen [and] for full participation in the U.S. marketplace" (Select Commission 1981, 289). At the same time, the majority expressed its acceptance of linguistic diversity and "the importance of ethnic languages and traditions" and recommended flexibility in exempting older persons from the requirement (290).

Concern was expressed in the 1980's and early 1990's about an insufficient rate of naturalization, especially among certain immigrant groups. The proportion of naturalized citizens among the foreign-born population has steadily decreased from its historical peak during World War II; estimated levels fell from 73.1 percent in 1950 to 63.6 percent in 1970 and 50.5 percent in 1980 (North 1987, 318–19).[16] Figures from the 1990 census indicate a level of 40.5 percent. The nearly 12 million alien residents would constitute 4.7 percent of the total U.S. population.[17] Rates of naturalization vary dramatically by nationality. A study conducted by the INS, involving the 1977 cohort of immigrants and using a conservative methodology, found that 37.4 percent had naturalized by 1990 but that while 57.2 percent of the immigrants from mainland China had naturalized by 1990, only 15.1 percent of the immigrants from Mexico had done so (INS 1992, 142).[18] Calculating these figures another way, the naturalizations occurring in 1990 represented 2.3 percent of the total noncitizen residents and 3.7 percent of the noncitizens who entered before 1985, while the Mexican naturalizations represented 0.5 percent of noncitizen residents from Mexico and 0.8 percent of those who entered before 1985.[19]

The reasons for low naturalization rates are disputed. Some have argued that U.S. law gives immigrants too few incentives to naturalize, because permanent resident aliens already enjoy nearly all the advantages that citizenship would entail (DeSipio 1987, 401; Schuck 1989, 10; Yang 1994, 453). (In fact, recent legislation changes that cut back sharply on alien residents' eligibility for welfare benefits appear to have increased naturalization rates;[20] poverty is not yet a ground for denial of naturalization in U.S. law.) Others emphasize barriers to return migration, such as geographical distance, underdevelopment, and political repression in home countries, as factors increasing the likelihood of naturalization (Pachon 1987, 304; Portes and Curtis 1987, 354; Yang 1994, 473). In addition to Mexico's proximity, fear of loss of property rights there has prompted immigrants to maintain their Mexican nationality (Pachon 1987, 305; DeSipio 1987, 401). The perception of discrimination in U.S. society discourages naturalization and counteracts the tendency of more educated immigrants to naturalize (Pachon 1987, 305; Portes and Curtis 1987, 361; Yang 1994, 470). Bureaucratic obstacles, including lengthy delays and inhospitable officials, have also been seen as a factor (Alvarez 1987, 339, 346; North

1987, 321–23; Pachon 1987, 305). The ability to meet the English language and civics requirements is also important; official figures indicating extremely high success rates of applications (ca. 95 percent) are misleading, because they report only final rejections, not applicants who were told to apply again after further study (North 1987, 324 [finding that more than 25 percent of applications were neither approved nor denied]).

Jus soli citizenship for children born to illegal aliens has provoked criticism in recent years, as concern about illegal immigration has grown. In 1985 Peter H. Schuck and Rogers M. Smith published a book arguing for a reinterpretation of the U.S. Constitution so that the Fourteenth Amendment would guarantee citizenship only to children born to U.S. citizens or alien residents, not to the children of temporary visitors or illegal aliens (Schuck and Smith 1985). Since I strongly criticized their argument about constitutional interpretation at the time (Neuman 1987; see also Carens 1987; Martin 1985), I will note here only the Clinton administration's agreement that the proposal is "not a plausible reinterpretation of the Constitution" (Dellinger 1995, 12). Schuck and Smith's policy arguments have persuaded some politicians, however, and interest in changing this rule by either constitutional reinterpretation or constitutional amendment has grown since the election of the Republican Congress in 1994.[21]

Schuck and Smith identified a number of linked disadvantages to birthright citizenship for the children of illegal aliens, and the proponents of constitutional amendments have picked up on their themes (Schuck and Smith 1985, 110–14; *Congressional Record* 139: H1005–6 [daily ed. 3 Mar. 1993] [remarks of Rep. Gallegly]). Schuck and Smith's first claim is that such automatic conferral of citizenship represents an unconsented increase in the citizenry. They regard this as offensive per se for reasons of political theory; it also uses up immigration slots that could be better allocated and provokes public resentment against immigration in general. The second argument is that these uninvited citizens impose financial costs on the nation, state, and locality in fields such as education, medical care, housing, and welfare. Third, the birth of citizen children makes it easier for illegal alien parents to remain in the United States. Fourth, several of these disadvantages are advantages to the parents, and so they operate, at least at the margin, as further incentives to illegal immigration.

In my opinion, the strongest response one can make to these arguments emphasizes the role of jus soli citizenship in preventing the reestablishment of a hereditary caste of subordinated denizens vulnerable to exploitation, which was the historical purpose of the Fourteenth Amendment (Neuman 1987). Compared to conditions in Germany, the realities of immigration enforcement in the United States make it far less likely that illegal aliens and their children could be successfully identified and deported. The United States has long wilderness borders, a highly diverse legal population, poorly policed rural and urban areas where people can go underground, and no population registry system.[22] Schuck has argued that the jus soli rule should not be altered without adequate alternative protections for illegal aliens' children, which do not currently exist (Schuck 1995, 9–10; Schuck and Smith 1985, 98–99).

One could respond briefly to the particular arguments as follows: First, whether the increase is unconsented depends precisely on whether the United States chooses to maintain its current constitutional rule; if so, consent is not lacking. Second, the net financial costs to the nation are empirically uncertain and must be balanced against the protective value of the Fourteenth Amendment. Third, it is overkill to deprive children of citizenship in order to deprive their parents of immigration benefits; if those advantages are too attractive, they should be changed directly. Fourth, modifying the jus soli citizenship rules would have an extremely modest effect on the incentives for illegal immigration (Martin 1985).

Rather than pursue these arguments further, it may be more useful to make two observations: First, there is no controversy in the United States about citizenship for the children of permanent resident aliens. In fact, there is little controversy about citizenship for the children of foreign tourists; Schuck and Smith objected to it purely on theoretical grounds, and some of the proposed constitutional amendments would not change that part of the rule.[23]

Controversy is decreased by a rule that Europeans may find unattractive, as some Americans do. The citizenship of U.S.-born children of aliens is not an obstacle to the deportation of their parents. When it becomes appropriate to deport the parents, the United States must choose among three values that cannot all be preserved: enforcement of the immigration laws, unity of the family, and the right of U.S. citizens to remain in the United States. In unusual cases, parents may be permitted to stay in order to avoid extreme hardship to their children. Ordinarily, however, the parents are deported and can choose whether to take their children with them or leave them behind. If the parents are deported and take the children, then the children can always return as U.S. citizens, if they wish; however, living in their parents' country may lead them to reject their U.S. citizenship or put them under pressure to renounce it. We do not really have empirical information on how often these different outcomes occur.

Second, there is little emphasis on the problem of dual nationality. Dual nationality as such is not perceived as a serious problem in contemporary U.S. politics.[24] This is partly due to the long experience with dual nationality in the United States, given the coexistence of our jus soli rule with jus sanguinis rules in many other countries, and partly due to some differences in other legal rules. Under ordinary conditions, dual nationality introduces few problems that are not already present when aliens reside permanently in the United States. U.S. rules of international private law (conflict of laws) usually make an individual's domicile rather than citizenship the factor on which choice of law turns, and so permanent residents already present almost as great a potential for conflict as dual nationals. The United States also maintains the practice of drafting resident aliens, with the result that conflicts or cumulative burdens of military conscription can befall permanent residents as well as dual nationals. In these areas, the costs of dual nationality are largely incremental. Of course, dual nationality can create tragic conflicts when war arises between the two countries. Those occasions are rare, and they do not currently dominate public attitudes toward dual nationality.

Nationality Law in the Federal Republic of Germany

A Sketch of German Nationality Law

German nationality law derives from a variety of sources: the constitution (*Grundgesetz*), statutes, and treaties. The central statutory source for German nationality law is the 1913 Reichs- und Staatsangehörigkeitsgesetz (which I will call the Nationality Act), as amended through the present.

Prior to unification, there was an important reason for preserving the Nationality Act of 1913 as the basis for nationality law in the Federal Republic. The Federal Republic maintained a legal claim to continuity with the predecessor German Empire. It never recognized East Germany as a foreign state and always regarded the citizens of East Germany as sharing a common nationality with West Germans; the 1913 act provided the juridical basis for that common nationality. Since unification, that function of the 1913 act has become obsolete, and the long-delayed recodification of nationality law has become a feasible project, though a politically divisive one. Some aspects of nationality law reform were addressed in the negotiations leading to the compromise among the major political parties on refashioning the asylum guarantee in Article 16 of the *Grundgesetz*; as will be specifically mentioned later, some of these have already been implemented, while others have been postponed.

Acquisition of Nationality at Birth

Under current law, German nationality is acquired at birth solely via jus sanguinis. Under the 1913 Nationality Act, legitimate children were born as German nationals if and only if their fathers were German nationals, and illegitimate children were born as German nationals if and only if their mothers were German nationals. Gender discrimination regarding legitimate children persisted until 1974, when the Federal Constitutional Court invalidated it as a violation of the constitutional guarantee of gender equality (Judgment of 21 May 1974, *BVerfGE* 37: 217). In response, the legislature amended the statute so that legitimate children inherit German nationality from a German parent of either gender, regardless of whether they also inherit another nationality from the other parent.

The gender discriminatory rule regarding illegitimate children persisted until 1993, when it was replaced by a provision that an illegitimate child may inherit German nationality from its mother, or, if only the father is a German national, from its father upon a legally binding determination of paternity (the proceedings for which must have begun before the child reaches the age of twenty-three). (Nationality Act §4[1]). Foundlings, i.e., children of wholly unknown parentage found in German territory at an early age, are regarded as children of German nationals until the contrary is demonstrated (Nationality Act §4[2]).[25]

Acquisition of German nationality by jus sanguinis is not affected by the possibility that the child may also acquire another nationality by jus soli (e.g., by birth to German parents in the United States) or jus sanguinis. Nor, under current law, is there any limit to the descent of German nationality through multiple generations of descendants who reside abroad, so long as the parents have not suffered loss of German nationality through such means as renunciation or voluntary naturalization. The interparty compromise of 1992 regarding asylum reform contemplated that, in a recodification of nationality law, limitations would be placed on the automatic heritability of German nationality by persons lacking real connections to German territory (Giesler and Wasser 1993, 228 [reprinting agreement]). Action on this aspect of the interparty compromise lies in the future.

Naturalization

German naturalization law has been significantly modified since 1989, and it is important to describe what preceded the change as well as what followed it. Section 8 of the 1913 Nationality Act, as amended, provides the framework for naturalization in the general case, while various other legal provisions address special cases.

Section 8 authorizes the naturalization, upon proper motion, of aliens who reside within the Federal Republic, have a fixed place of residence there, and are able to support themselves and their dependents; there is also a good moral character requirement, which until 1993 was defined with the phrase "leading an irreproachable life."[26] Section 8 does not confer an entitlement to naturalization but rather empowers officials to grant naturalization in their discretion once certain minimum criteria have been met. While discretionary naturalization regimes are not uncommon in Europe, the pre-1990 German law has been described as an extreme example (Brubaker 1989, 110–111).

The policies guiding the exercise of this discretion in recent years were formulated in the federal Naturalization Guidelines of 1977. These guidelines begin by pointing out that naturalization can be conferred only when the public interest would be served thereby; the personal wishes and economic interests of the applicant do not suffice to justify naturalization. (§2.2, reprinted in Hailbronner and Renner 1991, 624). Moreover, in a famous passage they assert, "The Federal Republic of Germany is not a country of immigration; it does not seek deliberately to increase the number of German citizens through naturalization" (§2.3). Among the additional desiderata for discretionary naturalization contemplated by the guidelines are a voluntary and lasting orientation (*Hinwendung*) to Germany (§3.1.1); oral and written mastery of German appropriate to the applicant's position in life (§3.1.1); knowledge of the Federal Republic's form of government and loyalty to its free democratic order (§3.1.2); and accommodation to living conditions in Germany, generally presumed after ten years' residence (§3.2.1).[27] The guidelines specifically identified political emigration activity as a factor negating *Hinwendung* to Germany (§3.1.1) and cautioned that years spent living in special housing for foreigners did not contribute to accommodation to German living conditions (§3.2.1). They also decreed that naturalization should be denied when it would disserve foreign policy goals, as when it contributed to the brain drain from developing countries (§§5.1, 5.2). The guidelines particularly emphasized the undesirability of multiple nationality, either for an individual or within a family and established a preference against naturalizing an individual if close family members were retaining foreign nationality (§4.1, 4.3).[28] And they required in most cases that naturalization applicants achieve legally effective release from their prior nationalities (§5.3.1).

Certain exceptional categories of naturalization applicants receive more generous treatment under separate legal provisions. For example, aliens who are married to Germans receive special consideration for naturalization under Nationality Act §9 and the guidelines.[29] Former German nationals who were denationalized under the Nazi regime on political, racial, or religious grounds, as well as their descendants, have a constitutional right to be renaturalized under Article 116 (2) GG. So-called Status Germans (see Citizenship v. Nationality: Article 116 GG, below) have a statutory right to naturalization, except for those who present a threat to the internal or external security of the state (Act of 22 February 1955 for the Regulation of Questions of Nationality §6[1], reprinted in Hailbronner and Renner 1991, 404). One may also consider as naturalization in a wider sense the acquisition of German nationality by force of law when a child is legitimated or adopted (Nationality Act §§5, 6).

The vast majority of resident aliens in the Federal Republic were ineligible for special naturalization provisions and thus relegated to the discouraging avenue of discretionary naturalization under section 8. This was true not only for immigrants but also for aliens born in the Federal Republic and their children born in Germany. After years of debate over relaxing the requirements for the naturalization of guest workers and their descendants, two new special provisions on naturalization were adopted as part of the recodification of the Aliens Act (not the Nationality Act) in 1990.

Section 86 of the act created a transitional rule aimed at the guest worker generation, establishing a window of opportunity (through 31 December 1995) in which aliens who had resided lawfully in the Federal Republic for fifteen years could apply for naturalization under relaxed criteria, with severe limits on official discretion to deny naturalization.[30] Other eligibility requirements included divestiture of prior nationality, absence of criminal convictions, and ability to support self and family.[31]

Section 85 of the act created a permanent rule aimed at later generations, giving them an opportunity to apply for naturalization under relaxed criteria on reaching maturity. The eligibility requirements included application at an age greater than sixteen and less than twenty-three, divestiture of prior nationality, eight years' lawful residence in the Federal Republic, six years' school attendance (including four years' general education), and absence of criminal convictions. As under section 86, discretion to deny the application was severely limited.

The requirement of divestiture of prior nationality under both provisions was qualified by section 87 of the act. Under section 87(1), this requirement was suspended where it was impossible or extremely difficult for the alien to give up prior nationality. Statutory illustrations included cases where the prior country afforded no legal avenue for release from its nationality; where the prior country regularly denies requests for release, and the alien has submitted such a request; where the prior country arbitrarily denies a request or fails to adjudicate a formally proper request within an appropriate time period; or where it would be unreasonably burdensome on the alien to submit such a request, as might be true for political refugees. Under section 87(2), officials had discretion to waive the requirement under certain conditions for aliens who had grown up in Germany, if the prior country refused to release an alien from its nationality until he or she had returned and performed military service.

Initial data suggest that the 1990 reforms have had very modest effects. Naturalization rates have increased, but they remain very low. As a result, further reform of naturalization criteria was negotiated as part of the asylum reform compromise of 1992, enacted in 1993. The most far-reaching change was the elimination of the 31 December 1995 deadline for naturalization under section 86. This revision not only gave the former guest worker population more time in which to naturalize under relaxed criteria but converted section 86 from a transitional provision directed at aliens who arrived in Germany before 1980 into a permanent provision relaxing naturalization criteria for all aliens after fifteen years' residence. At the same time, the remaining discretion to deny naturalization was eliminated from both sections 85 and 86, which were reformulated as entitlements, with one exception. That exception permits discretionary denial of naturalization if the alien is deportable as one who endangers the free democratic basic order of the Federal Republic of Germany or participates in, publicly incites, or threatens violence in the pursuit of political goals.[32] Finally, the

1993 reform also replaced the vague and demanding criterion of irreproachability in section 8 of the Nationality Act by a cross-reference to particular grounds of deportability, all of which involve violations of law.[33]

It is rather early to estimate the effects of the 1993 reforms; I have seen few subsequent statistics.

Loss of Nationality

Unlike the United States Constitution, the German *Grundgesetz* expressly prohibits involuntary deprivation of nationality. Article 16(1) GG provides that "No one may be deprived of his German nationality. Loss of nationality may arise only pursuant to a law, and against the will of the person affected only if such person does not thereby become stateless." This provision may be somewhat confusing to a U.S. audience, and not only because of the translation. Its legal significance entails a distinction between "deprivation" of nationality and "loss" of nationality. Deprivation of nationality, e.g., denationalization of political enemies or racial minorities, is never permitted. Loss of nationality, e.g., by renunciation in the course of naturalization elsewhere, is permitted, but only under circumstances specified by the legislature (not the executive).[34] As in former U.S. law, loss of nationality may occur against the subjective desire of an individual who voluntarily performs an expatriating act such as naturalizing in a foreign country or acquiring a foreign nationality by being adopted by an alien (Judgment of 22 June 1990, BVerfG [Kammer], in *Neue Juristische Wochenschrift* (1990): 2193; Nationality Act §§17, 25, 27).

The legal rules regarding loss of German nationality through naturalization elsewhere are somewhat complex. The Nationality Act imposes loss of nationality only when the naturalizing individual does not reside in Germany at the time of the naturalization (Nationality Act §25). However, as a result of Germany's adherence to the European Convention on the Reduction of Cases of Multiple Nationality, a supplementary rule will cause even individuals who reside in Germany to lose their German nationality if they naturalize in particular treaty partners. It is possible, however, for officials to grant a German national permission to retain his or her German nationality while naturalizing in another country, if that would be in the national interest or would avoid very serious disadvantages to the individual (Nationality Act §25[3]; Hailbronner and Renner 1991, 284–85; Kammann 1984, 211–12).

Citizenship v. Nationality: Article 116 GG

Further complexities of German nationality law result from Article 116 of the *Grundgesetz*. This article, designated as one of the "Transitional and Concluding Provisions" of the German Constitution, introduces two special rules and creates a technical distinction between nationals (*Staatsangehörige*) and citizens (*Staatsbürger*) quite different from the one in U.S. law. Since there will be a separate paper addressing policy aspects of the Article 116(1) phenomenon, I will discuss Article 116 here only for the light it sheds on other nationality issues in the Federal Republic.

Article 116(2) requires only brief mention here. It provides a right to reacquisition of German nationality for former German nationals (and their descendants) who were deprived of German nationality on political, racial, or religious grounds by the Nazi regime.

Article 116(1) has far greater importance. In form, it is only a definition, and a provisional one at that: "Unless otherwise provided by law, a German within the meaning of this Basic Law is a person who possesses German nationality or who has been admitted to the territory of the German Reich within the frontiers of 31 December 1937 as a refugee or expellee of German stock (Volkszugehoerigkeit) or as the spouse or descendant of such person." The original significance of this definition bears explanation: The population of West Germany at the time of the adoption of the *Grundgesetz* included persons who had been nationals of the former German Reich but also included large numbers of persons of German ancestry who were legally nationals of East European countries or were stateless. These persons had been expelled from their countries or had fled them as a result of measures of retaliation and dispossession directed against them as Germans. The purpose of the definitional provision Article 116(1) was to include these "Germans without German nationality" or "Status Germans" among the "Germans" to whom various civil rights were reserved by the *Grundgesetz*, pending alternative solutions to their problems. For example, although most fundamental rights in the *Grundgesetz* were framed as rights of persons, rights of geographical mobility, freedom of occupation, and rights of equal access to public employment were framed as rights of "Germans."

The effect of Article 116(1) and the legislation implementing it was to create a legal distinction between the categories of citizen and national. The Status Germans could enjoy the rights of citizenship without having German nationality under the Nationality Act or in the sense of international law. Thus German nationality effectively became a narrower category than German citizenship, a result opposite to the result in U.S. law, where the existence of "noncitizen nationals" makes the category of U.S. nationals broader than that of U.S. citizens.

From one perspective, the significance of Article 116(1) is rather limited. It provided a transitional definition of a constitutional term, serving to regulate the treatment of a large category of refugees and expellees who were already within Germany, and it was expressly subject to being superseded by a later statutory definition. In actuality, however, Article 116(1) and the legislation implementing it proved to have major significance in two ways. First, although Article 116(1) itself only specifies the treatment of individuals who are already within Germany, it became the basis for a statutory right for aliens of German ancestry to migrate from Eastern Europe and the Soviet Union to Germany. Although these statutes give ethnic Germans a preferred role in migration policy, they should not be confused with a jus sanguinis rule of nationality. If remote German ancestry entitled *Volksdeutsche* outside Germany to jus sanguinis, they would already be German nationals, and their right to enter Germany would not be subject to legislative control.

Second, the criteria of the definition posited the existence of a German *Volk*, or people, to which these aliens of German ancestry belonged, distinct from the populations of West Germany, East Germany, or any predecessor state (in other words, a *Volk* that is not a *Staatsvolk*). Article 116(1) can thus be interpreted as conferring constitutional legitimation on the notion of an ethnic rather than a political "German people." Administering the provision has also necessitated a continuing legal discourse over the criteria for membership in such a people.

Status Germans have a statutory right to naturalization, subject only to the exclusion of those who present a threat to the internal or external security of the state (Act of 22 February 1955 for the Regulation of Questions of Nationality §6[1], reprinted in Hailbronner and Renner 1991, 404). In particular, renunciation or divestiture of prior nationality is not a condition for their naturalization. This rule was consistent with the purpose of preserving the option for expellees to return to their former homelands in the future (Bergmann and Korth 1989, 81; Makarov 1966, 355–56). Naturalization provides a more secure status than remaining Status Germans does, because the Article 16 prohibition on deprivation of status applies only to actual nationality.[35]

Over the past decade, Article 116(1) and the statutes implementing it have been subject to two kinds of criticism. First, as the events of the 1940s have receded in time, the problems faced by *Volksdeutsche* in Eastern Europe and the (former) Soviet Union have become less acute and more distinguishable from the problems that originally motivated the provision. Second, some critics inside and outside Germany have been troubled by the degree of preferential treatment received by *Volksdeutsche* from Eastern Europe and the (former) Soviet Union in contrast to other migrants and refugees. These criticisms are beyond the scope of this paper.[36] It is enough to note that they have led to some tightening of the criteria and procedures for the reception of *Volksdeutsche* and the imposition of an annual quota (Alexy 1993; Gaa-Unterpaul 1993). On the other hand, the constitutional revisions accompanying and following the unification of Germany have not included a revision or removal of Article 116(1).[37]

The retention of Article 116(1) is potentially important to this paper because some participants in juristic debates over migration and nationality have emphasized the reference to *"deutsche Volkszugehörigkeit* as a clue to the constitutionally required understanding of German nationhood. Prior to unification, the idea of a prepolitical German people fortified West Germany's claim to eventual union with East Germany. In the 1980s, some authors contended that German nationality law and naturalization policy had to be guided by substantive criteria for membership in the German people; to grant German nationality to persons who were not sufficiently "German" was constitutionally impermissible. The favored principles might vary between preservation of the German *Kulturnation* and more restrictive criteria of descent (Bleckmann 1988 [*Kulturnation*]; Quaritsch 1988 [national homogeneity]; Uhlitz 1986 [descent]). These theories did not represent prevailing constitutional opinion in the Federal Republic, but they are not wholly implausible as an attempt at systematic interpretation of a constitution including both Article 116 and a Preamble declaring the goal of achieving national unity for the German people.

Now that the amended Preamble declares that the unity of Germany has been completed and that the constitution has been extended to the entire German people, one might hope that the German people could be equated with the citizenry of the Federal Republic. The idea that not all German nationals are true members of the German people, or that membership in the German people is properly defined by criteria that not all German nationals meet, can only lead to further trouble in the future.

Current Problems in German Nationality Law

The central problem in German nationality law is that the jus sanguinis rule has permitted the emergence of multiple generations of alien residents, resulting in the division of the resident population of the Federal Republic into two hereditary classes with differing sets of rights. If nothing changes, this problem will only grow worse over the next several decades, because the resident alien population has a positive natural growth rate and the resident national population has a negative natural growth rate. Proposals to reduce this division currently involve two options: increasing the rate of naturalization and modifying the jus sanguinis rule. Mass expulsion does not come into consideration, and efforts to induce voluntary emigration have had very modest success.

In the late 1980s one additional method was considered for conferring more of the rights of citizenship on resident aliens by granting them the right to vote and run for office. Two *Länder*, Hamburg and Schleswig-Holstein, implemented this proposal at the local level. The experiment, however, was blocked by the Federal Constitutional Court, which held that the principle of popular sovereignty in the *Grundgesetz* forbade the participation of aliens in elections, even at the local government level.[38] The Court maintained that the "people" in "popular sovereignty" were the people of the state (*Staatsvolk*). At the same time, it expressed approval of the theory

> that the democratic idea, and especially the notion of freedom that it contains, is served by making the possessors of democratic political rights congruent with those who are lastingly subject to a particular sovereignty. The starting point is correct, but it cannot lead to a dissolution of the connection between the characteristic of German [nationality] and membership in the citizenry [*Staatsvolk*] as possessor of the power of the state. The constitution blocks such an avenue. There remains under these circumstances under existing constitutional law only the possibility of addressing such a situation via corresponding rules of nationality law, perhaps by making the acquisition of German nationality easier for those aliens who have settled permanently in the Federal Republic of Germany and reside here lawfully and are therefore subject to German sovereignty in a manner comparable to German nationals. (*BVerfGE* 83: 52)

Actually, this decision was soon followed by the adoption of the Maastricht treaty on European union, which required the extension of voting rights in local elections to all member state nationals resident in another member state. To implement the Maastricht treaty, the *Grundgesetz* was amended to contain an explicit authorization for European nationals to vote in local elections. This amendment was drafted as narrowly as possible, so that it would comply with Maastricht but go no further.[39]

The first relaxation of naturalization standards in the 1990 Aliens Act, which preceded the court's decision by a few months, took effect at the beginning of 1991. Statistics suggest that it had rather modest effects (Beauftragte der Bundesregierung 1994, 43). The total number of discretionary naturalizations (the relevant category) increased from 20,237 in 1990 to 27,295 in 1991 and 37,042 in 1992. Among Turkish nationals, the relative increases were greater, from 2,016 in 1990 to 3,502 in 1991 and 7344 in 1992. Encouraging as these increases might seem, they must be measured against the relevant populations: total annual discretionary naturalizations increased from 0.4 percent to 0.5 percent and then 0.6 percent of the total population of foreign residents over the period from 1990 to 1992 (42); among Turkish nationals, discretionary naturalizations increased from 0.12 percent through 0.2 percent to 0.4 percent from 1990 to 1992 (author's calculations).[40] Looked at another way, in each year the number of children born as aliens in Germany far exceeded the number of aliens granted discretionary naturalization.[41] After the modest effect of the 1990 reform, the naturalization criteria were further amended in 1993, converting the special categories of 1990 into entitlements to naturalize. The statistics available to me do not isolate the effects of the 1993 amendments; however, they do indicate a total of 29,108 naturalizations under the relaxed standards of Aliens Act §§85 and 86, including 10,786 Turkish nationals (Beauftragte der Bundesregierung 1995, 126). The partly overlapping figure for discretionary naturalizations in 1993 was 44,950, or 0.65 percent of foreign population (19–20).

Various explanations have been offered for the low rates of naturalization for persons other than ethnic Germans. Opponents of liberal naturalization have contended that resident aliens do not want to naturalize because they have a healthy loyalty to their own national identities and do not want to become Germans and residence in the Federal Republic already offers them most of the benefits of citizenship with few of the burdens (Blumenwitz 1994, 248, 259; Quaritsch 1988, 502; Quaritsch 1989, 729; Uhlitz 1986, 144). This explanation is in some tension with survey data, in which alien residents have expressed interest in naturalizing, particularly if the criteria were changed (Bade 1994, 50–51; Hailbronner 1992, 9–10). Reluctance to naturalize may also result from social rejection, which has recently escalated into xenophobic violence (Bade 1994, 71; Rittstieg 1991, 1386).[42] Decades of restrictive naturalization policy may have lingering effects that do not disappear the moment naturalization criteria are relaxed (Bade 1994, 71).

The factor most prominently mentioned, however, is the insistence on avoiding dual nationality as a condition of naturalization. Survey data suggest the importance of this factor. Several elements, psychological or practical, have been identified as contributing to the desire to retain prior nationality. A foreign resident, even one born in Germany, may consider an association with the country of origin to be an important part of his or her personal identity and so may be reluctant to reject it (Wollenschläger and Schraml 1994, 228). Such an individual may also be reluctant to give offense to family members and peers by rejecting the country of origin; this problem may be especially serious for the second generation, children born in Germany to immigrant parents. Loss of prior nationality also leads to legal disabilities in the former country: for example, it may make it harder to travel there, impair the right to hold real property there, or bar rights of inheritance (Kiliç 1994, 70–72 [describing Turkish law];[43] Wollenschläger and Schraml 1994, 228). It has also been suggested that some residents perceive sacrifice of prior nationality as cutting off the avenue of retreat if xenophobic violence continues (Bade 1994, 71; Wollenschläger and Schraml 1994, 228).

As previously mentioned, German naturalization law requires actual divestiture of prior nationality where this is not waived; a unilateral act of renunciation does not suffice if it lacks legal effect in the former country. There are, however, exceptional circumstances in which retention of prior nationality is tolerated because the former country will not release its nationals or places unacceptable conditions on their release. Requiring a youth who has grown up in Germany to perform military service in the home country as a condition of release may amount to such an exception, but economic disadvantages ordinarily do not. In recent years, these provisions have been invoked in a majority of the cases of naturalization of Greek and Turkish nationals (Federal Government's Commissioner 1994, 110 [giving statistics on avoidance or toleration of multiple nationality for 1981–1991]).

The assumption that the insistence on avoiding dual nationality prevents the multiple generations of foreign residents from becoming German nationals has led to two kinds of proposals to change German nationality law. The first type involves much broader acceptance of dual nationality or even the total elimination of the avoidance policy. The second type circumvents the naturalization process by granting German nationality at birth to certain categories of children born to alien parents in the Federal Republic. These latter proposals are described as jus soli proposals, but some of them would apply to a very limited set of parents. For example, the Social Democratic caucus in the Bundestag[44] drafted a bill in 1993 under which a child would become a German national if one of its parents was born in Germany and possessed an unlimited residence permit or residence entitlement at the time of the child's birth (Blumenwitz 1993, 151; Wollenschläger and Schraml 1994, 226).[45] The same year the Bundesrat[46] submitted draft legislation under which children born in the Federal Republic would be German nationals if both parents (if living) were ordinarily resident there and at least one parent possessed an unlimited residence permit or a residence entitlement at the time (Wollenschläger and Schraml 1994, 225). The Bundesrat's draft also contemplated broad acceptance of dual nationality in naturalization, affording a right to naturalization to aliens after eight years' lawful ordinary residence in the Federal Republic. The prospects for these proposals currently appear dim, because they are vehemently opposed by the Right.

Objections to the Retention of Prior Nationality

Numerous objections have been made to permitting alien residents to naturalize without giving up their prior nationality. It is perhaps best to begin with two official sources, a statement by the federal government on naturalization policy and a dictum of the Federal Constitutional Court. In 1992 the federal government responded to a parliamentary inquiry on naturalization policy with the following explanation:

> The principle of avoidance of multiple nationality, which characterizes German naturalization law, is founded on the recognition that multiple nationality is in principle not in the interest of the state and the citizen. It leads to a conflict of duties under different legal orders and establishes a danger of legal uncertainty. On the other hand the possible accumulation of rights in certain areas can lead to an unjustified privileging of the multiple national.
>
> Diplomatic and consular protection abroad is restricted. The acquisition of German nationality on condition of loss of prior nationality is also preferable to multiple nationality on grounds of integration policy. These considerations have also led to the Council of Europe Convention on the Reduction of Cases of Multiple Nationality and Military Obligations in Cases of Multiple Nationality of 6 May 1963..., to which the Federal Republic of Germany has acceded.[47]

The Federal Constitutional Court had occasion to discuss multiple nationality in its important decision of 1974 invalidating gender discrimination in the descent of German nationality by jus sanguinis. When the government attempted to defend the descent of nationality to children of German fathers but not children with German mothers and alien fathers, on the ground that the latter would tend to increase dual nationality, the Court stated its agreement with the concern to reduce multiple nationality:

> It is accurate to say that dual or multiple nationality is regarded, both domestically and internationally, as an evil [Übel] that should be avoided or eliminated if possible in the interest of states as well as in the interest of the affected citizen: most international conventions in the field of nationality concern this subject or at least attempt to ameliorate the difficulties that arise out of the possession of several nationalities ... States seek to achieve exclusivity of their respective nationalities in order to set clear boundaries for their sovereignty over persons [i.e., prescriptive jurisdiction by reason of nationality]; they want to be secure in the duty of loyalty of their citizens—which extends if necessary as far as risking one's life—and do not want to see it endangered by possible conflicts with a loyalty owed to a foreign state. Accordingly, the duty of military service provides the principal reason for avoiding dual nationality. Conflicts between the two countries of nationality can also arise from such inconsistent duties and from competitive assertions of diplomatic protection; agencies and courts of third states face the problem of deciding which of the two nationalities they should give priority.[48]

This passage has become famous as the locus for the doctrine that multiple nationality is an evil to be avoided (*die "Übel-Doktrin"*).

These statements do identify practical disadvantages of multiple nationality, for the state, the individual, or both. (I hope it is not excessively liberal to wonder whether disadvantages for the individual might not be left to the individual to accept or reject.) The conflicts of laws and duties attributable to multiple nationality within the German context are somewhat greater than those within the U.S. context. First, U.S. law often relies on a party's residence as the basis for choice of law in situations where German law relies on the party's nationality. Second, the United States has maintained a practice of drafting resident aliens, while the Federal Republic imposes military obligations exclusively on nationals. Thus the United States accepts a level of "legal uncertainty" simply by admitting aliens as residents. The most intense form of conflict arising from dual nationality, of course, results when the two countries go to war against each other; the resulting dilemma is rare, but tragic when it occurs. Conflicts between states both wishing to engage in diplomatic protection of the same individual are probably not an everyday occurrence.

As the Federal Constitutional Court noted, international efforts have been made to defuse the conflicted situation of multiple nationals. For example, the European Convention on the Reduction of Cases of Multiple Nationality and Military Obligations in Cases of Multiple Nationality has more signatories to its provisions for resolving inconsistent claims to the military service of multiple nationals than to its provisions for decreasing the occurrence of multiple nationality (Hailbronner 1992, 24). The Council of Europe has also recently promulgated for signature a protocol to this convention that modifies its terms to tolerate multiple nationality in mixed marriages and when an alien acquires the nationality of the state where he or she was born or has resided as a minor.[49] If multiple nationality could be avoided altogether, states could save themselves the effort of arranging mechanisms for sorting out the consequences, but since those mechanisms must be created anyway, their extension to further categories of multiple nationals imposes incremental costs.

Opponents of dual nationality in naturalization have emphasized these practical disadvantages (Blumenwitz 1993; Löwer 1993; von Mangoldt 1993; Ziemske 1993), and some have also developed further the issue of conflicts of loyalty. These discussions sometimes repeat themes of the alien suffrage debate, moving beyond the question of the difficulty of complying with conflicting legal obligations to the proposition that a subjective disloyalty can be attributed to residents with dual nationality.[50] Some of these authors also place weight on the fact that the *Grundgesetz* would prohibit the Federal Republic from denationalizing dual nationals for acts of disloyalty, and they make inaccurate statements about U.S. nationality law to support a supposed connection between jus soli and flexible denationalization policy (Löwer 1993; Ziemske 1993). One also meets the claim that the true and exclusive national is characterized by the inescapability of his tie to the state, which alone gives sufficient motivation for responsible exercise of the franchise (Löwer 1993, 158; see Neuman 1992, 277–80 [discussing arguments concerning alien suffrage]; Rittstieg 1991, 1386 [criticizing this notion of inescapability]).

These arguments are vulnerable to the reproach of inconsistency. They attribute such negative characteristics to dual nationals that one wonders how the Federal Republic could ever tolerate the existence of dual nationality in any of its members—and yet the toleration of dual nationality is widespread (Hailbronner 1992, 17; Renner 1993; von Mangoldt 1993). As previously mentioned, *Aussiedler* have almost all the rights of citizenship without naturalizing; they can naturalize without giving up their prior nationality; despite the *"Übel-Doktrin,"* the legislature responded to the Federal Constitutional Court's decision by permitting all children born of German-alien marriages to retain both nationalities; children born to German parents in jus soli countries are dual nationals; dual nationality is tolerated in naturalization in exceptional cases; and even German nationals can naturalize in some other countries without endangering their German nationality, so long as they maintain residence in the Federal Republic or receive official permission. There is even a shadowy practice that lends a surreal flavor to this debate: it may be possible for a resident alien to take advantage of these rules by naturalizing and then reacquiring the former nationality (Martiny 1993, 1146).

This pattern of toleration and nontoleration of dual nationality further undermines a claim that looks odd to begin with: that permitting dual nationality in naturalization would amount to unconstitutional discrimination against native Germans. Some authors contend that increased toleration of dual nationality would reduce native Germans to second-class citizens in relation to the privileged foreigners (Löwer 1993, 158; Ziemske 1993, 336).[51] It appears that these authors know discrimination only as a formal concept and do not understand what it looks like in real life.

Ultimately, I find myself in agreement with Professor von Mangoldt's phrasing of the question, though not necessarily with his answer: whether dual nationality should be accepted depends on whether there is a sufficient countervailing interest to justify the disadvantages that it would entail.[52] German law does not provide the elements that would justify a doctrinaire rejection of dual nationality without regard to consequences. Striking the balance between advantages and disadvantages requires an empirical input and a valuative input. The first concerns the likely impact of tolerating multiple nationality on the trend of naturalization rates; the second concerns the value one places on naturalizing foreign residents.

The empirical question is complicated by the recency of the naturalization reforms. The 1990 amendments seem to have produced an upward trend in the rate of naturalization, which nevertheless has a long way to go before it substantially reduces the alien population. The 1993 amendments have only recently taken effect. If a satisfactory rate of naturalization could be achieved without dropping the objection to dual nationality, then that might furnish a reason not to incur the disadvantages. Currently available evidence gives no basis for optimism in this regard. One could wait and see, but only if one did not consider the problem urgent.

In the case of Turkish nationals, prediction is further complicated by an amendment to Turkey's nationality law in June 1995. First, the amendment repealed the former prerequisite that Turkish nationals must perform any required military service before they are eligible for release from Turkish nationality. This change will decrease the number of cases in which Germany permits naturalization without divestiture of prior nationality because of the difficulty of obtaining release; it will make naturalization easier to obtain, but only for those willing to give up their Turkish nationality. Second, the amendment mitigates the legal effects of loss of Turkish nationality. It provides that "persons who acquired Turkish nationality by birth, and who subsequently acquired a foreign nationality with a release from Turkish nationality by permission of the Council of Ministers, and their heirs, can enjoy the same rights accorded to Turkish nationals with respect to residence, travel, employment, inheritance, and the acquisition and transfer of personal and real property, subject to the provisions regarding the national security and public order of the Republic of Turkey." This rather vaguely worded provision may remove many of the legal and economic disincentives for Turkish nationals to naturalize in

Germany. What it will mean in practice, how it will be perceived by its beneficiaries, and what effect it will have on naturalization rates remain to be seen.[53]

While the empirical input is uncertain, the valuative question is evidently controversial. Some authors do not want foreign residents to naturalize until they have completed an unlikely process of cultural assimilation. They reject the idea of naturalization as an intermediate step in the social accommodation between the alien and national segments of the population. Others see the perpetuation of a hereditary distinction between German nationals and foreign residents as a serious fissure in the society, producing injustice and endangering social peace. Naturalization would not be a cure-all but could contribute to more equal relations. Nationality distinctions provide a basis for discriminations that are often not perceived as wrongful. If foreign residents were not voteless, politicians would hesitate more over their rhetoric.

Of course, the evaluation of a particular proposal depends on the available alternatives. If there were acceptable ways to classify applicants for the purpose of limiting acceptance of dual nationality to those applicants who would not otherwise naturalize, a better balance of advantages and disadvantages might be achieved. It might be appropriate, for example, to permit more rapid naturalization for those who give up other nationalities, while maintaining the lengthier residence period for those who do not. (At least prospectively. More than half the alien residents have already lived in Germany more than ten years; more than 25 percent have lived there more than twenty years [Beauftragte der Bundesregierung 1994, 40].) Similarly, the need for acceptance of dual nationality in naturalization depends on the rules for distribution of birthright citizenship.

Objections to Jus Soli Proposals

One objection raised against jus soli proposals has been that they result in dual nationality. I discussed most aspects of this issue in the preceding section. I turn now to other objections.

A second objection to jus soli involves the claim that a child's place of birth is coincidental and reflects no real tie to the state (Blumenwitz 1994, 255). Whatever degree of truth this claim might have with regard to the U.S. version of jus soli, it is wholly false as applied to the limited forms of jus soli under consideration in Germany, in which the parents not only must be lawful residents but must possess an aliens-law status that is distributed on a restricted basis, generally after five years' residence. It is even more grotesque when applied to third-generation jus soli proposals, which require one of the parents to have been born in Germany as well. In fact, these later generations of alien residents have stronger ties to Germany than do most jus sanguinis nationals born and living abroad.

A further objection to jus soli is the concern that it may fail to enlist the parents in the political integration of the child (Löwer 1993, 157, 159). In its decision invalidating gender discriminatory nationality rules, the Federal Constitutional Court described the effect of jus sanguinis as follows: "The principle of descent as the basis of acquisition of citizenship operates in two directions: first, the attachment to the state is mediated and guaranteed through the attachment to the independent social unit of the family, and, second, the common attachment to a particular state community supplies a part of the manifold close relations between parents and children and contributes to documenting and strengthening the cohesiveness of the family."[54] As a matter of probability, there may be some degree of accuracy in this reservation, although the United States offers numerous examples of well-socialized loyal citizens whose parents were unnaturalized aliens and whose families have not broken up over the difference in nationality. Moreover, the Court's reasoning seems persuasive only with regard to children who actually reside within the state of their parents' nationality, which is only one of the possible configurations to which jus sanguinis applies. Ultimately, however, the objection is an instrumental one, and it is unclear how Germany benefits from treating children as hereditary resident aliens rather than attempting to compensate for any absence of parental contribution to their political integration.

A final objection to jus soli, openly expressed by a few legal writers, is that it impairs the cultural or ethnic homogeneity of the Federal Republic. Some consider preservation of homogeneity as a constitutional requirement founded in Germany's identity as a *Nationalstaat*.[55] Ziemske has recently argued: "The jus sanguinis is based on the assumption that conflicts of loyalty can be minimized by common descent. For descent provides well-founded bases for the homogeneity of the community through common language, history, and culture and thus creates a natural attachment among citizens, whose relationship to the polity is ordinarily close enough that problems of loyalty will not arise at all."[56] Blumenwitz has maintained that to introduce jus soli would be to ignore the lessons of recent history, particularly the dissolution of the multinational states of the USSR and Yugoslavia, which have led in the 1990s to a reevaluation of the relationship between state and nation (*Staat und Nation*) (1994, 257). Yet surely if these are the lessons to be learned, they have been learned too late. Even if it might once have been desirable or acceptable to preserve an ethnic or cultural homogeneity in the Federal Republic, the opportunity has been missed. Alien residents have already been naturalized despite their ethnic difference and without adequate guarantees of their cultural fungibility. They are now part of the citizenry, entitled both morally and constitutionally to equal respect. Nationality law can no longer be predicated on the undesirability of their inclusion. That would be learning the wrong lesson from Yugoslavia.

Thus, among the arguments against jus soli nationality for children born to long-term resident aliens, several are weak or of dubious legitimacy, and the primary remaining argument is resistance to dual nationality. According to this argument, children born in Germany to two alien parents, unlike children born to one alien parent and one German parent, should be required to divest themselves of their other nationality.

"Kinderstaatszugehörigkeit"

Rejection of jus soli also appears to have a technical consequence: unless the parents themselves naturalize, the child will grow up as a resident alien and will not be able to acquire German nationality until it reaches maturity. Both the individual and the state suffer from this consequence. Most children who acquired dual nationality by the jus soli rules proposed in Germany would be likely to grow up in Germany and to feel primary identification with Germany. Unlike naturalizing immigrants, they would not have a prior exclusive nationality that had made an earlier claim on them. Granting nationality at birth gives the state a greater opportunity to weave itself into the person's identity, benefiting both the state and the child. Although from a formal perspective the state may seem to gain from the exclusive allegiance of the naturalized resident, the psychological tie of the jus soli national may in fact be stronger.

This phenomenon may have been taken into account in the creation of a rather strange compromise formation, the recent proposal for a provisional quasi-nationality for children, the *"Kinderstaatszugehörigkeit."* The 1994 parliamentary elections strengthened the Bavarian CSU (which has vehemently opposed jus soli and dual nationality) and weakened the liberal-centrist FDP. The new coalition agreement among the CSU, CDU, and FDP proposes the enactment of this provisional quasi-nationality, though only for certain children of the third generation (ZAR 1995, 2). The status would reportedly ensure national treatment in most respects. To be eligible, the child would have to be born in the Federal Republic to alien parents, at least one of whom was born in the Federal Republic and both of whom had already lived in the Federal Republic for ten years (perhaps with a particular aliens-law status) before the birth of the child. This quasi-nationality would only be granted if the parents applied for it before the child's twelfth birthday. It would later ripen into actual German nationality if the child successfully divested itself of all other nationalities but would expire on the child's nineteenth birthday if the child had not so divested him- or herself by that time.

In order for the status to be provisional and thus to expire, it must be made different enough from actual nationality to circumvent the constitutional prohibition on deprivation of nationality.[57] It is not clear whether the provisional nationality would supply a child with a secure basis for forming an identification with the country and planning its life there. Nor is it clear whether adults and other children with secure German nationality would regard a child whose German nationality was provisional and insecure as their full equal. The requirement that the child successfully divest him- or herself of prior nationality by the age of nineteen would be very disturbing if it really contemplated extinguishing the status because of factors beyond the child's control.

Thus, even if this proposal were more generally applicable, it is not clear why parents who decline to naturalize would choose it for their children. The fact that the proposal is limited to a specific subcategory of the third generation makes it an obstacle to reform rather than a reform.

Conclusion

A comparative paper should compare in both directions. The United States jus soli rule (which is neither exclusive nor total, but which is very broad) operates to prevent the emergence of a hereditary subordinated class of noncitizens in the resident population. The realities of migration enforcement in the United States make this principle applicable even to the children of illegal aliens, and the United States should retain its traditional rule. The realities of migration enforcement and policing in the Federal Republic are quite different, and so broad a rule could not be recommended there.

In the absence of jus soli nationality, a hereditary subordinated class of noncitizens has emerged in the Federal Republic. Some people wish they would just leave, but there is a fairly broad recognition that their status represents a major social problem, for the present and especially for the future. The question is what to do about it. It currently appears that the major stumbling block to reform is the policy of avoiding dual nationality in naturalization.

The debate about dual nationality involves both practical and conceptual dimensions. In part, it flows from the conflict between a pluralistic conception of nationality as one allegiance among others and a monistic conception of nationality as an exclusive loyalty that admits no degrees or rivals. Some pluralists find the acceptance of multiple nationality liberating, part of a process of transcending the nation-state. Monists find the acceptance of multiple nationality threatening, undermining the supposed certainty of the nation-state. Pluralists win the conceptual battle. The monists who insist on exclusivity as an essential characteristic of nationality are elevating their own ideal types over the complexity of human reality, and over the flexibility of their own legal system.

On the practical dimension, I will retreat to empiricism and be tentative. Dual nationality has practical disadvantages, which depend on context. The United States' acceptance of dual nationality among its jus soli citizens moderates the effect of its insistence on renunciation of prior nationality when the immigrant generation seeks to naturalize. It may be that the low propensity of Mexican immigrants to naturalize has serious negative effects that could best be addressed by accepting dual nationality, but that has not yet been demonstrated. In the meantime, I would regard this as a transition problem, which is cured in the next generation. Germany, in contrast, currently rejects dual nationality (in the overwhelming majority of cases) both for immigrants and for succeeding generations born to alien parents in its territory. Without a change in this approach, there is no solution in sight. On the available evidence, it appears that a change in policy is desirable. The prospective adoption of a supplemental jus soli rule would address the problem after a long delay. Modification of naturalization practice would be necessary to address the population already living. Both deserve serious consideration.

Notes

1. I wish to express my thanks to Professor Kay Hailbronner and especially to Professors Jochen Abraham Frowein and Rüdiger Wolfrum, whose hospitality at the Max-Planck-Institut für ausländisches öffentliches Recht und Völkerrecht enabled me to write this article.
2. Actually, this phrasing cheats in one respect. German law includes a category of persons who are not considered either aliens (*Ausländer*) or nationals but have most of the rights of nationals: the "Status-Germans." See Citizenship v. Nationality: Article 116 GG, below.
3. Under current German law, European Union nationals do have rights to participate in local elections but not in state or federal elections. Other aliens cannot vote even in local elections (Constitution [GG] art. 28[1]).
4. *Elk v. Wilkins*, 112 U.S. 94 (1884). This rule only applied to tribes that had not otherwise been granted citizenship by statute or treaty.

5. 8 U.S.C. §§1408, 1101(a)(29) (defining "outlying possession of the United States"). The survival of this exception may result partly from a perception by the American Samoan political elite that under current conditions it facilitates local control and legal preferences for Samoans over other U.S. nationals (Leibowitz 1989, 447–51). This perception may not accurately reflect legal doctrine, yet it may still accord with political realities.

6. A series of recent cases have held unconstitutional the continuing effects of the pre-1934 rules on persons born prior to 1934 to alien fathers and U.S. citizen mothers (*Wauchope v. U.S. Dep't of State*, 985 F.2d 1407 [9th Cir. 1993]; *Elias v. U.S. Dep't of State*, 721 F.Supp. 243 [N.D.Cal.1989]). In 1994 Congress amended the Immigration and Nationality Act in order to grant citizenship to most such persons (Pub. L. 103-416, §101[a], 108 Stat. 4306 [adding 8 U.S.C. §1401(h)]), although the statute made an exception to avoid having to confer citizenship on persons who had participated in genocide (Id. §101[c][2]).

7. See *Rogers v. Bellei*, 401 U.S. 815 (1971) (upholding this requirement); Act of 10 October 1978, Pub. L. No. 95-432, 92 Stat. 1046 (repealing this requirement). An amendment in 1994 makes it possible for citizens to regain citizenship lost as the result of a failure to comply with this residence requirement, unless they come within the ideological grounds of disqualification for naturalization (Pub. L. No. 103-416, §103, 108 Stat. 4308 [1994] [adding 8 U.S.C. §1435(d)]).

8. Sometimes the term is used more broadly to include conferral of citizenship by jus sanguinis, because this is a legislative supplement to the constitutional jus soli rule.

9. See, e.g., 8 U.S.C. §§1427(f) (naturalization of persons making extraordinary contributions to national security), 1430 (three-year residence period for spouses of U.S. citizens), and 1439 (naturalization of aliens who serve in U.S. armed forces); INS 1991, 145 (listing five naturalizations by private law in fiscal year 1989, four in 1990, and none in 1985–1988). Roughly 90 percent of all naturalizations take place under the general provisions.

10. In their current form, the English language and civics requirements do not apply to those who cannot meet them because of physical or developmental disability or mental impairment (Pub. L. No. 103-416, §108, 108 Stat. 4310 [adding 8 U.S.C. §1423(b)]). The English-language requirement is also waived for persons of advanced age who have lived in the United States for many years (fifty years old and twenty years' residence or fifty-five years old and fifteen years' residence), and the attorney general is instructed to give "special consideration" in applying the civics requirement to persons over the age of sixty-five who have resided in the United States for twenty years.

11. 8 U.S.C. §1426. The "unless" clause was added in 1990. Resident aliens are not generally exempt from military service but may be exempted under bilateral treaties. Of course, there is currently no mandatory military service for citizens or aliens in the United States.

12. *Rogers v. Bellei*. As previously mentioned, this "condition subsequent" was removed from the statute by a later Congress.

13. Misunderstanding of this point in Germany may result from a combination of several factors: the complexity of the sources of law; the delay between the Supreme Court's decisions and the amendment of the U.S. Code to

restate the governing rule; the unusual form in which the code now expresses the rule; and reliance on out-of-date secondary writings, such as Bar-Yaacov 1961.

14. See, e.g., *Price v. INS*, 962 F.2d 836 (9th Cir. 1992), cert. denied, 114 S. Ct. 683 (1994) (applying only rationality test to naturalization inquiry challenged on First Amendment grounds); *Trujillo-Hernandez v. Farrell*, 503 F.2d 954 (5th Cir. 1974) (finding challenge to English-language requirement wholly nonjusticiable). In *Wauchope v. U.S. Dep't of State*, the court applied a rationality test to the pre-1934 gender-discriminatory rule for descent of citizenship but invalidated the statute nonetheless.

15. The 1990 U.S. census estimated that over 17 million persons over the age of five spoke Spanish at home, out of a total population of nearly 249 million (230 million over the age of five). The next most common non-English language, French, had only a tenth as many speakers (1.7 million) (Bureau of the Census 1993, 51–52).

16. Census figures must be read with caution, however, because they are estimates based on samples and status is self-reported and not confirmed.

17. Author's calculations based on table PB01, "Foreign Born Population," from the 1990 census.

18. The methodology was conservative because it relied on actual matching of immigration records. Immigrants whose naturalization records were not found, or who had died, or who had emigrated were counted as nonnaturalized. The rate of naturalization found for Mexico still exceeded the rate for most West European countries, Japan, Canada, and Australia (which had the lowest rate: 6.3 percent). Follow-up figures through fiscal year 1993 are slightly higher and consistent, indicating that 41.5 percent of the immigrants had naturalized, including 60.9 percent of the immigrants from mainland China, 17.6 percent of the immigrants from Mexico, and 7.8 percent of the immigrants from Australia (INS 1996, 156).

19. Author's calculations, based on census figures for foreign-born residents and figures for naturalization in fiscal year 1990 from INS 1991. In addition to other qualifications of these figures, it should be noted that 1990 is one of a series of atypical years, because aliens legalized under the 1986 amnesty, more than half of whom were from Mexico, were not yet eligible for naturalization.

20. Fear of deterioration in resident aliens' rights appears to have contributed to a great increase in naturalization applications in 1995 (Paral 1995, 938). Other factors include the increased pool of eligible residents (a delayed consequence of the 1986 amnesty) and the agency's requirement that permanent residents replace their green cards with newer, more secure versions. Apparently this procedural burden creates an incentive to naturalize for many who were otherwise held back by inertia (Paral 1995, 938–39; INS 1996, 126–27).

21. See H.R. 705, 104th Cong., 1st sess. (1995) (statutory proposal); H.R. 1363, 104th Cong., 1st sess. (1995) (statutory proposal); H.J. Res. 56, 104th Cong., 1st sess. (1995) (proposed amendment); H.J. Res. 64, 104th Cong., 1st sess. (1995) (proposed amendment); H.J. Res. 87, 104th Cong., 1st sess. (1995) (proposed amendment); H.J. Res. 93, 104th Cong., 1st sess. (1995) (proposed amendment).

22. At present. There is in fact a danger that efforts to control legal immigration will lead to population control systems that will threaten the civil liberties of citizens; the United States lags far behind the Federal Republic in the field of data protection (Strojny 1995; U.S. Commission on Immigration Reform 1994, 12–17).

23. H.J. Res. 87 ("persons born within the United States and to a parent who was lawfully present in and subject to the jurisdiction of the United States at the time of that parent's entry into the United States"); H.J. Res. 93 ("No person born in the United States ... unless the mother or father of the person is a citizen of the United States, is lawfully in the United States, or has a lawful status under the immigration laws of the United States, at the time of birth").

24. I do not mean to imply that the U.S. government officially favors dual nationality. See Nash 1993, 601. Also, while this chapter was in press, a controversy has begun to develop, focusing specifically on changes in Mexican law that would permit Mexicans to retain their nationality after naturalizing in the United States.

25. A similar rule operates in the United States, on the opposite rationale: a person of unknown parentage found in the United States while under the age of five years is a U.S. citizen until shown, prior to attaining the age of twenty-one, not to have been born in the United States (8 U.S.C. §1401[f]). The German rule is not a jus soli rule. It creates a presumption of German parentage for children of unknown parentage, but not for children born in Germany to known parents who have undetermined nationality or are stateless (Hailbronner and Renner 1991, 142–43).

26. Nationality Act §8. For further discussion of these criteria, see Hailbronner and Renner 1991, 171–78. I have subsumed under *proper motion* a technical requirement addressing the alien's legal capacity to act (Nationality Act §8[1]). The vague and demanding criterion of irreproachability was replaced in 1993 by a cross-reference to particular grounds of deportation (see note 33 and the accompanying text).

27. When an alien naturalizes, his or her children may be naturalized simultaneously regardless of length of residence, and a spouse may be naturalized simultaneously on the basis of five years' residence (Guidelines §§3.2.2.4, 3.2.2.5).

28. The 1992 asylum reform compromise led to an agreement that differing nationalities within a family would no longer be treated administratively as an obstacle to naturalization (Bundestag-Drucksache 12/4152, reprinted in Giesler and Wasser 1993, 284). No statutory change was required to implement this policy.

29. The guidelines shortened the presumptive residence period to five years for spouses of German nationals and to two years if in addition the applicant comes from another German-speaking country (§6.1.3).

30. Aliens Act §86 (1990 version). If the requirements were met, naturalization was to be granted "as a general rule" (*in der Regel*); in other words, there was no absolute entitlement, but naturalization could only be denied because of exceptional circumstances arising in each particular case. Family members could also be naturalized along with the principal applicant without meeting the fifteen years' residence requirement.

31. Aliens Act §86(1)(1, 2, 3) (1990 version). More specifically, the applicant had to be able to support both self and family members entitled to support, without using welfare benefits (*Sozialhilfe*) or unemployment benefits, unless the inability resulted from reasons for which the alien could not be considered responsible.

32. Aliens Act §§85(2), 86(3) (1993 version). This change was accomplished by cross-reference to the deportation provision, Aliens Act §46(1). The 1993 revision also clarified that an alien must have a residence permit (*Aufenthaltserlaubnis* or *Aufenthaltsberechtigung*) to be entitled to naturalization.

33. The designated grounds include endangering the free democratic basic order of the Federal Republic of Germany or participating in, publicly inciting, or threatening violence in the pursuit of political goals; committing violations of law or of a legal order that are not isolated or insignificant; being convicted of intentional crimes, for which the punishment is not suspended; violating regulations or orders concerning prostitution; using heroin, cocaine, or similarly dangerous narcotics and refusing rehabilitation; or violating laws concerning the distribution of narcotics (Aliens Act §§46[1, 2, 3, 4], 47[1, 2]).

34. Hailbronner and Renner indicate that the application of these categories to denaturalization (in the U.S. sense of withdrawal of a defectively conferred or fraudulently obtained naturalization) is disputed. The Nationality Act itself contains no procedure for denaturalization, which may instead be governed by rules of general administrative procedure (1991, 233–35, 322–23).

35. Again, if Status Germans enjoyed jus sanguinis nationality, naturalization would be superfluous, their status could not be withdrawn, and those presenting security threats could not be extradited or deported.

36. I do note, however, that U.S. immigration laws have provided favorable treatment for children facing discrimination in Vietnam because they were apparently fathered by Americans during the Vietnam War era. The solicitude expressed in these provisions does share some features with the solicitude expressed in the *Volksdeutsche* policy, although of course the details differ.

37. It has been suggested that Article 116(1) was retained for fear that its modification or removal would be misunderstood in Eastern Europe and the Soviet Union as a signal that the door was closing for the *Volksdeutsche* and thus trigger a huge wave of migration at a time when the Federal Republic was attempting to moderate the pace of their entry.

38. Judgment of 31 October 1990, *BVerfGE* 83: 37 (Schleswig-Holstein); Judgment of 31 October 1990, *BVerfGE* 83: 60 (Hamburg). For commentary in English, see Neuman 1992. This decision was consistent with mainstream legal opinion.

39. GG art. 28(1). It has been argued that the government could go no further, because lifting the citizens' monopoly on voting rights in *Land* or federal elections would go beyond the unamendable core of the popular sovereignty guarantee and because only the Federal Republic's participation in the transnational European Union made it permissible to let European nationals vote even in local elections. The Federal Constitutional Court had

pointed to the possibility of a constitutional amendment of the type required by Maastricht in its decision (*BVerfGE* 83: 59).

40. Actually, the percentages of total annual discretionary naturalizations could be regarded as slightly understated, because the denominators include asylum seekers, whose numbers increased dramatically over that period. For example, if the 1991 percentage were calculated using aliens with residence permits or residence entitlements as the denominator, it would change from 0.5 percent to 0.7 percent. The understatement is smaller for the Turkish population.

41. The birth statistics were 86,320 (1990), 90,763 (1991), and 100,118 (1992) (Beauftragte der Bundesregierung 1994, 31).

42. It is worth noting here that U.S. studies have concluded that perceptions of social discrimination decrease the probability of naturalization in the United States. See Current Problems in U.S. Nationality Law, above.

43. But see below, where I describe changes in Turkish law.

44. The Bundestag is the parliament proper, elected by the citizenry through a somewhat complicated system of proportional representation. The Bundestag elects the chancellor (prime minister).

45. The forms of authorization to reside in Germany are graduated; most non-European Union aliens must spend five years living under durationally limited residence permits (*befristete Aufenthaltserlaubnisse*) before being granted a durationally unlimited residence permit (*unbefristetes Aufenthaltserlaubnis*) and ultimately a residence entitlement (*Aufenthaltsberechtigung*), the form offering greatest security.

46. The Bundesrat may be thought of, very loosely, as the upper house of the German legislature, comparable to the U.S. Senate. It does not consist of members elected by the citizenry but rather of delegates of the *Länder* governments, who cast votes on behalf of their governments, weighted by population. In recent years the Social Democrats, with coalition partners, have controlled enough *Länder* to achieve a majority in the Bundesrat, while the Christian Democrats, with coalition partners, have controlled a majority of the Bundestag.

47. Bundesregierung 1992, 2 (citation omitted); see also Naturalization Guidelines §5.3.1, reprinted in Hailbronner and Renner 1991, 633 (identifying legal uncertainty, conflict of duties, and restricted availability of diplomatic protection abroad as reasons for the policy of avoiding dual nationality).

48. Judgment of 21 May 1974, *BVerfGE* 37: 217, 254–55. The Court concluded, however, that the gender discriminatory rule was not a necessary means for carrying out this policy.

49. Second Protocol amending the Convention on the Reduction of Cases of Multiple Nationality and Military Obligations in Cases of Multiple Nationality, 2 February 1993, European Treaty Series 149. New Article 1(5) of the convention will provide: "Notwithstanding the provisions of paragraphs 1 and, where applicable, 2 above, where a national of a Contracting Party acquires the nationality of another Contracting Party on whose territory either he was born and is resident, or [*sic*] has been ordinarily resident for a period of time beginning before the age of 18, each of these Parties may provide that he retains the nationality of origin."

50. Löwer 1993, 157, 159 (unable to imagine a German-Turkish policeman protecting Kurdish demonstrators against Turkish counterdemonstrators);

Quaritsch 1989, 738; von Mangoldt 1993, 967. Some proponents of multiple nationality have seen this insistence on exacting a subjective loyalty going beyond legal duties of compliance as reflecting an outdated, authoritarian conception of the relation between state and individual (Rittstieg 1991, 1385–86; Zünkler and Findeisen 1991, 253).

51. Von Mangoldt 1993, to the contrary, sees dual nationals as second-class citizens because of the accompanying disadvantages (967).

52. Perhaps this reflects an idiosyncratic reading of the analysis in von Mangoldt 1993.

53. The amendment, Act No. 4112, 7 June 1995, was published in Resmi Gazete [Turkey] No. 22311, 12 June 1995, at 8; a discussion with German translation appears in Cebecioglu 1995. I thank Elif Uras for helping me compare the translation with the Turkish original.

54. Judgment of 21 May 1974, *BVerfGE* 37: 217, 246. The Court also observed that it was "doubtful whether going over to a pure jus soli without any special rules for birth abroad—which in practice exists in no state—would be constitutionally permissible in view of the essence of nationality in a democratic state and in consideration of Article 6, paragraphs 1 and 2 [guaranteeing state protection to the family]" (249). This passage, however, expresses constitutional concerns about eliminating altogether German nationality for children born to German nationals abroad and does not question the propriety of a supplementary rule granting citizenship to children born to alien parents within Germany.

55. Bleckmann 1990, 1398–99 (German nationality can only be conferred on those who are sufficiently integrated into the German *Kulturnation*, as a result of the *Nationalstaat* principle); Ziemske 1994 (see text following); Blumenwitz 1994, 251–52 (relying on both Bleckmann and Ziemske). Quaritsch (1988) argued that national homogeneity must be maintained in order to ensure compliance with the constitutional requirement of reunification of Germany; this objection to jus soli is fortunately moot.

56. Ziemske 1994, 232 ("Dem ius sanguinis liegt die Vermutung zugrunde, Loyalitätskonflikte könnten durch die gemeinsame Abstammung vermindert werden. Denn die Abstammung gibt begründete Anhaltspunkte einer gemeinschaftlichen Homogenität durch gemeinsame Sprache, Geschichte und Kultur, und schafft so eine natürliche Verbundenheit der Staatsangehörigen, deren Näheverhältnis zum Staatsverband im Regelfall eng genug ist, Loyalitätsprobleme erst gar nicht aufkommen zu lassen").

57. From a U.S. perspective, a provisional nationality is somewhat unusual but not a contradiction in terms. The United States itself has experimented with provisional nationality—ironically, in the area of jus sanguinis. See *Rogers v. Bellei*, discussed above.

References

Alexy, Hans. 1993. "Zur Neuregelung des Aussiedlerzuzugs." *Neue Zeitschrift für Verwaltungsrecht* 12: 1171–73.

Alvarez, Robert. 1987. "A Profile of the Citizenship Process Among Hispanics in the United States." *International Migration Review* 21: 327–51.

Bade, Klaus J. 1994. *Ausländer-Aussiedler-Asyl: Eine Bestandsaufnahme*. Munich: Beck.

Barbalet, J. M. 1988. *Citizenship: Rights, Struggle, and Class Inequality*. Milton Keynes: Open University Press.

Bar-Yaacov, Nissim. 1961. *Dual Nationality*. London: Praeger.

Bauböck, Rainer. 1994. *Transnational Citizenship: Membership and Rights in International Migration*. Aldershot: Edward Elgar.

Beauftragte der Bundesregierung für die Belange der Ausländer. 1995. *Bericht der Beauftragte der Bundesregierung für die Belange der Ausländer über die Lage der Ausländer in der Bundesrepublik Deutschland*. Bonn: Beauftragte der Bundesregierung.

———. 1994. *Daten und Fakten zur Ausländersituation*. 14th ed. Bonn: Beauftragte der Bundesregierung.

Bergmann, Wilfried, and Jürgen Korth. 1989. *Deutsches Staatsangehörigkeits- und Paßrecht*. 2d ed. Cologne: Heymann.

Bleckmann, Albert. 1990. "Anwartschaft auf die deutsche Staatsangehörigkeit?" *Neue Juristische Wochenschrift* 43: 1397–1401.

———. 1988. "Das Nationalstaatsprinzip im Grundgesetz." *Die Öffentliche Verwaltung* 41: 437–44.

Blumenwitz, Dieter. 1994. "Abstammungsgrundsatz und Territorialitätsprinzip." *Zeitschrift für Politik* 41: 246–60.

———. 1993. "Territorialprinzip und Mehrstaatigkeit." *Zeitschrift für Ausländerrecht und Ausländerpolitik* 13: 151–56.

Brubaker, William Rogers. 1992. *Citizenship and Nationhood in France and Germany*. Cambridge: Harvard University Press.

———. 1989. "Citizenship and Naturalization: Policies and Politics." In *Immigration and the Politics of Citizenship in Europe and North America*, ed. William Rogers Brubaker. Lanham, Md.: University Press of America.

Bryde, Brun-Otto. 1994. "Die bundesrepublikanische Volksdemokratie als Irrweg der Demokratietheorie." *Staatswissenschaften und Staatspraxis* 5: 305–30.

Bundesregierung. 1992. *Antwort der Bundesregierung auf die Kleine Anfrage der Abgeordneten Ulla Jelpke und der Gruppe der PDS/Linke Liste*. Bundestag Drucksache 12/2035.

Bureau of the Census. 1993. *Statistical Abstract of the United States*. Washington: U.S. Government Printing Office.

Carens, Joseph H. 1987. "Who Belongs? Theoretical and Legal Questions about Birthright Citizenship in the United States." *University of Toronto Law Journal* 37:413–43.

Cebecioglu, Tarik. 1995. "Änderungen im Staatsangehörigkeitsrecht der Türkei." *Informationsbrief Ausländerrecht* 17: 297–98.

Dellinger, Walter, 1995. "Statement of Walter Dellinger, Assistant Attorney General, Office of Legal Counsel, Before the Subcommittees on Immigration and Claims and on the Constitution of the United States House of Representatives, Committee on the Judiciary, Concerning Proposed Legislation to Deny Citizenship at Birth to Certain Children Born in the United States." Available in Lexis CNGTST file.

DeSipio, Louis. 1987. "Social Science Literature and the Naturalization Process." *International Migration Review* 21: 390–405.

Federal Government's Commissioner for Foreigners' Affairs. 1994. *Report by the Federal Government's Commissioner for Foreigners' Affairs on the Situation of Foreigners in the Federal Republic of Germany in 1993*. Bonn: Federal Government's Commissioner.

Franke, Dietrich, and Rainer Hofmann. 1992. "Nationale Minderheiten—ein Thema für das Grundgesetz?" *Europäische Grundrechte-Zeitschrift* 19: 401–9.

Frowein, Jochen Abr. 1994. "Rechtliche Aspekte der Ausländerpolitik und des Staatsangehörigkeitsrechts." In *Migration und Integration in Brandenburg*, ed. Brandenburgische Landeszentrale für politische Bildung. Potsdam: Brandenburgische Universitätsdruckerei.

Gaa-Unterpaul, Birgitta. 1993. "Das Kriegsfolgenbereinigungsgesetz und die Änderungen für das Vertriebenenrecht." *Neue Juristische Wochenschrift* 46: 2080–82.

Giesler, Volkmar, and Detlef Wasser. 1993. *Das neue Asylrecht: Die neue Gesetzestexte und internationale Abkommen mit Erläuterungen*. Cologne: Bundesanzeiger.

Gonzalez Cedillo, Ricardo. 1983. "A Constitutional Analysis of the English Literacy Requirement of the Naturalization Act." *St. Mary's Law Journal* 14:899–936.

Grawert, Rolf. 1987. "Staatsvolk und Staatsangehörigkeit." In *Handbuch des Staatrechts*, ed. Josef Isensee and Paul Kirchhof. Heidelberg: Müller.

Haberland, Jürgen. 1994. "Der Asylkompromiß vom 6. Dezember 1992—ein Jahr danach (1. Teil)." *Zeitschrift für Ausländerrecht und Ausländerpolitik* 14: 3–9.

Habermas, Jürgen. 1994. "Struggles for Recognition in the Democratic Constitutional State." Trans. Shierry Weber Nicholsen.

In *Multiculturalism*, ed. Charles Taylor and Amy Gutmann. Princeton: Princeton University Press.

Hailbronner, Kay. 1992. *Rechtsfragen der doppelten Staatsangehörigkeit bei der Erleichterten Einbürgerung von Wanderarbeitnehmern und ihren Familienangehörigen.* Hamburg: Der Ausländerbeauftragte.

_____. 1989. "Citizenship and Nationhood in Germany." In *Immigration and the Politics of Citizenship in Europe and North America*, ed. William Rogers Brubaker. Lanham, Md.: University Press of America.

Hailbronner, Kay, and Günter Renner. 1991. *Staatsangehörigkeitsrecht: Kommentar.* Munich: Beck.

Immigration and Naturalization Service (INS). 1996. *1994 Statistical Yearbook of the INS.* Washington: U.S. Government Printing Office.

_____. 1992. *1991 Statistical Yearbook of the INS.* Washington: U.S. Government Printing Office.

_____. 1991. *1990 Statistical Yearbook of the INS.* Washington: U.S. Government Printing Office.

Kammann, Karen. 1984. *Probleme mehrfacher Staatsangehörigkeit: Unter besonderer Berücksichtigung des Völkerrechts.* Frankfurt am Main: P. Lang.

Kanstroom, Daniel. 1993. "Wer Sind Wir Wieder? Laws of Asylum, Immigration and Citizenship in the Struggle for the Soul of the New Germany." *Yale Journal of International Law* 18: 155–211.

Kettner, James H. 1978. *The Development of American Citizenship, 1608–1870.* Chapel Hill: University of North Carolina Press.

Kiliç, Memet. 1994. "Rechtsfragen einer deutsch-türkischen Doppelstaatsangehörigkeit." *Zeitschrift für Türkeistudien* 7: 59–80.

Kymlicka, Will, and Wayne Norman. 1995. "Return of the Citizen: A Survey of Recent Work on Citizenship Theory." In *Theorizing Citizenship*, ed. Ronald Beiner. Albany: SUNY Press.

Leibowitz, Arnold H. 1989. *Defining Status: A Comprehensive Analysis of United States Territorial Relations.* Dordrecht: Martinus Nijhoff.

Löwer, Wolfgang. 1993. "Abstammungsprinzip und Mehrstaatigkeit." *Zeitschrift für Ausländerrecht und Ausländerpolitik* 13: 156–60.

Makarov, Alexander N. 1966. *Deutsches Staatsangehörigkeitsrecht: Kommentar.* Frankfurt am Main: A. Metzner.

Marshall, T. H. 1965. *Class, Citizenship and Social Development.* New York: Doubleday, Anchor.

Martin, David A. 1985. "Membership and Consent: Abstract or Organic?" *Yale Journal of International Law* 11: 278–96.

Martiny, Dieter. 1993. "Probleme der Doppelstaatsangehörigkeit im deutschen Internationalen Privatrecht." *Juristenzeitung* 48: 1145–50.

Nash (Leich), Marian. 1993. "Contemporary Practice of the United States Relating to International Law: Loss of Nationality." *American Journal of International Law* 87: 598–604.

Neuman, Gerald L. 1994. "Justifying U.S. Naturalization Policies." *Virginia Journal of International Law* 35: 237–78.

_____. 1992. "'We are the People': Alien Suffrage in German and American Perspective." *Michigan Journal of International Law* 13: 259–335.

_____. 1987. "Back to Dred Scott?" *San Diego Law Review* 24: 485–500.

North, David S. 1987. "The Long Grey Welcome: A Study of the American Naturalization Program." *International Migration Review* 21: 311–26.

Pachon, Harry. 1987. "An Overview of Citizenship in the Hispanic Community." *International Migration Review* 21: 299–310.

Paral, Rob. 1995. "Naturalization: New Demands and New Directions at the INS." *Interpreter Releases* 72: 937–43.

Perea, Juan F. 1992. "Demography and Distrust: An Essay on American Language, Cultural Pluralism, and Official English." *Minnesota Law Review* 77: 269–373.

Portes, Alejandro, and John Curtis. 1987. "Changing Flags: Naturalization and Its Determinants Among Mexican Immigrants." *International Migration Review* 21: 352–71.

Preuß, Ulrich K. 1993. "Staatsbürgerschaft und Zivilgesellschaft." *Kritische Justiz* 26: 232–35.

Quaritsch, Helmut. 1989. "Die Einbürgerung der 'Gastarbeiter.'" In *Staat und Völkerrechtsordnung: Festschrift für Karl Doehring*, ed. Kay Hailbronner, Georg Ress, and Torsten Stein. Berlin: Springer.

_____. 1988. "Einbürgerungspolitik als Ausländerpolitik?" *Der Staat* 27: 481–503.

Renner, Günter. 1993. "Verhinderung von Mehrstaatigkeit bei Erwerb und Verlust der Staatsangehörigkeit." *Zeitschrift für Ausländerrecht und Ausländerpolitik* 13: 18–25.

Rittstieg, Helmut. 1991. "Staatsangehörigkeit und Minderheiten in der transnationalen Industriegesellschaft." *Neue Juristische Wochenschrift* 44: 1387–90.

Schuck, Peter H. 1995. "Statement of Peter H. Schuck Before the Subcommittee on Immigration and Claims and Subcommittee on the Constitution, Committee on the Judiciary, U.S. House of Representatives. To be published in official text of hearings.

_____. 1989. "Membership in the Liberal Polity: The Devaluation of American Citizenship." *Georgetown Immigration Law Journal* 3: 1–18.

Schuck, Peter H., and Rogers M. Smith. 1985. *Citizenship Without Consent: Illegal Aliens in the American Polity*. New Haven: Yale University Press.

Select Commission on Immigration and Refugee Policy. 1981. *U.S. Immigration Policy and the National Interest: Final Report and Recommendations*. Washington: Select Commission on Immigration and Refugee Policy.

Strojny, Andrew M. 1995. "Papers, Papers, ... Please: A National ID or an Electronic Tatoo?" *Interpreter Releases* 72: 617–22.

Uhlitz, Otto. 1986. "Deutsches Volk oder 'Multikulterelle Gesellschaft'?" *Recht und Politik*: 143–52.

U.S. Commission on Immigration Reform. 1994. *U.S. Immigration Policy: Restoring Credibility: Executive Summary*. Washington: U.S. Government Printing Office.

von Mangoldt, Hans. 1994. "Ius sanguinis- und ius soli-Prinzip in der Entwicklung der deutschen Staatsangehörigkeitsrechts." *Das Standesamt* 47: 33–42.

_____. 1993. "Öffentlich-rechtliche und völkerrechtliche Probleme mehrfacher Staatsangehörigkeit aus deutscher Sicht." *Juristenzeitung* 48: 965–74.

Wollenschläger, Michael, and Alexander Schraml. 1994. "Ius soli und Hinnahme von Mehrstaatigkeit." *Zeitschrift für Rechtspolitik* 27: 225–29.

Yang, Philip Q. 1994. "Explaining Immigrant Naturalization." *International Migration Review* 28: 449–77.

Zeitschrift für Ausländerrecht und Ausländerpolitik (ZAR). 1995. "Koalitionsvereinbarung zum Ausländerrecht." *ZAR* 15: 2.

Ziemske, Burkhart. 1994. "Verfassungsrechtliche Garantien des Staatsangehörigkeitsrechts." *Zeitschrift für Rechtspolitik* 27: 229–32.

_____. 1993. "Mehrstaatigkeit und Prinzipien des Erwerbs der deutschen Staatsangehörigkeit." *Zeitschrift für Rechtspolitik* 26: 334–36.

Zünkler, Martina, and Michael Findeisen. 1991. "Einbürgerung ist das Zeichen der Demokratie." *Informationsbrief Ausländerrecht* 13: 248–54.

Notes on Contributors

Richard D. Alba received his undergraduate and graduate education at Columbia University. After completing his Ph.D. in 1974, he taught at Lehman College and the City University Graduate Center in New York City and at Cornell University. He is now professor of sociology and public policy at the State University of New York at Albany where he has been since 1980. He also serves as chair of the Sociology Department and previously founded and directed the university's Center for Social and Demographic Analysis. His teaching and research focus mainly on race/ethnicity and international migration, in the United States and in the Federal Republic of Germany, where he has twice been a Fulbright scholar. His books include *Ethnic Identity: The Transformation of White America* (1990), *Italian Americans: Into the Twilight of Ethnicity* (1985), and *Right Versus Privilege: The Open Admissions Experiment at the City University of New York* (with David Lavin and Richard Silberstein, 1980). He has published numerous articles in the major journals of sociology, most recently with John Logan and others on racial and ethnic residential patterns in the metropolitan United States.

Nathan Glazer, professor of education and sociology emeritus at Harvard University and coeditor of the quarterly of public policy *The Public Interest*, has written and edited books on ethnic issues in the United States, on immigration, on urban problems, and on social policy. Among them are *Beyond the Melting Pot*, with Daniel P. Moynihan (1963); *Affirmative Discrimination* (1975); *Ethnic Dilemmas*, 1964–1982(1983); *Clamor at the Gates* (1985); and *The Limits of Social Policy* (1988).

Johann Handl (born 1947) has received degrees in sociology, economics, and statistics. He is currently Professor for Statistics and Social Science Research Methods at the University of Mannheim. He has published on methodological and substantive problems in several areas of social structural analysis, e.g., labor force participation of women, demographic problems, and ethnic inequality structures. His recent publications include a book with Christa Herrmann, *Soziale und berufliche Umschichtung der Bevölkerung in Bayern*(Munich 1994), as well as the articles "Sozialstruktureller Wandel und Flüchtlingsintegration" (with Christa Herrmann, in the *Zeitschrift für Soziologie*, 1993); and "Hat sich die berufliche Wertigkeit erwerbstätigen, deutschen Berufsanfänger auf der Basis von Mikrozensusergebnissen" (ölner *Zeitschrift für Soziologie und Sozialpsychologie*, 1996).

Walter Müller is professor of sociology at the University of Mannheim. His main research interest lies in the comparative study of social inequality in industrial societies, and his publciations include several books and numerous articles on education, stratification, and research methods, for example, "Social Selection in Educational Systems in Europe," with Wolfgang Karle (*European Sociology Review*, 1993) and "Class Origin, Class Destination, and Education," with Hiroshi Ishada and John Ridge (*American Journal of Sociology*, 1995). He is currently researching institutional factors that affect national differences in the links between education and labor market position in various European societies.

Rainer Münz, born in Basel, Switzerland, in 1954, is professor of demography at the Humboldt University, Berlin. Until 1992 he was director of the Institute for Demography of the Austrian Academy of Sciences, Vienna. His main fields of research are European migration, ethnic and linguistic minority issues, and the impact of demographic change on social policy.

Gerald L. Neuman is professor of law at the Columbia University School of Law, where he specializes in constitutional law, immigration law, and comparative German and U.S. constitutional law. His recent writings include *Strangers to the Constitution: Immigrants, Borders, and Fundamental Law* (1996); "Casey in the Mirror: Abortion, Abuse and the Right to Protection in the United States and Germany" (*American Journal of Comparative Law*, 1995); and "Aliens as Outlaws: Government Services, Proposition 187, and the Structure of Equal Protection Doctrine" (*U.C.L.A. Law Review*, 1995).

Rainer Ohliger studied history and demography at the University of Freiburg in Germany and the University of Michigan in Ann Arbor. He now works as a scientific assistant at the Humboldt University in Berlin, within the interdisciplinary research project Gesellschaftsvergleich (Research Group for Comparative Studies of Societies), which is sponsored by the German Research Foundation. His research focuses on ethnic relations, historical demography, and migration issues.

Alejandro Portes was born in Havana, Cuba, and educated in universities in Havana, Buenos Aires, and the Midwest. He received his Ph.D. from the University of Wisconsin–Madison in 1970 and has taught at the University of Illinois, University of Texas, Duke, and Johns Hopkins. He is currently John Dewey Professor of Sociology and International Relations at Johns Hopkins. His recent books include *City on the Edge: The Transformation of Miami*, with Alex Stepick (1993), *En Torno a La Informalidad* (Mexico City, 1995), *The Economic Sociology of Immigration* (1995), and *Immigrant America, a Portrait*, 2d edition, with Rubén Rumbaut (1996).

Peter H. Schuck, coeditor and contributor to this volume, is the Simeon E. Baldwin Professor of Law at Yale Law School. His main fields of teaching and scholarship include the law and policy of immigration and refugees, torts, and public administration. In the field of immigration, his many published books and articles include *Citizenship Without Consent: Illegal Aliens in the American Polity* (with Rogers M. Smith); "The Transformation of Immigration Law" (*Columbia Law Review*, 1984); "Alien

Rumination" (*Yale Law Journal*, 1996); and *"The Politics of Rapid Legal Change: Immigration Policy in the 1980s"* (*Studies in American Political Development*, 1992). Before joining the Yale faculty in 1979, Professor Schuck was Deputy Assistant Secretary for Planning and Evaluation in the U.S. Department of Health, Education, and Welfare and practiced "public interest" law in Washington, D.C., and private law in New York City. He is a graduate of Cornell University (B.A.), Harvard University (J.D., M.A.), and New York University (Ll.M.).

Wolfgang Seifert was born in 1959 in Ostrach, Germany. He studied sociology, political science, and pyschology at the Freie Universität Berlin from 1979 to 1985, receiving his Ph.D. from that institution in 1994, with a dissertation entitled "Occupational, Economic, and Social Mobility of Mediterranean Immigrants in German." From 1986 to 1995 he worked at the Wissenschaftszentrum Berlin, and since April 1995 he has participated in a research project funded by the German Research Foundation (DFG) at the Humboldt University. His fields of research are migration, the integration of migrants into host societies, and the effects of migration. Publications include *Die Mobilität der Migranten: Die berufliche, ökonomische und soziale Stellung ausländischer Arebitnehmer in der Bundesrepublik* (1995) and, with Heinz Warner, "Die integration ausländischer Arbeitnehmer in den Arbeitsmarkt" (*Beiträge zur Arbeitsmarkt- und Berufsforschung* 1994).

Index